UNEQUAI

UNEQUAL CITIZENS
A Study of Muslim Women in India

Zoya Hasan and Ritu Menon

OXFORD
UNIVERSITY PRESS

OXFORD
UNIVERSITY PRESS

Oxford University Press is a department of the University of Oxford.
It furthers the University's objective of excellence in research, scholarship,
and education by publishing worldwide. Oxford is a registered trademark of
Oxford University Press in the UK and in certain other countries

Published in India by
Oxford University Press
YMCA Library Building, 1 Jai Singh Road, New Delhi 110001, India

First Edition published in 2004
Oxford India Paperbacks 2006
Fourth impression 2014

ISBN-13: 978-0-19-568459-9
ISBN-10: 0-19-568459-1

Typeset in Garamond (TIF) in 10.5/12
by Excellent Laser Typesetters, New Delhi
Printed in India by Ram Printograph, Delhi 110 051

Contents

Acknowledgements

This book owes its existence to the kinds of conversations that routinely take place among those of us concerned with issues of gender, community, identity politics, law, and so on, and their impact on women. Fortunately for us, we found a listening ear and helping hand in Maja Daruwala, then a Program Officer with the Ford Foundation in India, who generously agreed to support a rather ambitious project that sought to map the diversity of Muslim women's lives in India. We are grateful to Maja, Gowher Rizvi, the then Regional Representative of Ford Foundation, Mallika Dutt, Maja's successor, and the staff of Ford for all their help during the four years of the project.

The Nehru Memorial Museum and Library provided a most congenial environment for locating and working on the project. We would like to record our gratitude to Professor Ravinder Kumar, former Director, for his warm encouragement and to the present Director, Dr O. P. Kejariwal for his constant and unstinting support to this project, and to Deshraj, N. Balakrishnan, and Liaqat Ali for facilitating it at every stage.

An enterprise like this is a truly collaborative one, and we would have been unable to realize it without the active participation of numerous friends and colleagues. So, for many hours of advice and discussion, for helpful pointers and valuable suggestions, especially during the formulation of the project, we would like to thank Bina Agarwal, Martha Nussbaum, Amrita Basu, Imtiaz Ahmed, Patricia and Roger Jeffery, Abusaleh Shariff, Syeda S. Hameed, Ratna Sudershan, Vina Mazumdar, Indu Agnihotri, Uma Chakravarti, Vasanth and Kalpana Kannabiran, and Indira Jaising. For issues related to the

Survey, from sampling to data analysis, we owe a special debt to Aijazuddin Ahmed, Sachidananda Sinha, Yogendra Yadav, and S. N. Jha for their help in drawing up the sample frame for this study. We are enormously grateful to Mary John, Pratap Bhanu Mehta, A. K. Shiva Kumar, and Ghanshyam Shah for their helpful comments on the manuscript, and to Vasundhara Sirnate for her help with the tables and charts in the book.

We owe the deepest gratitude to Ashwini Deshpande for her participation in various stages of this project. Her excellent tabulation and statistical interpretation of this large data set were of great importance, and made a significant contribution to our own understanding and analysis of the issues. For administering the questionnaire and conducting the Survey itself, we must acknowledge and thank ORG-MARG, and especially Deepali Nath, P. K. Chopra, Lalitendu Jagatdeb, and Ashish Panigrahi for their patience and perseverance in carrying out what for them, must have been a most unusual survey design.

We would also like to thank our research associates, Nita Mishra, Aarti Saihjee, Chanda Akhouri, R. Brevin, Adnan Faruqui, and Nissim Mannathukkaren for their assistance. And without Seema Sagar, who played a most helpful role in the administration and logistical arrangements of this project, we would have been quite lost.

How could we not thank the Oxford University Press for their exemplary support and efficiency in handling the production of this volume. Special and heartfelt thanks are due to all at OUP for their expertise in making a book out of a mass of data, tables, charts, and text.

Finally, for their faith in our ability to get the job done, as well as for their friendship and support, we would like to thank: Krishna Menon, Mushirul Hasan, Kamla Bhasin, Anuradha Chenoy, Tani and Rajeev Bhargava, Tanika Sarkar, Pamela Philipose, Praful Bidwai, and Achin Vanaik.

ZOYA HASAN
RITU MENON

Tables

xii □ *Tables*

Figures

Introduction

Few issues have attracted greater interest among academics and activists in India than those concerning women and Islam, but much of this interest is caught up in misconceptions that usually leave Muslim women invisible. Their experiences are commonly viewed as synonymous with those of Muslim men, or women generally, thus reifying the categories of community and gender; their invisibility is compounded by the fact that when they do become visible in their own right, then religion is seen to be the primary force influencing every aspect of their lives, from poverty and unemployment to family structure, marriage, divorce, education, etc. However, this invisibility is not a recent phenomenon for, as Gail Minault has noted, imperial discourse in colonial India also ignored Muslim women because '*purdah* removed' women from scrutiny, both literally as well as figuratively'.[1]

In the post-colonial period, at least two misunderstandings have dominated academic discussions and debates on Muslim women. First, it is commonplace to view Muslims and Muslim women as a monolithic category; writings on Muslims in general, and Muslim women in particular, make broad generalizations about what is, in reality, a highly differentiated and heterogeneous community. Such a reductive thesis is based on a complete misapprehension of Islamic history, culture, and politics, and totally obscures or denies the rich and diverse traditions that make up Muslims and Muslim discourses. Nasreen Fazalbhoy writes that this is so because the analysis of Muslims has been concentrated on a few areas, and has been largely defined by attitudes prevalent in the larger social milieu.[2] Thus, the absence and presence of certain issues as the focal point of the studies is revealing of a larger political and social dynamic. This, in turn, has restricted the development of the study of Muslims and has channelled their study in a specific direction. With a few notable exceptions, the spotlight has always been on the role of religion in Muslim life and culture, largely producing sociologies of religion (often distorted and in the abstract) rather than a sociology of Muslims. In this perspective, Muslims were typically seen as a monolithic entity in terms of an Islam that is all-pervasive and primarily prescriptive, ignoring data on the heterogeneity of Muslim communities, their culture, and their social organization.

The second misinterpretation stems from the weight given to Muslim personal law in defining women's status, resulting in a disproportionate emphasis being placed on it, and a great deal of heated discussion about the gender bias of personal law and the appeasement of Muslims.[3] Many studies fixed on Islam and personal law as either the oppressor[4] or saviour, and most of them attribute women's low status to ignorance, traditional beliefs, and the inequities of personal laws. The defining factors are popularly believed to be segregation, the male privilege of unilateral divorce, high fertility, the ubiquitous veil, and conformity to the strict confines of womanhood within a fundamentalist religious code. Moreover, just as the focus in these studies and debates is not on women *per se*, but on Shariat and the legal codes that are biased *against* women, so too, the appeasement is of religious leaders rather than of women. In any event, Islamic practice does not and cannot constitute the whole of women's lives. Nonetheless, Muslim personal law is a contentious issue. Eradicating the gender bias of personal laws is undoubtedly important, but even a complete revamp of personal laws cannot radically improve the status of Muslim women, a status based on achieved relations established on the basis of a person's involvement in the country's economic, social, or political life.[5] Legal equality is one of the fundamental rights of women, but this alone is inadequate and cannot ensure them a fair stake in economic and social development,[6] nor can it lead to a major improvement in the lives of the majority unless the structures that generate disadvantage and discrimination are dismantled.

Feminist analyses of the past decade or more, too, have either centred on Muslim women's status within the religious community, or on their relationship with a secular state as citizens equal before the law. On the one hand, Muslim women have been viewed as wards of their community, and on the other, as independent, freely-choosing subjects entitled to rights, resources, and protection, irrespective of sex or religion. In most analyses, as well as in much of the campaigning and struggle, greater attention has been paid to the question of Muslim personal law and its curtailment of rights *vis-à-vis* women, and on *legal* equality in the matter of personal law as a minimum guarantee of equal citizenship, than on socio-economic, historical, or local factors.

A more deliberate engagement with the secular discourse of development and empowerment, it seems to us, might be one way out of the current impasse. It would allow us, first, to address the 'structural forms of marginalization that have gone into the making of the "Muslim"',[7] as well as to examine the embeddedness of institutionalized inequalities in Indian society and the structures of domination that perpetuate social injustice. It would also enable us to better understand Muslim women by locating them within the broader context of economic, political, and other interests, and recognize that disadvantage, discrimination, and disempowerment are experienced at specific and particular intersections of class, caste, gender, and community.

The Muslim Women's Question

Currently available fragmented, statistical, and micro studies on Muslim women reiterate that the majority are among the most disadvantaged, economically impoverished, and politically marginalized sections of Indian society today. These studies suggest that, like other women, Muslim women too are not homogeneous, and are differentiated along the fault-lines of class, caste, community, and region. Their lives are similarly located at the intersection of gender, family, and community within the dynamic context of Indian society, polity, and economy. At the same time, however, their minority location does qualitatively transform women's experiences and perceptions in very distinct ways, and this transformation is central to understanding the development of women's subjectivity and consciousness. Social commentators have observed that the gendered politics of minority location have become more acute and complex in the last 15 years, following the intensification of communal politics in India and the consolidation of fundamentalist factions across religions in the wake of the Shah Bano controversy in 1985–6, the Deorala Sati in 1987, and the tragedy of the Babri Masjid in 1992 (see Hasan 1994; Butalia and Sarkar 1996; Jeffery and Basu 1999). All these have had significant consequences for the articulation of gender identity for, as well as by, women in contemporary India.

Stereotypes of Muslim women, entrenched by the trinity of multiple marriages, triple *talaq*, and purdah, have held them hostage for so long that they have become difficult to dislodge. But any discussion of Muslim women must speak to two simultaneous projects: a critique of cultural essentialism/reductionism as pointed out earlier, and the formulation of historically and socially grounded concerns and strategies.[8] The first project is one of dismantling, while the second is one of building and constructing. It is to the second project that we address ourselves in this study. We wish to go beyond the societal stereotype of 'praying men and veiled women' by delineating the locus of Muslim women as constituted by class, gender, or sexual difference. By doing so, we also hope to move away from the conventional dichotomy/dualism between inside/outside or public/private distinctions as the major axes of gender discrimination in Indian society,[9] for 'private' and 'public' form a field influenced by wider gender relations of power and domination in society, the economy, and polity.

In examining the impact of development on any society or group the question that proponents of a gender approach ask is: who benefits, who loses, what is the resulting balance of rights, power, and privilege between men and women, and between given social groups? Although the question of gender inequality has been addressed, resulting in a large body of information and analysis on the status of Indian women,[10] there is a paucity of community-disaggregated data on women's status. The increasing documentation of gender inequities and women's economic and social subordination has thus left Muslim women out of this discussion. Virtually nothing is known about the social and economic status of Muslim women; no nationwide, comprehensive surveys of Muslim women have been undertaken, with the result that there is little understanding of the specific factors that keep a large population in a state of poverty and subordination.[11] One reason for the gap is that government agencies do not assess the role of social inequality, and particularly of religion, in access to opportunities, livelihood, and services. This gap is most evident in the Census. Disaggregated community data are collected by census enumerators, but (barring tables on fertility) are not accessible to the public; they remain unpublished and thus outside the public domain. The National Council of Applied Economic Research's

(NCAER's) rural survey of 1999 is a significant exception, but its scope is limited to the conventional census categories of literacy, educational level, work, fertility, and so on. The National Family Health Surveys (NFHSs, first and second rounds) which, in their sampling of 90,000 households, extended their enquiry to include data on exposure to media, contraception, violence, and autonomy; and the Women's Research and Action Group's (WRAG's) study of 15,000 Muslim women, eliciting information on their response to Muslim Personal Law, are very important additions to our knowledge; they have made a definite contribution to closing the information gap and demystifying widely-held assumptions about the conservatism and ingrained backwardness of the community. Like the earlier NCAER study, however, they remain sharply focused on a few issues—law, fertility, reproductive health, education. It is in this context that the present study assumes significance as possibly the first of its kind to address, and assess, the existential, lived reality of Muslim women's lives in all its diversity.

At the conceptual level, this study seeks to investigate the status of Muslim women within a theoretical framework of social inequality and inter-group disparity. In India, social inequalities revolve around religion, caste, and gender, as evident from state policy and the conflicts witnessed in the recent past. In some cases, the differences between groups are sharply marked, with major disparities in social conditions and access to society's material and cultural resources—income, employment, education, health, and so on. These inequalities are rooted in property, income, wealth, and employment relations; to be more precise, the focus is on both inter-group and intra-group diversities and disparities. The upper castes are the most advantaged in India while the Scheduled Castes and Tribes are among the poorest and most disadvantaged. Although caste disadvantage has been well documented as an important and pervasive axis of social inequality in India, disadvantage and discrimination do not end with the Scheduled Castes and Tribes. Religious minorities are also disadvantaged, but this fact is less well documented and recognized; and though Muslims are a heterogeneous minority, they have had a historically 'other' status which has made them vulnerable to discrimination in, for example, access to health and education, as recent studies have shown.[12] Thus, frequently, the identities of class, gender, and religious community overlap to create discrimination and inequality in most spheres of life.

The focus of this study is on the disparity deriving from an overlap between gender, class, and religious community, all of which are important indicators; and between gender, class, community, and patriarchy, the last dominating the other three categories. Some women are more disadvantaged, historically and structurally, than others; all women do not suffer economic discrimination, which reinforces other discriminations and perpetuates their low status. We know, for instance, that any account of women's employment will require an exploration of how far class, gender, and community, for example, impinge in different combinations on women's employment status. Disadvantage can be group-based, which is why higher investment in education or a greater effort to open up jobs and careers that, rightly or wrongly, have remained closed to such groups, may be required. Similarly, as far as women are concerned, a greater determination to remedy structural inequality, of which legal reform is one important dimension, may be necessary.

At the empirical level, this study attempts to generate a national profile of Muslim women in all their heterogeneity through a survey carried out across the country. The Muslim Women's Survey (MWS) focuses on several aspects of Muslim women's lives: socio-economic status, work, education, marriage, mobility, media access, political participation, decision-making, and domestic violence. Quantitative data cannot of course measure crucial dimensions of equality such as human dignity, self-respect, and social and emotional security, but they are a useful starting point for assessing trends, principally because very little is known about the impact of uneven development, biases in the social sector, education, employment status and income, social mobility or political participation, by community.

With the possible exception of Scheduled Caste women, Muslim women probably comprise the poorest and most disadvantaged group in the country. The overall negative impact of this on Muslim women can scarcely be overstated, with the majority of them being among the poorest of the poor in India. A detailed examination of their status assumes importance in the light of this singular and significant fact. There are, however, other reasons, for attempting a serious consideration of the socio-economic status of Muslim women in India, partly because these indicators of inequality are important in their own right, and partly because they shed light on other aspects of gender relations, and through them on a number of interlinked features of Indian society. As such, they provide a rich base from which to draw lessons on poverty, patriarchy, equity, and social hierarchies, including gender hierarchies, disadvantage, and discrimination. As mentioned earlier, the focal point is the intersection of gender, class, and patriarchy in the creation of inequalities and subordination.

Of interest, too, is our attempt to compare the status of Muslim and Hindu women. Are Hindu and Muslim women legitimately comparable? Our own emphasis on Muslim women and intra-Muslim variations does not preclude inter-group analysis. We have done a purposive sampling of the Muslim community to generate a national profile of Muslim women in all their heterogeneity through a survey carried out in 40 districts spread across 12 states of the country. Eighty per cent of our sample was Muslim and 20 per cent Hindu, but all estimates presented here are weighted estimates, which is why a limited comparison with Hindus has been made based on the distribution of the Muslim population (see the section on the methodology adopted).

We are aware that neither Hindu nor Muslim women can be seen as a collective entity, and that it would therefore be inappropriate to make comparisons of unified collectivities. As the Hindu community is caste stratified, with vastly different standards of living between castes, we have disaggregated Hindu women along variables of caste, class, and region. Muslims have been disaggregated by class and region only, because there is no official recognition of caste among Muslims. Muslims are frequently distinguished in terms of *ashraf* (high-born) and *aijlaf* (low-born) groups, which is not comparable with caste differences among Hindus, but despite these differences in the social character of the two communities, we believe that comparison is worthwhile for two reasons. First, inter-group disparities are politically salient and consequential; second, it makes a difference to our conception of welfare when we choose to treat community as the basic unit of disaggregation. Specifically, it provides a more nuanced and accurate picture of where the Muslim community is located *vis-à-vis* the Hindu community in terms of the standard of living, and it highlights the importance of gender inequalities in both communities.

Making Muslim women visible and extrapolating the developmental policy, and gender implications of such an enquiry is one of the central objectives of this study. The MWS data on a multitude of basic indicators will hopefully encourage governments to confront the question of opportunities, disadvantage, and discrimination as they differentially affect women and communities. Mainstream policies have generally been adept at sidelining this reality by deflecting attention to conservative personal laws; without denying the role played by religious conservatism or personal laws, we would nevertheless like to emphasize the complex interplay of systemic and structural forces which reinforce the multiple hierarchies that govern women's lives, and of which religion is only one.

This apart, our investigation of Muslim women reflects both a political as well as an intellectual engagement with the question of women's continuing subordination in India, and their lack of access to the opportunities, services, resources, and benefits of a secular, democratic, and constitutionally egalitarian society. Several decades of grass-roots development work by governmental and non-governmental agencies among the urban and rural poor, have highlighted the extent of women's disempowerment and marginalization. Sustained campaigning by the women's movement as well as other social movements, and targeted government programmes of education, income generation, improved health, self-help, and credit facilities, together with important legal and policy amendments and provisions, have effected some improvement in their condition; it is necessary to bear in mind, however, that deepening and widening economic inequalities and an increase in the number of the absolute poor have had an alarming impact on women, resulting in what many gender analysts have termed the feminization of poverty. If this is the situation of women in general in the country, one can assume that the situation of Muslim women is even more disadvantaged and depressed. Finally, our study attempts to integrate the conceptual and empirical evidence within a secular discourse of empowerment that is sensitive to differences of caste, class, and community, and yet is committed to a larger emancipatory politics.

The Muslim Women's Survey

The aim of our survey was first, to describe the status of Muslim women from a gender and social equity perspective; second, to portray the diversity in the status of women and situate them in a class, community, and regional context; and third, to analyse social inequality and disadvantage, and suggest some directions for empowerment based on the status of Muslim women in India.

The MWS is the first comprehensive baseline survey of Muslim women in India, indeed of women anywhere, covering a wide range of issues, and conducted in the year 2000 with 9541 Muslim and Hindu women respondents. The survey design, identification of districts, and selection of the sample follow logically from our reconceptualization of 'the issue; i.e. avoiding essentialism and moving beyond religious community in order to situate women in a socio-economic, regional, and political context; and equally, to avoid the polarization of the public and private, by which most investigations (particularly those that rely on survey data) either focus on the more public, hence quantifiable variables, or selectively assess only particular dimensions of the private. A full picture thus eludes both.

A word about the several connected and often overlapping elements of our survey, and the questions and concerns that undergird the areas it explores, is in order. The most basic of these is to present primary data on Muslim women's socio-economic status, and conventional status indicators like literacy, education, marital status, and work. Following on from this, however, are several questions that bedevil us about women's persistent low status and the reasons for it. Material considerations apart, such as poverty, poor education, ill-health, economic dependency, and gender discrimination, should we be looking at other factors that correlate with these objective ones—factors that might help explain the existential reality of Muslim women's lives? For instance, are increasing literacy rates a sufficient index of women's improved educational status, or is the educational level attained a more accurate assessment? If so, what sorts of constraints operate or impede their attaining these higher levels? Are they economic, social, or cultural? Do they have to do with class, community, or region? How far are they gendered? Does early marriage, for instance, have a bearing on the high incidence of dropping out among Muslim girls, or can it be accounted for by factors like the availability of sex-segregated neighbourhood schools, financial pressures, number of siblings, and medium of instruction?

Similarly, is early marriage a consequence of conservatism within the Muslim community, or a result of socio-cultural factors that make for sharp differences between regions, irrespective of religious community? Is it a function of poverty or of the general devaluation of women, Hindu or Muslim? Conversely, does late marriage, or even marriage after the legal age, make a significant difference to women's educational or work status? Alternatively, as we hope to elaborate, are mobility and autonomy more important than either education or marital status as far as women's work status and economic independence are concerned? Does the attainment of school education, better health, employment, and a measure of economic self-sufficiency necessarily pave the way for empowerment? What place would any consideration of empowerment accord to the severe curtailment of women's mobility, and to pervasive and wide-ranging domestic violence? We hope to demonstrate that it is only by evaluating objective indices like literacy, education, and work, together with marital status and motherhood, the more elusive factors like decision-making, control over income, mobility, and violence and how they intersect with class, community, religion, and region, that we can arrive at a more informed understanding both of women's actual status and the extent to which empowerment has been achieved.

Questions related to attitudinal and perceptual matters formed an essential aspect of our survey design, as important indicators of social and other change. Census data, as well as findings from various surveys, have established the increased enrollment of girls in schools, which is a significant development. Our attempt through this survey, however, was to probe the high drop-out rates for girls, the practice of seclusion and how it impacts girls' education, parental opposition to girls' higher education, as well as attitudes regarding co-education for girls. Is there, for instance, a perceptible generational, attitudinal shift with regard to working outside the home? Does employment outside the home encourage later marriage? Do women themselves prefer late marriage, which is to say, the legal age of marriage, and if so why?

Related considerations guided the questions asked of respondents on work, autonomy, and decision-making, access to welfare and development programmes, and political participation. For example, how significant was the respondents' information on, and recourse to, schemes to benefit single mothers, widows, or those below the poverty line? Do women support reservations for themselves all the way up to Parliament and the state legislature, or are local elections more important?

It is generally accepted that women are not very forthcoming in their responses to questionnaires, especially when those administering them are unfamiliar or unsympathetic. There are, however, other reasons for their reticence. For example, a tendency to devalue their work, to disregard their contribution to the household economy, often leads to their answering in the negative when asked about income and employment. Similarly, questions on mobility and decision-making need to be detailed in such a way that they capture the unsaid or implicitly stated; when correlated with other variables, such as early marriage or education or poverty, they may yield to an analysis that would otherwise remain elusive. The *interconnectedness* of both issues and questions in our survey reflects the interconnectedness of virtually every aspect of women's lives, approximating, more, a life-cycle approach to the problem than a purely 'objective' one. At the same time, the more obvious assumptions have deliberately been avoided in formulating the questions themselves; this is especially so with regard to decision-making, mobility, and domestic violence.

Two areas of concern are notably absent in the MWS: personal laws and fertility, and it is necessary to explain the survey's silence on these issues. Two recent national-level surveys—the Women's Research and Action Group (WRAG) survey on personal laws and the National Family Health Survey (NFHS) I and II on family health—have presented their findings on both aspects. The NFHS, in particular, has correlated variables such as education, marital and work status, decision-making, and mobility to assess their impact on women's reproductive behaviour. Similarly, the WRAG survey details the incidence of divorce and remarriage by respondents' educational status, and assesses their response to the desirability or otherwise of maintaining personal laws. Both surveys are comprehensive and current in their findings, obviating the need for further data collection on these two issues, at least for the time being.

A few methodological issues need to be clarified. The MWS is focused on women, not on men or on male–female disparities, nor is it principally a study of inter-community disparities; rather, the survey and analysis offered here attempt to do two things: present a more accurate assessment of Muslim women's status in a social, economic, and regional context; and provide some indication of where they stand in relation to Hindu women.

It is no doubt true that a properly gendered analysis of our data would benefit from a male–female comparison, demonstrating more sharply the extent and nature of women's subordination and of social or communitarian bias. This is especially true in areas such as education and work, for example. Information on why Muslim boys have such high drop-out rates would not only enable us to speculate on their impact on Muslim girls' discontinuing school education, but indicate community apprehensions of, and experiences with, employment prospects—continuing or higher education may not have the obvious job-related benefits for them as they do for others. Following from this, one may then relate the high incidence of self-employment and artisanal or semi-skilled occupations to generally low levels of educational attainment among Muslim boys. Conversely, an improvement on this front may have a positive impact on Muslim women, but we are unable to confirm this on the basis of our data.

Notwithstanding the above, however, it bears repeating that while a gendered comparison is an important consideration in appreciating the status of Muslim women, it cannot displace the women-specific features and disabilities that are responsible for their continuing subordination even when other indicators show some improvement. Why, for instance, should sex discrimination almost always work in women's disfavour—after all, men are poor too. But poverty intersects with patriarchy to perpetuate gender hierarchies and systemic discrimination based on gender, as well as caste and community. Similarly, empirical studies have shown that even when women's educational or work status improves, it is not necessary that there will be a corresponding improvement in their decision-making capacity or result in greater autonomy and empowerment. Thus, the absence of data on men and on male–female disparities does not detract from the significance of the extensive qualitative and quantitative information that has been analysed and presented. The comparison with Hindu women, moreover, underlines the shared discrimination and subordination of women in both communities, while simultaneously noting important social and economic community differences and their differential impact on Hindu and Muslim women.

Methodology

Universe of the Study: The Muslim and Hindu female population (aged 18+ years) of the country constitutes the universe of the study.

Sample Size: A sample of 10,000 households was selected for the study from 40 districts in 12 states with a large Muslim population. A total of 9541 households were interviewed from a sample of 10,000 households selected for the study. Within each area, 80 per cent of the sample constituted Muslim, and 20 per cent Hindu, households. The proportion of urban–rural households selected was 60:40. The sample size for Hindus is appropriately weighted to enable inter-community comparisons. The remaining households of the targetted 10,000 either refused to provide information or had no adult respondent available at home on the day of the field visit. A detailed distribution of the urban–rural sample selected is given in Annexure I.

Sample Design: A multi-stage sampling procedure was followed to select the required sample. In the first stage, districts were selected, followed by a selection of villages/towns/cities and households.

Selection of Districts: At the national level, all districts were stratified according to a two-fold criteria, namely the proportion of Muslims in the district and the Relative Development Index (RDI) provided by the Centre for Monitoring the Indian Economy (CMIE). Based on the Muslim population, districts were stratified into three groups, with density of Muslim population being:

• High (30 per cent or more);
• Medium (10 to 30 per cent);
• Low (less than 10 per cent).

The districts in each group were further divided into three sub-groups, based on the Relative Development Index as:

• High (score of 140 or more);
• Medium (score of 70–139);
• Low (score less than 70).

This procedure divided all the districts in the country into nine groups. The sample of 10,000 women was then allocated to each of the nine groups in proportion to its Muslim population. A sample of 250 women was allocated to each selected district. This decision was taken in order to work out the number of districts to be selected from each group; the required number of districts from each group was selected using a Probability Proportion to Sampling (PPS) random sampling procedure. Three sets of sample districts were selected, following the above procedure. Of the three, one set of districts that closely *satisfied* the Gender Sensitivity Index for backwardness, created by the Centre for Women's Development Studies (Delhi), was selected.

The sample of 250 women in a selected district was further allocated to rural and urban areas in the ratio of 40:60; however, where the district was either fully rural or fully urban, obviously no rural/urban allocation was resorted to.

Selection of Cities: In each selected district, all the towns were arranged according to the proportion of Muslim population, and were further divided into two strata. Stratum I comprised towns with a Muslim population of one lakh and above, and stratum II of towns with a population of Muslims below one lakh. The urban sample for each stratum was allocated proportionately. From each stratum, one or two towns were selected using the PPS method. The number of towns to be selected from each stratum was estimated by allocating a minimum sample of 40 household to each town.

Selection of Villages: It was decided to conduct 20 interviews in selected villages, based on which the number of villages to be covered in each district was calculated. In each district, two blocks with a concentration of Muslims were randomly selected; in each selected block, all the villages with a high concentration of Muslims were listed, and two to three villages per block were selected randomly, taking care that villages with a population of 5000 and below were covered by the study.

Selection of Census Enumeration Blocks (CEBs): In each selected town, before selecting the households, CEBs were selected. The number of CEBs to be selected was worked out by fixing a sample of 15–20 households per CEB. A list of CEBs belonging to the wards/ localities with a predominantly Muslim population was prepared as a sampling frame in each selected town, and the required number of CEBs was randomly selected.

Selection of Households: In each selected village, a voters' list was obtained, from which separate lists for Hindu and Muslim households were prepared. Using these lists as the sampling frame, the required number of Muslim and Hindu households was selected following a systematic random sampling procedure. In the event of the required number of households not being available in the selected village/CEB, a neighbouring village/CEB was selected to complete the number of interviews. In each village, a sample of 20 households was allocated to Muslim and Hindu households in the ratio of 80:20.

Selection of Respondents: In each selected household, information on ,age, gender, marital status, etc. was collected for each member. All women aged 18+ years were identified as eligible respondents for detailed interview, and one woman was selected using KISH methods.

As the objective was to assess the status of Muslim women, the sample selected was purposive and biased towards the Muslim population. According to the 1991 census, Muslims constitute 11.4 per cent of India's population, of which 64 per cent live in rural India, and 35.47 per cent in urban areas. With some exceptions, proportionately a larger number of Muslims, than members of other religions, live in urban areas. For example, in all South Indian states with the exception of Kerala, the percentage of Muslims living in urban areas is more than double that of Hindus, and substantially higher than the state average in Rajasthan, Gujarat and Uttar Pradesh, whereas in West Bengal, Bihar, and Jammu and Kashmir, the proportion in urban areas is lower than or about the same as the state average.[13] In a number of cities throughout the country, Muslims constitute over 20 per cent of the population: Hyderabad (38 per cent), Kanpur (20 per cent), Lucknow (29 per cent), Varanasi (26 per cent), and Allahabad (24 per cent). Muslims constitute more than their national average in the cities of Kolkata, Mumbai, Bangalore, Ahmedabad, Agra, Jaipur, Indore, and Jabalpur.[14] Given such high levels of Muslim concentration in urban India, we decided to assign greater proportions to the urban population. The difference in the universe and the sample is, therefore, the result of a purposeful decision to focus greater attention on the urban population, with the sample allocated to urban and rural areas in the ratio of 60:40. Apart from this basic difference, other background information, such as age, gender, religion, education, main occupation, and caste and community groups point to the wide coverage and representativeness of the sample.

Endnotes

1. Gail Minault, *Secluded Scholars: Women's Education and Muslim Social Reform in Colonial India*, Oxford University Press, New Delhi, 1998.
2. Nasreen Fazalbhoy, 'Sociology of Muslims in India: A Review', *Economic and Political Weekly*, 28 June 1997, pp. 1547–51.

3. On some aspects of gender and personal law issues, see Zoya Hasan (ed.), *Forging Identities: Gender, Communities and the State*, Kali for Women, New Delhi, 1994.

4. Shibani Roy's study of Muslim women makes an explicit link between Islam and women's subordinate status. Shibani Roy, *Status of Muslim Women in North India*, B. R. Publishers, New Delhi, 1979.

5. Ibid., p. 51.

6. On the importance of economic equality, see Irene Tinker, 'The Making of a Field: Advocates, Practitioners and Scholars', in Nalini Vishvanathan, Lynn Duggan, Laurie Nisonoff, and Nan Wiegersma (eds), *The Women, Gender and Development Reader*, Zed Books, London, 1997, pp. 33–41.

7. Mary John, 'Feminism, Internationalism and the West: Questions from the Indian Context', Occasional Working Paper No. 27, Centre for Women's Development Studies, New Delhi, 1998.

8. The idea of two projects is borrowed from Chandra Talpade Mohanty, 'Under Western Eyes: Feminist Scholarship and Colonial Discourses', in Nalini Vishvanathan et al., op cit., pp. 79–86.

9. On this, see Mary E. John, 'Gender, Development and the Women's Movement', in Rajeswari Sunder Rajan (ed.), *Signposts: Gender Issues in Post-Independence India*, Kali for Women, New Delhi, 1999, p. 118.

10. Mahbub ul Haq Development Centre, *Human Development in South Asia, 2000: The Gender Question*, Oxford University Press, Karachi, 2000.

11. *Towards Equality*, cited earlier, was the first to attempt a partial survey across the country, based on interviews and questionnaires. Two others, the WRAG and NFHS Surveys, deal primarily with personal law and reproductive health respectively, but make important intercommunity comparisons, as well as correlate significant variables.

12. Roger Betancourt and Suzanne Gleason, 'The Allocation of Publicly Provided Goods to Rural Households in India: On Some Consequences of Caste, Religion and Democracy', *World Development*, (28)12, 2000.

13. Abusaleh Shariff, 'Socio-economic and Demographic Differentials between Hindus and Muslims in India', *Economic and Political Weekly*, vol. 46, 18 November 1995, p. 2948.

14. Fifty-two per cent of India's total Muslim population is concentrated in the three states of Uttar Pradesh, Bihar, and West Bengal. Muslims form a majority in Jammu and Kashmir (64 per cent). In five states, their population is above the national average: Assam (28.43 per cent), Kerala (23 per cent), West Bengal (23.16 per cent), Uttar Pradesh (17 per cent), and Bihar (14 per cent). Another state with a sizeable Muslim population is Karnataka (11 per cent).

MUSLIM WOMEN SURVEY
List of Selected Districts

S. No.	State	District
1.	Andhra Pradesh	Hyderabad
		Rangareddy
		Chittoor
2.	Assam	Tinsukia
		Dhubri
		Nagaon
3.	Bihar	Katihar
		Darbhanga
		Madhubani
		Sahibganj
4.	Gujarat	Kutch
		Valsad
		Nanded
5.	Karnataka	Dakshan Kannad
		Kolar
6.	Kerala	Malappuram
		Kasaragod
		Thrissur
7.	Madhya Pradesh	Morena
		Raigarh
8.	Maharashtra	Greater Bombay
		Nashik
9.	Orissa	Sundargarh
10.	Tamil Nadu	Chennai
		Thanjavur
11.	West Bengal	Haora
		North Twenty-Four Parganas
		Maldah
		Murshidabad
		Jalpaiguri
		South Twenty-Four Parganas
12.	Uttar Pradesh	Lucknow
		Bijnor
		Muzaffarnagar
		Firozabad
		Shahjahanpur
		Azamgarh
		Budaun
		Gonda
		Banda

1
Socio-economic Status
of Households

In studies of stratification and women's status, an important question
has been whether the individual or the household should be taken
as the unit of analysis. This debate has been prompted in recent years
by feminist criticism of those conventional approaches to stratification that have allocated women to social classes in accordance with
the occupational position of the head of the household or husband.
Proponents of this approach claim that this can adequately approxi-
mate women's class status. Critics have argued that women's work
and income must be considered independently in determining women's
position in the stratification system.

In India, however, information on the economic status and standard
of living of women has often to be inferred from equivalent information on households. Even the most comprehensive databases on living
standards do not contain information that would enable the classification of individuals on the basis of his or her occupation or make an
inter-gender comparison of entitlements *within* households. This is
due to several reasons: most women under-report their involvement
in productive work and thus often get classified as non-workers. The
extent of control that women have over their earnings and income
varies considerably and thus, self-reported earnings of women often
tend to be inaccurate. However, data on household entitlements can
form the starting point of an assessment of living standards of women.
The household questionnaire of the Muslim Women's Survey (MWS)
collected information on a number of economic variables from each
household. These include housing conditions, ownership and posses-
sion of house, ownership of productive and non-productive assets,
type of employment, and so on.

To assess socio-economic status, we constructed an index using several indicators of standard of living from the survey data. The Standard of Living Index (SLI) is a composite of the following variables: type of house, type of toilet, type of lighting, type of cooking fuel used, source of drinking water, ownership of certain consumer durables, and ownership of dwelling. In addition, for rural respondents, we have included information on the ownership of agricultural land (with additional points for irrigated land) and ownership of livestock. Thus, while the creation of the index was necessitated by the absence of income data, given the multifaceted composition of this index, it is likely that it yields a more comprehensive picture of the standard of living of different groups, than one that would emerge from income figures alone. Also, income distribution is only one factor among many that influence status and inequality or the real opportunities people enjoy, which are influenced by a range of individual circumstances and the social environment.[1]

The focus here is on the socio-economic status of Muslim households and on comparing this status with that of Hindus. The MWS provides disaggregated information on communities and for the Hindu community, membership of specific caste groups: Scheduled Castes and Tribes, Other Backward Classes (OBC), and others (that is, upper castes). Although, as noted in the Introduction, Muslims are also stratified in terms of ashraf and aijlaf categories, these are not strictly comparable to the *varna jati* system. We, therefore, decided to focus on economic stratification among Muslims rather than social stratification. However, as the Hindu community has a well-defined pattern of social stratification that is recognized by state agencies, we have followed the accepted classification (in addition to an economic classification).

Before we begin a discussion of the socio-economic status, two clarifications are relevant. First, the analysis is based on household standard of living indicators and not income or earning data. Second, the chapter presents data on inter-group variations and differences, that is, differences between Muslims and Hindus and variations among Muslims across class and region. Initially the analysis for all the chapters was done with a five fold classification of communities, however, in certain areas (for example, decision making, mobility, access to basic amenities and women's participation in the political process) we found the community difference among Hindus to be insignificant, hence, we collapsed these into Hindus and Muslims for simplification of presentation.

All-India Standard of Living and Socio-economic Status

The SLI[2] is the sum of points based upon ten variables indicative of the standard of living.

The following variables are used in the creation of the SLI:

1. House type: 4 points for *pucca*, 2 points for semi-pucca, 0 point for *kachha*.

2. Toilet facility: 4 points for own flush toilet, 2 points for public flush toilet, 1 point for pit toilet, 0 point for no facility.

3. Source of lighting: 2 points for electricity, 1 point for kerosene/gas/oil, 0 point for others.

4. Main fuel for cooking: 2 points for electricity/LPG/biogas, 1 point for coal/coke/charcoal/kerosene, 0 point for wood/crop residue/dung cake/others.

5. Source of drinking water: 2 points for piped water/hand pump/well, 0 point for standpost/spring/river/stream/others.

6. Ownership of agricultural land: 4 points for 5 acres or more, 3 points for 2.0–4.9 acres, 2 points for less than 2 acres, 0 point for no agricultural land.

7. Ownership of irrigated land: 2 points if some irrigated land is owned, 0 point for no irrigated land.

8. Ownership of livestock: 2 points for owned livestock, 0 point if no livestock owned.

9. Ownership of durable goods: 4 points for car/tractor, 3 points for moped/scooter/motorcycle/telephone/refrigerator/colour television, 2 points for bicycle/electric fan/radio/transistor/sewing machine/black and white television/water pump/bullock cart/thresher, 1 point for mattress/pressure cooker/chair/bed/table/clock.

10. Ownership of house: 2 points for yes, 0 point for no.

Higher points indicate better living standards.[3]

We have divided the SLI into five socio-economic status (SES) categories: low, lower middle, middle, upper middle, and high. At the all-India level, around 34 per cent of Muslims belong to the low and lower middle categories of SES, a proportion that is nearly double that of upper caste Hindus (18 per cent).[4]

There are major variations in the socio-economic status of communities. The all-India summary of the community variations in SLI is given in Figure 1.1.[5] Most significant are the differences between upper

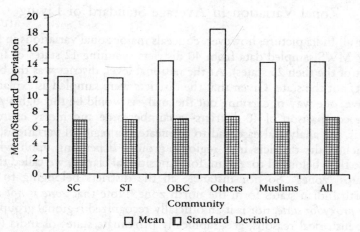

FIGURE 1.1: Summary of SLI

castes and Scheduled Castes and between upper castes and Muslims. In the country as a whole, the Scheduled Castes and Tribes groups within the Hindu community have the lowest average SLI. Given that due to lack of data we have aggregated the Muslim community into one group, when, in fact, the Muslims themselves are highly differentiated by SLI as well as by status, this comparative picture understates the disparity between the poorer Muslims and the Hindus at the upper end of the SLI spectrum. In other words, if we were to compare the richer strata among the Hindus with the poorer Muslims, the gap in average standard of living would in fact be much larger than what is indicated by Figure 1.1. Despite that, it is instructive that Muslims, 50 years after independence, on the whole have an average SLI (14.1) less than even the OBCs, and well below upper caste Hindus, who have an average SLI of 18.15. *The community level differences in the mean SLI are statistically significant.* The standard deviation measures the dispersion around the average SLI and is a very rough indicator of polarization *within* the group. Figure 1.1 indicates that the maximum polarization is *among* the Hindu upper castes (7.36).

The all-India SLI underscores the lower standard of living of Muslims, below that of the Hindu lower castes and significantly less than that of the Hindu upper castes. Thus, on the whole, they are just slightly better off than the Scheduled Castes population, a section of the Hindu community that has remained very poor even after half a century of independence.[6]

Zonal Variation in Average Standard of Living

The all-India picture, however, conceals major zonal variations in SLI. The MWS sampled data from 40 districts spanning 12 states of India (out of the then 25 states). At the national level, district was the basic unit, not the state. Given that the districts were sampled as explained above, one way of carrying out the analysis would be through a *pairwise* comparison of 40 districts—a cumbersome and messy exercise. Thus, for analytical ease and to delineate the regional variations, we bunched the districts into regional groups, depending upon which state they belonged to. Again, for expositional clarity, we called these groups 'zones'. So, for instance, all the districts belonging to the North Indian states form the north zone. Note that *zone is not used as a proxy for state*, nor is it an officially recognized regional grouping. For historical reasons, geographically proximate states of India (that are distinct states today, following the linguistic reorganization of states, and containing territories that today belong to different states, but were often a part of one common state as recently as 50 years ago), share certain common socio-economic features, which provided another motivation behind the construction of zones.

For the purpose of regional analysis, districts were divided into four zones (although, as mentioned above, sampling was done on a district basis): (i) north zone: Uttar Pradesh and Bihar; (ii) south zone: Andhra Pradesh, Karnataka, Kerala, and Tamil Nadu; (iii) east zone: Assam, Orissa, and West Bengal; and (iv) west zone: Gujarat, Maharashtra, and Madhya Pradesh.

The all-India averages (see Figure 1.1) are a useful benchmark against which to assess the regional variation. Given that the zonal picture is differentiated further by the rural–urban divide, Figures 1.2 and 1.3 present the averages for each zone, separately for rural and urban areas. The rural–urban disparity in living standards in India is well known; the MWS findings reiterate this disparity. Figures 1.2 and 1.3 reveal that both for urban and rural areas (except the rural east), upper caste Hindus across all zones have the highest average SLI.

The SLI for rural Muslims in the north is low and even lower than their urban counterparts. More important, the SLI for Muslims in the rural north (12.74) is lower than their all-India average (14.27), which means that Muslims in the rural north are very poor indeed. The east zone, on the whole, has a standard of living lower than the all-India average for all communities. It is noteworthy that in the rural

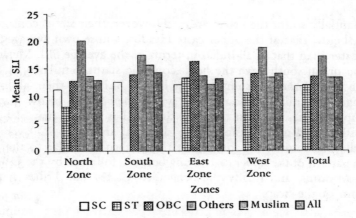

FIGURE 1.2: Regional Variation in Mean SLI: Rural

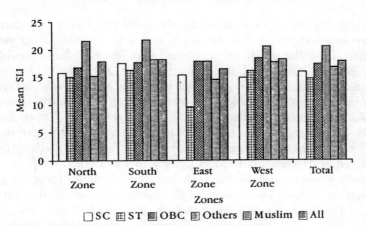

FIGURE 1.3: Regional Variation in Mean SLI: Urban

areas in the east zone, the Muslims have an SLI lower than the Scheduled Tribes. The tribes in this region are very poor and are battling poverty themselves, and in this context the relative backwardness of the Muslims acquires significance. Within the Hindus in this region, the OBCs seem to be at the top in rural areas and very close to the top in urban areas. Significantly, urban Muslims in the east zone have an SLI lower than the urban Scheduled Castes.

By contrast, in the south zone, Muslims have a relatively higher standard of living, an average SLI above the all-India average, substantially so for the urban areas.[7] However, their status continues to be below that of the upper caste Hindus, whose own average SLI is greater than that of all-India. In terms of the average SLI, Muslims in the urban south have the best economic status. Similarly, in the urban west zone, Muslims have a higher SLI than their all-India average, but unlike the south zone where their SLI is below that of the upper castes only, in the west their SLI is below that of both the OBCs and upper caste Hindus. In rural areas, the SLI averages for all communities are lower, but the pattern is similar to the all-India pattern of the upper caste being best off, followed by the OBCs, then Muslims, and finally the Scheduled Castes and Tribes at the bottom of the heap.

SLI and State Domestic Product

Aggregating for rural–urban areas, the zonal averages for all groups taken together reveal that the south and west zones typically have higher SLI, followed by the north and then the east. If we compare this ranking to that of the states based on their State Domestic Product (SDP), the most common indicator of economic development of a society, available from other sources, it transpires that the MWS SLI accurately reflects the ranking of states based upon their SDP. Of course, we need to note that our sample is not drawn from each state of the country. Hence, for instance, based on SDP, we find two distinct trends in the north. Two of the richest states in the country—Punjab and Delhi, with net state domestic product per person in 1998–9 14274 and 24133 respectively—are in the north. But the north zone also comprises Uttar Pradesh (SDP 5447) and Bihar (SDP 3215). Given that our sample is drawn from the latter two states, not surprisingly, the SLI that we have calculated is lower than the all-India average. In other words, if our sample had included the two richest states, then we might well have obtained an SLI for the north zone that would be higher than the MWS-generated SLI. If we examine the average SLI figures in the context of our sample, we do capture, broadly speaking, the ranking of states based upon their SDP.

The east zone comprises the poorest states in India—Assam and Orissa, with SDP 5165—and the relatively better-off West Bengal (SDP 8814). Our SLI averages reflect this pattern of relative economic backwardness of the east zone. The MWS sample is drawn from all the four states of the south: Kerala SDP 9619, Tamil Nadu (SDP 11817), Karnataka 10607, and Andhra Pradesh (SDP 9162). Thus, the south zone comprises states in the upper half of the SDP ranking, and this is also reflected in the SLI trends. Finally, in the west, our data comes from Maharashtra (SDP 13941), Gujarat (SDP 13493), and the relatively poorer Madhya Pradesh (SDP 7609).[8] Notwithstanding the presence of the latter, the averages continue to be high, which could be due to the dominating effect of the relative prosperity of the former two states.

Geographically, the groups of developed states fall in the western and southern parts and the groups of backward states are in the northern and eastern parts of the country. Among development indicators, sex ratio and literacy are perhaps the most important indicators of social development and the most telling index of gender disparity among states.[9] Among the states considered in our study, two of the developed states, i.e. Kerala (1036) and Andhra Pradesh (972), have sex ratios above the national average (846.3), while even Maharashtra and Gujarat have sex ratios only marginally higher than the national average. Gender equality in Uttar Pradesh (879) is among the worst, reflected in an unfavourable sex ratio, which is the second worst in the country among the major states. Equally, female literacy in the entire first set of states except Andhra Pradesh is higher than the national average of 39.3 per cent, whereas only West Bengal and Assam, in the second group, have female literacy above the national average. Female literacy in Bihar and Uttar Pradesh is below 30 per cent. Female literacy as a percentage of male literacy varies from 91.6 per cent in Kerala to 36.5 per cent in Uttar Pradesh. Significantly, Kerala, which has made the greatest progress in social development, has a per capita income below the national average. Tamil Nadu, Maharashtra, and Gujarat have per capita incomes above the national average, while all the states in the backward group have per capita incomes below the national average.[10]

For the Muslim community, the best outcomes on most indicators are in the urban west and urban south zones, with the highest SLI, and both regions also significantly exceed the all-India average for the Muslim community. South India or the south zone is a relatively advanced part of India. The relative development and growth of the region also has had some impact on the economic status of the Muslims. By the same token, in the north and the east, the lower SLI of the Muslim community reflects the relative poverty and underdevelopment of the regions. The highest poverty is recorded in Bihar and Uttar Pradesh with 55 per cent and 40 per cent of the population, respectively, below the poverty line, with the corresponding percentages in West Bengal and Assam being 35.7 and 40 per cent respectively. The inter-zonal variations in the level and social differentials are in all likelihood caused by distinctive historical trajectories of development and state-specific public policies and programmes.

Variation in Selected Indicators Comprising SLI

To understand the variation in SLI, we have focused on three components that differ significantly by region and community. These are house-ownership, land-ownership, and ownership of consumer durables (see Table 1.1). The rural–urban divide is marked in all regions and for all communities, and therefore, for all these indicators, it is necessary to look separately at the rural–urban SLI. Ownership of consumer durables is on average much higher for urban areas (for all communities) than for rural.

TABLE 1.1
Variation in Indicators Comprising SLI

Group	Own house					Do not own house				
	North	South	East	West	Total	North	South	East	West	Total
Rural										
SC	12.47	14.37	12.32	17.13	12.84	6.31	10.00	9.33	4.29	7.04
	3.73	4.11	3.74	7.13	3.95	1.88	4.15	2.17	0.57	2.19
	0.50	0.68	0.34	0.67	0.49	0.24	0.00	0.33	0.00	0.18
ST	11.00		13.19	13.22	12.99	5.80		13.78	7.14	9.59
	2.50		3.62	3.78	3.55	1.80		6.00	0.86	3.24
	0.00		0.84	0.89	0.77	0.00		0.22	0.57	0.28
OBC	13.60	16.97	16.16	17.27	14.66	9.52	11.14	16.67	6.70	10.08
	3.99	6.14	5.26	6.77	4.68	2.97	4.03	6.33	1.40	3.33
	0.79	0.42	1.32	0.64	0.76	0.75	0.08	1.67	0.70	0.51
Others	20.81	21.00	13.66	22.33	17.83	11.00	14.64	12.00	3.00	11.86
	7.87	9.11	4.77	8.62	6.66	3.25	5.91	5.33	0.00	4.44
	1.20	0.78	0.18	1.23	0.73	0.50	0.18	0.00	0.00	0.19
Muslims	14.64	18.40	12.42	16.43	13.90	8.38	13.06	10.21	8.92	10.16
	4.47	7.47	3.43	6.16	4.22	2.54	5.58	3.83	2.98	3.73
	0.83	0.24	0.56	0.44	0.66	0.53	0.06	0.58	0.58	0.43

TABLE 1.1 (contd.)

Group	Own house					Do not own house				
	North	South	East	West	Total	North	South	East	West	Total
Total	14.20	16.91	13.15	17.65	14.41	7.94	11.66	12.04	5.99	9.27
	4.43	6.09	4.07	6.78	4.66	2.43	4.40	4.59	1.03	3.12
	0.73	0.52	0.49	0.80	0.65	0.47	0.08	0.47	0.42	0.35
Urban										
SC	16.07	18.37	15.77	18.90	16.87	13.67	16.45	13.33	11.17	13.65
	6.15	7.45	6.04	7.19	6.55	4.07	7.36	6.33	4.48	5.64
	0.24	0.05	0.15	0.19	0.17	0.40	0.00	0.25	0.30	0.21
ST	15.80	18.20	9.80	21.33	16.29	13.00	11.50	9.00	12.00	11.78
	4.60	7.40	3.20	9.33	6.16	7.00	5.00	1.00	4.75	4.86
	0.00	0.00	0.00	0.67	0.14	0.00	0.00	0.00	0.00	0.00
OBC	17.51	21.62	18.79	20.61	18.88	11.53	15.11	15.42	15.12	14.54
	7.25	9.23	8.43	8.90	7.97	5.74	6.86	7.33	6.58	6.65
	0.51	0.08	0.36	0.32	0.39	0.41	0.04	0.42	0.08	0.13
Others	22.05	23.67	19.29	20.67	21.21	19.61	19.29	14.52	19.18	17.93
	9.91	11.06	7.60	8.60	9.16	8.66	8.93	5.74	9.36	7.93
	0.48	0.44	0.09	0.38	0.37	0.63	0.00	0.00	0.00	0.22
Muslims	16.21	20.96	15.09	19.87	17.97	11.74	16.40	12.50	13.20	14.65
	6.28	9.07	5.75	8.17	7.26	4.58	7.13	5.07	5.68	6.25
	0.16	0.04	0.19	0.08	0.12	0.09	0.05	0.09	0.03	0.06
Total	18.32	20.75	17.33	20.27	18.96	14.83	15.91	14.17	14.02	15.04
	7.64	8.88	6.89	8.42	7.88	6.41	7.15	6.02	6.09	6.62
	0.41	0.11	0.16	0.29	0.29	0.43	0.03	0.14	0.12	0.15

Note: Average SLI, Average P 9 (index for ownership of consumer durables), average P 6 (index of ownership of total land owned). Note that these are not the average values of the actual ownership of land and consumer durables, but the average value of the index that forms a part of the overall SLI. Thus, what appears in the first row for any community is the average SLI. What appears in the second row is the average value of the *index* for consumer durables. The third row is the average value of the index of landownership.

The average values of SLI differ sharply for all communities, and for all zones, ownership of house makes a significant difference, with the average SLI of house-owners being in some cases up to 10 points higher than the corresponding figure for non-house-owners. For instance, for upper castes in the rural north the average SLI of house-owners and those who don't own houses is 20.1 and 22.23. This suggests that ownership of house makes a significant difference to the standard of living. This can be further seen in the rural population, where the all-India average SLI of house-owners is 14.41 as opposed to 9.27 for non-house-owners. The corresponding urban figures are 18.96 and 15.04. The gap is higher for rural than for urban areas, indicating that house-ownership makes an even greater difference in rural areas than in urban areas. For Muslims in the rural south, the non-house-owners have an SLI that is lower than that of the house-owners, but is higher than the SLI of the house-owning Muslims in the rural east. *To express this differently, although not owning a house, Muslims in the rural south are better off than those owning a house in the rural east.* The difference in status could be due to the greater ownership of consumer durables by rural Muslims in the south zone than those in the other zones. In sum, for all groups and for all regions, ownership of consumer durables seems to be positively associated with house-ownership.

Comparing rural Muslims with rural Hindu upper castes, the interesting fact that emerges is that the disparity between the SLI of these two groups is greater (across zones) for the house-owners than for the non-house-owners. Given that the house-owning group would be, on average, richer than the non-house-owning group, this suggests that while both groups are better off in absolute terms, the gap between the two groups *increases* at the upper end of the SLI spectrum. However, this picture does not quite hold in the urban areas. Here the total gap (across all zones) is not significantly different between house-owning and non-house-owning Muslims and Hindu upper castes, while in specific zones, the difference is significant. It is not, however, true that the gap is always larger for house-owners than for the non-house-owners.

It is interesting to note that ownership of agricultural land does not play a significant role in the high SLI of Muslims in the south zone. Amongst rural Muslims, it is only in the north zone that land-ownership, or the absence of it, matters in explaining significant disparity in the SLI, both for house-owners and for non-house-owners.

Regional Variation in SES Classes

The SLI takes values from 1 to 48. Broadly dividing the population into five socio-economic classes, we get five SES groups: low SLI (1–7), lower middle (7–10), middle (10–16), upper middle (16–21), and high (22–48). The all-India picture can be seen in Figure 1.4. (Numbers

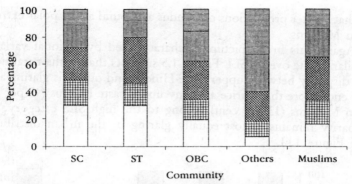

SES Classes: ☐ Low ▦ Lower Middle ▨ Middle ▥ Upper Middle ▤ High

FIGURE 1.4: SES by Community

in each cell are percentages; for instance, 29.77 per cent of Scheduled Castes belong to SES category 1 and so on.)

At the lower end (SES categories 1 and 2), we can see from Figure 1.4 that the Scheduled Castes and Tribes groups have large shares, with close to 50 per cent in this category, followed by Muslims and OBCs. However, at the upper end, we see that the OBCs and upper caste Hindus have the highest percentages in categories 4 and 5. Corresponding to the earlier discussion of the SLI, the distribution for Muslims lies somewhere between that for the Scheduled Castes and Tribes, on the one hand, and the OBCs/upper caste, on the other. The upper caste Hindus are more equally distributed over the five SES groupings than are the Muslims who show greater concentration at the low and lower middle levels (close to 67 per cent of all Muslims are in SES categories 1 to 3).

The highest proportion of Muslims in the high SES category is in the urban west (26 per cent). Here, however, the corresponding proportion for upper caste Hindus is 41 per cent, so the relative disparity remains (see Figure 1.12). The disparity increases at the upper end: only 14 per cent Muslims are in the high SES category, in comparison to 33 per cent upper caste Hindus, and 16 per cent OBCs (see Figure 1.4). If we were to sum up the material condition of the majority of Muslims, the survey findings unequivocally demonstrate that nearly 66 per cent belong to the low to middle SES categories. On the whole, Hindus have a higher standard of living. Also, Hindus are more polarized in terms of SLI than the Muslims, in that greater proportions of Hindus are found at the polar extremes than Muslims.

Again, this broad picture is characterized by regional variation, similar to the overall SLI. Figure 1.5 suggests that in the rural north, the disparity between upper caste Hindus and others is glaring at the top end. More than thrice as many upper caste Hindus (47 per cent) than Muslims (13 per cent) belong to the high SES category. This disparity remains almost equally glaring in the urban distribution (see Figure 1.6).

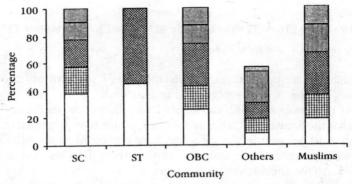

SES Classes: ☐ Low ⊞ Lower Middle ▩ Middle ▥ Upper Middle ▤ High

FIGURE 1.5: SES by Community: Rural North

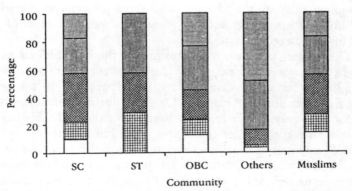

SES Classes: ☐ Low ⊞ Lower Middle ▩ Middle ▥ Upper Middle ▤ High

FIGURE 1.6: SES by Community: Urban North

In the south zone (see Figures 1.7 and 1.8), Muslims are concentrated in the middle and upper middle brackets, confirming the trend that we have seen from the averages. As we have noted earlier, in the rural south, Muslims tend to exhibit a higher SLI than the OBCs and have a distinctly better distribution than the Scheduled Castes, in contrast to the all-India picture. The urban south is clearly a region of relative prosperity, as can be seen by the lower proportion of Muslims in the low SES category for all social groups. While a far greater proportion of Muslims is concentrated at the upper end in

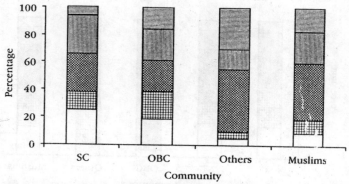

SES Classes: ☐ Low ⊞ Lower Middle ▨ Middle ▥ Upper Middle ▦ High

FIGURE 1.7: SES by Community: Rural South

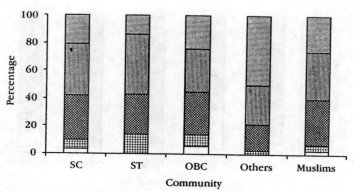

SES Classes: ☐ Low ⊞ Lower Middle ▨ Middle ▥ Upper Middle ▤ High

FIGURE 1.8: SES by Community: Urban South

comparison to the rest of the country, it must be noted that the proportion is just above half that of upper caste Hindus.

Reflecting the relative poverty of the region, in the rural east zone (see Figure 1.9), the proportions for all groups in the upper end are lower than in the urban south and present a stark contrast to that in the urban east, where the OBC group has the highest percentage in the uppermost SES. It is important to note that the Muslims and STs have the lowest percentage in the upper end amongst all the groups. Corresponding more to the all-India trend in the SES intervals, Muslims are concentrated in the low and lower middle ranges of SES. In the urban east (see Figure 1.10), the trend is similar

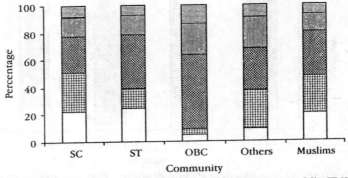

SES Classes: □ Low ⊞ Lower Middle ▓ Middle ▥ Upper Middle ▤ High

FIGURE 1.9: SES by Community: Rural East

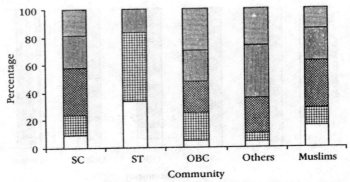

SES Classes: □ Low ⊞ Lower Middle ▓ Middle ▥ Upper Middle ▤ High

FIGURE 1.10: SES by Community: Urban East

to rural areas, except that proportions in the upper end are higher, given that urban areas in general are more prosperous. In the urban west zone (see Figures 1.11 and 1.12), the proportion of Muslims in the highest SES category (26 per cent) is marginally higher than in the urban south. At the upper end, Muslim distribution is closer to upper caste Hindu distribution in comparison to the urban south. In other words, the noteworthy point is that while there is some disparity between Hindus and Muslims in the urban west zone in the higher SES category, the disparity is smaller for the urban west

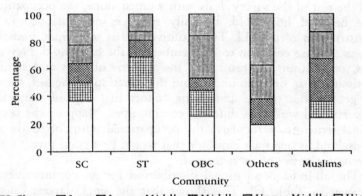

SES Classes: ☐ Low ▦ Lower Middle ▨ Middle ▥ Upper Middle ▤ High

FIGURE 1.11: SES by Community: Rural West

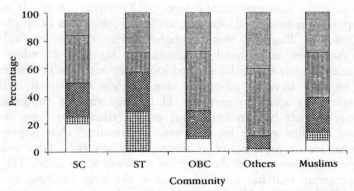

SES Classes: ☐ Low ▦ Lower Middle ▨ Middle ▥ Upper Middle ▤ High

FIGURE 1.12: SES by Community: Urban West

than for the urban south. This has more to do with the proportion of upper caste Hindus in the high SES category (50 per cent in the urban south versus 41 per cent in the urban west). On the whole, the urban west distribution for all groups is significantly better than the all-India one, suggesting that Muslims do well in conditions of relative prosperity than otherwise.

Occupational Distribution of Head of Household

As the rest of the survey deals with women alone, the occupation of the head of household, typically male, is not included in the construction of the SLI. The intuitive idea is to include household assets that are common to all members of the household. Nevertheless, occupations are central to the analysis of class and status of households. In order to understand the variation in the SLI, we need to get an idea of the underlying factors that explain the relative poverty and wealth of different communities. Mapping the occupational structure, particularly the occupational status of the head of household, is one such indicator that would be a good proxy for the *purchasing power of the household*.

The all-India occupational distribution for all communities can be seen in Table 1.2. This shows that the single largest category for Muslims is unskilled labour (21 per cent). The next most important category is small business (18 per cent). Agriculture (15 per cent) and skilled labour (13 per cent) come next. Agricultural labour is the next important category (12 per cent). A much smaller proportion is in salaried jobs such as clerical jobs, Class IV employees, or teachers. Basically, this occupational pattern can be explained by the lower educational attainment of Muslims or when they cannot compete in regular salaried jobs, they are in self-employment where they have an advantage due to their traditional skills or networks or access to markets. Thus, they are not shunning the labour market by remaining out of it; rather they have merely found another avenue for economic sustenance.[11] *Not surprisingly, occupations at the top end of the earnings spectrum (large business, professionals) are more or less confined to Hindu upper castes.* The only other group that has some presence in the large business sector is the Hindu OBCs. Hindu upper castes also constitute the single largest component of small business (although OBCs are very close behind) and skilled labour. Within the skilled labour category,

TABLE 1.2

Main Occupation of the Head of the Household by Community

Caste	1	2	3	4	5	6	7	8	9	10	11	12	Total
SC	10.94	25.24	21.18	9.32	0.38	9.27	0.34	2.75	2.18	3.29	4.05	10.50	100
ST	13.85	23.13	32.85	4.83	0.00	5.39	0.00	0.35	1.82	3.11	4.73	9.96	100
OBC	14.17	13.11	18.97	10.62	0.32	19.05	2.32	2.25	0.49	4.84	2.75	11.00	100
Others	14.26	7.39	13.87	13.86	2.29	20.55	4.37	2.50	1.62	6.36	2.70	10.22	100
Muslims	14.58	11.86	20.08	13.32	0.67	18.23	1.41	3.10	1.85	2.67	2.02	9.91	100
Total	13.26	16.09	19.61	10.87	0.72	15.53	1.85	2.46	1.46	4.26	3.14	10.50	100

Note: 1–Agriculture; 2–Agricultural labour; 3–Unskilled labour; 4–Skilled labour; 5–Doctor, engineer/lawyer; 6–Small business; 7–Large business; 8–Driver; 9–Teacher; 10–Clerical job; 11–Class IV Services; 12–Others.

Hindu upper castes and Muslims have almost identical percentages. *In sum, the bulk of Muslims are absent from the wealth-creating occupations.*

Regional Variation in Occupational Distribution of the Head of Household

Both agriculture (24 per cent) and agricultural labour (14 per cent) are important occupational categories for Muslims in the rural north as almost 40 per cent are engaged in agriculture-related activities. Here, Muslims have a lower SLI because fewer among them own land (see Table 1.3). Unskilled labour is the next largest category for Muslims (23 per cent), a higher proportion than the all-India average, followed by small business (13 per cent), and skilled labour (11 per cent). By comparison, agriculture is the single most important occupational category (41 per cent) for Hindu upper castes, as against agricultural labour, which is insignificant. In all the urban areas, agriculture and agricultural labour categories are naturally insignificant. For Muslims in the urban north (see Table 1.4), the largest categories seem to be small business, unskilled labour, and skilled labour, in that order. The gap between upper castes and Muslims in large business is very large (13 per cent and 2 per cent respectively) and is one of the highest gaps in the country. Clearly, the respondents in the urban north represent small business to a significant extent, as this category is large and significant for all communities, albeit in varying degrees.

Neither agriculture nor agricultural labour is a significant occupational category for Muslims in the rural south, and yet they have a high SLI owing to the existence of a significant group of small business (17 per cent) among them, even though they are more or less absent from large business (see Table 1.5). As elsewhere in the country, the proportion of upper castes who are professionals (doctor/engineer/lawyer) is far higher than that for the other communities. The urban south is the region where Muslims do markedly better than in the rest of the country (see Table 1.6). This is largely because their presence in the large business community is appreciably greater than elsewhere. In addition, they are concentrated in the skilled labour categories to a substantial extent. Small business continues to be an important category as is the case in the rest of India.

TABLE 1.3

Main Occupation of the Head of the Household by Community: Rural North

Caste	1	2	3	4	5	6	7	8	9	10	11	12	Total
SC	15.92	33.33	22.89	5.47	0.00	4.98	0.00	2.99	2.99	1.99	2.99	6.47	100
ST	0.00	66.67	0.00	0.00	0.00	22.22	0.00	0.00	11.11	0.00	0.00	0.00	100
OBC	18.85	21.99	22.51	6.28	0.00	16.23	2.09	1.05	0.00	2.09	1.57	7.33	100
Others	41.38	3.45	10.34	6.90	3.45	20.69	3.45	0.00	0.00	3.45	0.00	6.90	100
Muslims	23.80	13.97	23.02	11.06	0.22	13.41	1.01	1.12	1.56	2.23	2.12	6.26	100
Total	20.45	24.25	20.95	6.44	0.41	12.14	1.27	1.68	1.53	2.18	1.98	6.70	100

Note: 1–Agriculture; 2–Agricultural labour; 3–Unskilled labour; 4–Skilled labour; 5–Doctor, engineer/lawyer; 6–Small business; 7–Large business; 8–Driver; 9–Teacher; 10–Clerical job; 11–Class IV Services; 12–Others.

TABLE 1.4

Main Occupation of the Head of the Household by Community: Urban North

Caste	1	2	3	4	5	6	7	8	9	10	11	12	Total
SC	3.28	3.28	22.13	9.02	0.00	18.03	0.82	2.46	3.28	15.57	11.48	10.66	100
ST	0.00	28.57	28.57	0.00	0.00	42.86	0.00	0.00	0.00	0.00	0.00	0.00	100
OBC	6.82	5.30	12.12	10.61	0.76	31.82	4.92	0.76	1.52	10.23	1.52	13.64	100
Others	1.58	1.05	5.79	4.74	4.21	31.05	12.63	2.63	4.21	15.26	1.58	15.26	100
Muslims	3.40	3.07	23.07	19.50	1.83	26.56	1.99	2.49	2.66	3.82	1.74	9.71	100
Total	4.19	3.69	13.58	9.52	1.73	28.56	6.00	1.80	2.73	11.83	3.39	12.96	100

Note: 1–Agriculture; 2–Agricultural labour; 3–Unskilled labour; 4–Skilled labour; 5–Doctor, engineer/lawyer; 6–Small business; 7–Large business; 8–Driver; 9–Teacher; 10–Clerical job; 11–Class IV Services; 12–Others.

TABLE 1.5

Main Occupation of the Head of the Household by Community: Rural South

Caste	1	2	3	4	5	6	7	8	9	10	11	12	Total
SC	9.38	15.62	28.12	9.38	3.12	3.12	0.00	3.12	0.00	3.12	3.12	18.75	100
ST													
OBC	9.59	6.85	26.03	15.07	0.00	10.96	0.00	4.11	0.00	4.11	1.37	21.92	100
Others	20.00	0.00	15.00	20.00	0.00	20.00	10.00	0.00	0.00	0.00	0.00	15.00	100
Muslims	5.25	4.03	28.02	12.96	0.35	16.81	1.58	4.55	1.58	3.15	1.23	19.96	100
Total	10.67	7.65	25.09	14.27	0.76	10.97	1.60	3.32	0.14	3.20	1.57	20	100

Note: 1–Agriculture; 2–Agricultural labour; 3–Unskilled labour; 4–Skilled labour; 5–Doctor; engineer/lawyer; 6–Small business; 7–Large business; 8–Driver; 9–Teacher; 10–Clerical job; 11–Class IV Services; 12–Others.

TABLE 1.6

Main Occupation of the Head of the Household by Community: Urban South

Caste	1	2	3	4	5	6	7	8	9	10	11	12	Total
SC	1.61	1.61	19.35	14.52	3.23	12.90	0.00	4.84	1.61	9.68	8.06	20.97	100
ST	0.00	0.00	57.14	14.29	0.00	14.29	0.00	14.29	0.00	0.00	0.00	0.00	100
OBC	2.88	0.72	13.67	14.39	1.44	20.86	5.04	7.19	0.00	7.91	5.04	19.42	100
Others	3.12	9.38	9.38	12.50	9.38	12.50	6.25	9.38	6.25	6.25			100
Muslims	2.00	2.60	12.33	15.71	0.95	23.35	3.12	10.24	1.74	5.12			100
Total	2.40	2.19	15.14	14.47	2.53	18.66	3.63	7.71	1.35	7.36			100

Note: 1–Agriculture; 2–Agricultural labour; 3–Unskilled labour; 4–Skilled labour; 5–Doctor; engineer/lawyer; 6–Small business; 7–Large business; 8–Driver; 9–Teacher; 10–Clerical job; 11–Class IV Services; 12–Others.

In the rural east (see Table 1.7), Muslims are equally distributed over agriculture, agricultural labour, unskilled labour, and small business (roughly 17 per cent each). The next most important category is skilled labour (12 per cent). In a departure from the trend in the rest of the country, the proportion of upper castes in the agricultural labour category is significantly large. Here, in the large business and clerical jobs categories, the largest proportion is that of OBCs. This is the other important departure from all-India trends (except for the urban east, as explained below). Note that a sizeable proportion of Scheduled Castes households are engaged in small business. In the urban east (see Table 1.8), as in its rural counterpart, the proportion of OBCs in the large business category is very high (higher than the rural proportion). In this category, the gap between upper castes and Muslims is one of the smallest in the country. Almost half the Muslim households are distributed equally between unskilled labour and small business. Skilled labour is the other important category for Muslims. The professional category is insignificant for all groups. For upper castes, the most important categories are small business, skilled labour, and unskilled labour, in that order.

The single largest category for Muslims in the rural west is agricultural labour, followed by small business (see Table 1.9). The next most important category is that of small business. Note that the proportion of Muslims in large business is insignificant, but this has to be seen in the context of the fact that for the other groups, the proportion is zero. Both unskilled and skilled labour categories have equal proportions of Muslim households. About 8 per cent of Muslims self report themselves as drivers. For Hindu upper castes, small business is the single largest category. In the urban west (see Table 1.10), small business is the single largest category for Muslims, followed by skilled labour. The proportion of Muslims in clerical jobs is higher in this region than the all-India average. For upper castes, the single largest category is that of skilled labour, followed by small business. The next most important categories for upper castes are clerical jobs and professional categories along with class IV services. For Muslims, the most significant categories seem to be small business, agriculture, and skilled labour, in that order. Notice once again the small presence of the Muslims in the large business and the professional categories. *Clearly, therefore, the high proportions in categories 1 (Agriculture), 2 (Agricultural labour), 3 (Unskilled labour) reflect the primacy of agriculture to both communities and also indicate the large proportion of poverty in the sample.*

TABLE 1.7
Main Occupation of the Head of the Household by Community: Rural East

Caste	1	2	3	4	5	6	7	8	9	10	11	12	Total
SC	7.04	19.72	14.08	16.90	0.00	18.31	1.41	0.00	1.41	0.00	2.82	16.90	100
ST	14.63	9.76	39.02	7.32	0.00	0.00	0.00	0.00	0.00	4.88	7.32	17.07	100
OBC	22.73	4.55	0.00	13.64	0.00	27.27	4.55	0.00	4.55	9.09	9.09	4.55	100
Others	4.62	16.92	23.08	21.54	0.00	12.31	1.54	1.54	1.54	3.08	4.62	9.23	100
Muslims	17.56	17.56	17.97	11.70	0.92	17.15	1.13	1.23	2.05	1.33	1.54	9.65	100
Total	11.3	15.62	20.02	15.12	0.20	14.35	1.42	0.66	1.63	2.65	4.26	12.32	100

Note: 1–Agriculture; 2–Agricultural labour; 3–Unskilled labour; 4–Skilled labour; 5–Doctor; engineer/lawyer; 6–Small business; 7–Large business; 8–Driver; 9–Teacher; 10–Clerical job; 11–Class IV Services; 12–Others.

TABLE 1.8
Main Occupation of the Head of the Household by Community: Urban East

Caste	1	2	3	4	5	6	7	8	9	10	11	12	Total
SC	4.69	0.00	28.12	14.06	0.00	21.88	1.56	0.00	3.12	1.56	6.25	18.75	100
ST	0.00	0.00	83.33	0.00	0.00	0.00	0.00	0.00	0.00	0.00	16.67	0.00	100
OBC	2.50	0.00	2.50	12.50	0.00	42.50	7.50	0.00	2.50	10.00	10.00	0.00	100
Others	0.00	2.97	13.86	16.83	0.99	26.73	3.96	2.97	3.96	7.92	4.95	14.85	100
Muslims	2.81	4.07	25.07	17.42	0.58	23.43	3.00	2.90	1.36	3.10	2.71	13.07	100
Total	2.02	1.78	18.97	15.06	0.49	26.94	3.68	1.62	3.05	5.75	6.10	14.47	100

Note: 1–Agriculture; 2–Agricultural labour; 3–Unskilled labour; 4–Skilled labour; 5–Doctor; engineer/lawyer; 6–Small business; 7–Large business; 8–Driver; 9–Teacher; 10–Clerical job; 11–Class IV Services; 12–Others.

TABLE 1.9
Main Occupation of the Head of the Household by Community: Rural West

Caste	1	2	3	4	5	6	7	8	9	10	11	12	Total
SC	0.00	36.36	18.18	13.64	0.00	9.09	0.00	4.55	0.00	9.09	4.55	4.55	100
ST	25.00	37.50	31.25	0.00	0.00	6.25	0.00	0.00	0.00	0.00	0.00	0.00	100
OBC	21.87	12.50	15.62	15.62	0.00	18.75	0.00	3.12	0.00	6.25	3.12	3.12	100
Others	6.25	18.75	12.50	0.00	0.00	25.00	0.00	2.50	0.00	12.50	6.25	6.25	100
Muslims	11.14	24.46	13.08	13.32	0.73	18.89	0.73	7.99	2.42	3.15	0.48	3.63	100
Total	13.81	24.42	18.32	9.51	0.04	15.31	0.04	4.82	0.13	6.78	3.33	3.50	100

Note: 1–Agriculture; 2–Agricultural labour; 3–Unskilled labour; 4–Skilled labour; 5–Doctor; engineer/lawyer; 6–Small business; 7–Large business; 8–Driver; 9–Teacher; 10–Clerical job; 11–Class IV Services; 12–Others.

TABLE 1.10
Main Occupation of the Head of the Household by Community: Urban West

Caste	1	2	3	4	5	6	7	8	9	10	11	12	Total
SC	2.27	13.64	13.64	13.64	0.00	15.91	0.00	11.36	0.00	6.82	11.36	11.36	100
ST	0.00	0.00	28.57	14.29	0.00	0.00	0.00	0.00	14.29	14.29	14.29	14.29	100
OBC	1.47	0.00	14.71	20.59	2.94	27.94	1.47	4.41	1.47	8.82	8.82	7.35	100
Others	1.41	0.00	9.86	29.58	5.63	23.94	0.00	4.23	1.41	11.27	5.63	7.04	100
Muslims	0.32	3.06	14.12	20.55	0.42	30.03	1.16	10.01	1.79	5.80	3.06	9.48	100
Total	1.34	3.14	13.34	21.81	2.64	24.03	0.65	6.59	1.62	8.78	7.41	8.62	100

Note: 1–Agriculture; 2–Agricultural labour; 3–Unskilled labour; 4–Skilled labour; 5–Doctor; engineer/lawyer; 6–Small business; 7–Large business; 8–Driver; 9–Teacher; 10–Clerical job; 11–Class IV Services; 12–Others.

Conclusion

In the preceding sections, in distinguishing socio-economic status, we have investigated social inequalities while assessing the relative importance of several indicators of standard of living in the classification of socio-economic status across zones and rural–urban residence. We have considered differences in the standard of living by classifying the population into five socio-economic classes. We have also gauged differences in the standard of living by focusing on three key components of standard of living: ownership of house, land, and consumer durables, and looked at the occupation of the head of the household. Although these indicators point to some variations in the status of Muslims across zones, the unmistakable fact is that they are generally poor and disadvantaged. They are at the bottom of the economic hierarchy and a wide disparity separates the poorer Muslims from Hindus at the upper end of the SLI spectrum.

Undoubtedly, the Scheduled Castes are worse off. Large sections of them are uniformly disadvantaged and deprived. Even 50 years after independence they are the poorest on most social and economic indicators. Therefore, when we think of disadvantage and deprivation we continue to think of the Scheduled Castes and Tribes, but the MWS shows that Muslims are only slightly better off than the Scheduled Castes. Thanks to reservation policies, the educational status and job opportunities of the Scheduled Castes and Tribes has registered a significant improvement. Any analysis of socio-economic status and the influence of jobs and occupations on status must take into account the effects of reservation in public sector jobs in offsetting some of the disadvantage that deprived groups may face in salaried employment. Recent comparative studies have emphasized the acute inter-group disparities and inequalities in access to political and economic resources: for instance, the NCAER survey of socio-economic status (rural) notes that Scheduled Castes and Tribes are the poorest, and Muslims are only next to them.[12] The overlap between particular social groups and the category of the poor is obvious. Yet, the economic and social vulnerability of Muslims is not well documented or acknowledged, let alone addressed.

Three key factors contribute to the low socio-economic status of Muslims: educational attainment; occupational profile; the concentration of large proportions of Muslims in the economically and socially backward regions of the country—a point stressed by the

National Commission on Minorities (NCM) which notes that 'a rather alarming percentage of the minority, particularly the poorer section among Muslims, live in these states'.

Inequalities in education are important, as these are central to the reproduction of inequalities in life chances. In this context, the low levels of education needs no underscoring. The government too has recognized the Muslims as an educationally backward community, and this is partly responsible for the under-representation of Muslims in public employment. The NCM Report, 1998–9, notes that: 'The enormous Muslim population of India is terribly under-represented in all public services both at the national and state levels. Their presence in the general education institutions of the country is also much below their population ratio—and is often found to be nil. Educational backwardness is both the main cause and the inevitable effect of under-representation of Muslims in public employment and resources generating bodies.'

The MWS occupational distribution demonstrates that the bulk of the Muslims are absent from the wealth-creating occupations. Occupations at the top end of the earnings spectrum (large business, professionals) are more or less confined to the Hindu upper castes. Muslims in urban areas are at a distinct disadvantage in formal jobs; in fact, their overall exclusion from the formal job market is conspicuous. Recent empirical studies have confirmed that the Muslim share in regular worker category and regular wage-salary occupations in the organized sector is minimal as opposed to other communities.[13] For instance, the NSS 50th Round shows that though Muslims comprise 10 per cent of the sample, they make up 17 per cent of the non-farm self-employed. By contrast, the Scheduled Castes and Tribes are proportionately fewer in numbers in this category. Muslims conversely are more likely to be self-employed and under-represented in regular salaried work in the government sector. These latter types of jobs comprise principally teachers, clerks, security personnel, and office attendants, which are not necessarily high status occupations, but the lower middle classes including Muslims desire these jobs. Thus, the concentration of Muslims in self-employment is not simply because of their preference for self-employment, but it could be a means to circumvent the disadvantage they face in the formal job market.[14] Self-employed Muslims predominantly are tailors, weavers, transport workers, car mechanics, rickshaw pullers, carpenters and masons, etc.

Horizontal inequalities typically translate into disadvantage for minorities. Other groups in Indian society, viz. Scheduled Castes and Tribes have to countenance discrimination and disadvantage; however, as pointed out earlier, reservations appear to mediate the disadvantage for Scheduled Caste and Tribe men.[15] On the other hand, whether Muslims are discriminated against or not in public employment is not documented, although the writings of Muslim scholars and intellectuals put emphasis on discrimination against them in formal jobs, giving rise to a push out of formal employment. In any event, very little effort is made to further their public employment even as there is a strong opposition to the demand for reservation of jobs for Muslims.[16] Also no serious effort to implement the provision for special consideration to be given to minorities in public appointments under the 15-point programme of the Union Ministry of Welfare has ever been properly implemented.

Finally, the accessibility to economic opportunities varies from region to region. There are important regional differences between states in terms of organization of agriculture, the level and extent of economic and industrial development, and employment opportunities. These differences may then be reflected in variations in the nature of the regimes, the character and extent of political mobilization, organization of civil society, which in turn are radically influenced by caste and communal politics. These social and political differences may well exercise a substantial impact on group disparities and the position of Muslims. From the foregoing discussion, it is clear that the major factors explaining group inequalities are structural and influenced by the socio-political context of different regions.

In the southern states, the status of Muslims is generally better. In Kerala, for example, Muslims are relatively better off: Gulf employment, reservation in education, and higher educational attainment has contributed to this. In Karnataka too, they have experienced modest success in business and trade. In western India, the Bohra, Khoja, and Memon communities continue to play trading and mercantile roles. Though still under-represented in the professions and in private sector and government employment, they have made their mark in textile, transport, and petty trading and shopkeeping. In Uttar Pradesh, however, the circumstances of Muslims were adversely affected by the huge migration of middle classes large numbers of professionals, academics, and administrators to Pakistan in the aftermath of Partition. The elimination of Urdu as a language of administration and education further aggravated the problems facing Muslims, particularly for the lower middle classes seeking jobs in government and educational institutions. It deprived them of networks and influence that usually are important ingredients of success in conditions of scarce opportunities. Nevertheless, some Muslims have flourished during the recent decades, owing to the expansion of the tertiary and service sectors in medium-sized urban cities. A new middle class has emerged in several Uttar Pradesh towns in the informal economy, especially small industry. The size of this class expanded in the post-1973 Gulf boom in the wake of changes brought about by large-scale migration of Muslims to the Gulf and the Middle East, that is to say some of this prosperity has come through business and professional links with the Arab world.

In sum, the analysis of socio-economic status indicates the particularly low status of Muslims in the less developed regions. Remedial measures would have to be taken by the state governments to reduce disparities, contingent as they are on the specific regional histories. However, regional variation also suggests that disadvantage may not be endemic to Muslims in India, rather a certain conjuncture of historical and political circumstances could, and do, lead to substantially different outcomes. But in the context of Indian society, incorporation of minorities requires a more liberal and enlightened view of sharing economic and political resources than just a rhetorical emphasis on democracy and development that will accommodate all interests.

Endnotes

1. Amartya Sen, *On Economic Inequality*, Oxford University Press, New Delhi, 1997.
2. The Standard of Living Index is based on *National Family Health Survey 1998-9*.
3. Maximum SLI = 48;
   Minimum SLI = 1;
   Mean SLI = 17.06164;
   Median SLI = 17;
   Mode SLI = 19.
4. The SLI for the five SES categories are as follows:
   (1) 1-8: Low SLI;
   (2) 9-15: Lower middle SLI;
   (3) 16-22: Middle SLI;
   (4) 23-32: Upper middle SLI;
   (5) 32-48: High SLI.

5. All figures reported henceforth are weighted appropriately.

6. This is corroborated by the NCAER rural survey on socio-economic status, which reveals that Scheduled Castes and Scheduled Tribes are the poorest group, with the Muslims only slightly above them.

7. The rural sample does not have any Scheduled Tribes households in the south zone.

8. The NSDP (net state domestic product) for 1998–9 in 1993–4 prices *indicate* relative prosperity or backwardness of states in terms of their domestic product. All figures in rupees. 'Domestic Product of States of India, 1960–1 to 2000–1', *Economic and Political Weekly Research Foundation*, June 2003.

9. N. J. Kurian, 'Widening Regional Disparities in India: Some Indicators', *Economic and Political Weekly*, 35(7), 12 February 2000, pp. 539–41.

10. Ibid., p. 541.

11. Maitreyi Bordia Das, 'Employment and Social Inequality in India: How Much do Caste and Religion Matter', Ph.D. Dissertation submitted to the University of Maryland, USA, 2002, p. 169. (Unpublished)

12. Abusaleh Shariff, *India Human Development Report: A Profile of Indian States in the 1990s*, Oxford University Press, New Delhi, 1999.

13. Maitreyi Bordia Das, 'Employment and Social Inequality in India', p. 254.

14. Abusaleh Shariff, 'Socio-economic and Demographic Differentials between Hindus and Muslims in India', *Economic and Political Weekly*, 30(46), 18 November 1995, p. 2948.

15. The *Human Development Report 2000* observes that: 'The Achilles heel of majoritarian democracies: the exclusion and marginalization of minorities. The scale and extent of discrimination differ, but the histories of India, Israel, Nigeria, Spain, Sri Lanka, Turkey, Uganda, the United Kingdom, the United States, to name a few, show that minorities suffer serious discrimination in several countries, including India.' UNDP, *Human Development Report 2000*, Oxford University Press, New Delhi, 2000.

16. Naseem Zaidi, 'Muslims in Public Service', *Economic and Political Weekly*, 36(38), 22 September 2001, pp. 3592–5.

2
Education

As far back as 50 years, the Constitution of India promised to provide universal education to all children up to the age of 14 years. This goal was to be achieved by 1960. While considerable progress has been made in this regard in the decade of the 1990s, much still remains to be done for girls' education.[1] Enrolment rates at the primary level have risen considerably, but many of the students who enrol drop out and only a very small number manage to get beyond the primary stage. Gender inequality in education is one important aspect of educational disparity. Inequality and differences between communities is another critical aspect of this broader phenomenon of disparity in India. Though the Census reports remain silent on the educational status of Muslims, it is well known that the literacy and educational levels of Muslims is below the national average.[2] Even so, the inter-community disparity has not received the attention it deserves in the studies of educational impoverishment, which for the most part focus on Scheduled Castes, women, and the poor, with the latter two seldom being disaggregated by religious community. Inter-group disparity remains significant despite the acknowledgment by the National Policy of Education (1986) that the central issue was the 'removal of disparities and to equalize educational opportunity by attending to the specific needs of those who have been denied equality so far'. Notwithstanding rapid improvements, the overwhelming reality is the persistence of inter-group disparity in educational attainments and pockets of persistent educational backwardness. In this scenario, the educational backwardness of Muslim women is a matter of particular concern, especially the high drop-out rate, resulting in substantially fewer proportions of them managing to complete high school, and even less availing of higher education. Not surprisingly, Muslim women account for the lowest levels of educational attainment.

This chapter reports trends in literacy, enrolment, educational attainment, and most important, factors and attitudes responsible for low schooling and the high level of drop-outs. To assess enrolment, we asked: Have you ever attended school? Which type of school have you attended? To ascertain the educational level of the respondent, we asked a range of questions: What is the highest grade completed and are you currently studying? To understand the high drop-out rate of Muslim responderts, we asked the following set of questions on reasons for dropping out and attitudes to schooling: Why did you not continue further studies? What obstacles did you overcome to continue your schooling? Up to what standards should girls and boys study? Should girls be sent to co-educational schools and if yes, up to what standard?

We explore some of these issues to understand how and why Muslim women fail to gain access to or benefit from the education available. What are the principal reasons for their low educational attainment? Is it that disadvantaged groups, such as Muslims, do not care for schooling? Or do underlying socio-economic reasons constrain them? Finally, are there gender biases that restrict the educational progress of Muslim women?

Literacy Levels

The MWS reports a high level of illiteracy (57.55 per cent). The average conceals major differences in literacy rate across communities, castes, and regions. Close to 60 per cent Muslim respondents self-report themselves to be illiterate, lower than the Scheduled Castes and Tribes' proportion, but slightly higher than that for the OBCs (see Table 2.1).

TABLE 2.1
Women's Education Level by Community

Community	1	2	3	4	5	6
SC	68.79	0.93	6.47	12.36	7.19	4.25
ST	71.73	0.00	9.45	8.46	8.99	1.37
OBC	56.63	0.93	6.71	17.96	12.34	5.43
Others	36.32	0.56	7.42	27.15	16.87	11.68
Muslim	57.66	1.80	10.51	16.75	9.71	3.56
Total	57.55	1.80	7.43	17.27	11.08	5.74

Note: 1–Illiterate; 2–Non-formal; 3–Primary; 4–Middle; 5–Secondary and higher secondary; 6–Graduate and above.

Rural illiteracy rates are higher. The proportion of Muslim respondents who are illiterate is substantially higher for the rural north than for all India—84 per cent report themselves to be illiterate in the rural north (see Table 2.2). At one end is the rural north with Muslim respondents reporting near universal illiteracy, and at the other end is the urban south (see Table 2.5) with only 22.14 per cent illiterate Muslim women; that is to say, the percentage of literate Muslim women in the urban south is nearly four times more than that in the rural north. In the north, the overall illiteracy is significantly lower in urban areas (see Table 2.3) (48 per cent), but the community differences are significant, with a striking disparity between Muslims (75 per cent) and upper castes (26 per cent); that is, the percentage of illiterate Muslim women in the rural south is three times more than that of the upper castes and remains significantly behind the proportion for the Scheduled Castes (65 per cent). Interestingly, the rural–urban distribution in the south is the same for Muslim respondents and, more important, unlike the rural north, Muslim respondents (22 per cent) in the rural south (see Table 2.4) report significantly lower illiteracy levels than the Scheduled Castes (47 per cent), but in the urban areas they have a higher illiteracy rate than the Scheduled Castes. Patterns of illiteracy in the rural east (see Table 2.6) and west (see Table 2.8) are similar to the national average. Significantly in the rural east, Scheduled Tribes report the highest illiteracy levels, followed by Muslims and Scheduled Castes, while the Scheduled Tribes report the highest illiteracy levels in the rural west followed by Scheduled Castes and Muslims. In the rural north, the lowest illiteracy figures are reported by upper caste Hindu women, followed by OBCs and Muslims—a major reversal from the trends in other parts of the country. While the percentage of illiterate women is higher in the urban west zone than in the urban south, the relative positions of the communities in the latter are more in line with the all-India trends. These trends indicate major regional variations in illiteracy patterns, with the south zone on the whole reporting high literacy for Muslim respondents. Furthermore, the high levels of illiteracy of Muslim women in the north zone indicates the failure of government policy on adult literacy as well as mass literacy campaigns supported by the Central government both financially and at the policy level.

School Enrolment and Educational Attainment

The MWS indicates that Muslim girls' schooling is poor. The findings of the MWS are revealing, though not surprising. Two important facts

TABLE 2.2
Regional Distribution of Women's Education Level: Rural North

Community	1	2	3	4	5	6
SC	88.06	1.00	1.99	4.98	1.99	1.99
ST	88.89	0.00	0.00	11.11	0.00	0.00
OBC	82.72	0.00	1.57	10.47	2.09	3.14
Others	58.62	0.00	3.45	17.24	10.34	10.34
Muslim	83.58	3.02	2.35	4.58	4.25	2.23
Total	82.29	0.71	2.00	8.46	3.18	3.35

TABLE 2.3
Regional Distribution of Women's Education Level: Urban North

Community	1	2	3	4	5	6
SC	65.57	1.64	4.10	12.30	9.02	7.38
ST	85.71	0.00	0.00	14.29	0.00	0.00
OBC	51.14	0.76	4.92	18.18	11.36	13.64
Others	25.26	1.05	3.16	12.11	21.58	36.84
Muslim	74.36	2.74	2.57	4.56	6.97	8.80
Total	49.37	1.22	3.94	13.74	13.25	18.47

TABLE 2.4
Regional Distribution of Women's Education Level: Rural South

Community	1	2	3	4	5	6
SC	46.88	3.12	12.50	18.75	12.50	6.25
ST						
OBC	24.66	1.37	16.44	30.14	23.29	4.11
Others	20.00	0.00	5.00	40.00	25.00	10.00
Muslim	23.64	0.70	14.01	39.23	18.21	4.20
Total	29.07	1.52	13.64	29.73	20.57	5.48

TABLE 2.5
Regional Distribution of Women's Education Level: Urban South

Community	1	2	3	4	5	6
SC	17.74	1.61	8.06	22.58	33.87	16.13
ST	14.29	0.00	14.29	28.57	42.86	0.00
OBC	19.42	0.00	9.35	29.5	31.65	10.07
Others	15.62	0.00	3.12	28.12	34.38	18.75
Muslim	22.14	1.04	11.02	35.85	20.83	9.11
Total	19.09	0.54	8.87	29.16	30.51	11.83

TABLE 2.6
Regional Distribution of Women's Education Level: Rural East

Community	1	2	3	4	5	6
SC	45.07	0.00	16.09	25.35	8.45	4.23
ST	65.85	0.00	14.63	4.88	12.20	2.44
OBC`	22.73	4.55	13.64	22.73	36.36	0.00
Others	35.38	1.54	15.38	36.92	10.77	0.00
Muslim	50.10	0.82	19.51	18.58	9.65	1.33
Total	45.12	0.96	16.44	23.30	12.32	1.86

TABLE 2.7
Regional Distribution of Women's Education Level: Urban East

Community	1	2	3	4	5	6
SC	34.38	0.00	20.31	21.88	17.19	6.25
ST	33.33	0.00	33.33	33.33	0.00	0.00
OBC	20.00	2.50	12.50	32.50	17.50	15.00
Others	23.76	0.00	8.91	25.74	28.71	12.87
Muslim	41.72	1.45	16.26	25.46	10.84	4.26
Total	28.60	0.61	14.09	25.98	20.73	10.00

TABLE 2.8
Regional Distribution of Women's Education Level: Rural West

Community	1	2	3	4	5	6
SC	63.64	0.00	0.00	13.64	18.18	4.55
ST	87.50	0.00	0.00	12.50	0.00	0.00
OBC	56.25	3.12	9.38	15.62	12.50	3.12
Others	37.50	0.00	0.00	43.75	12.50	6.25
Muslim	56.66	1.45	14.29	20.10	5.08	2.42
Total	60.27	1.18	4.05	19.78	11.29	3.43

TABLE 2.9
Regional Distribution of Women's Education Level: Urban West

Community	1	2	3	4	5	6
SC	40.91	0.00	0.09	25.00	0.09	15.91
ST	42.86	0.00	14.29	0.00	42.86	0.00
OBC	36.76	2.94	8.82	22.06	16.18	13.24
Others	23.94	0.00	9.86	25.35	26.76	14.08
Muslim	34.88	1.79	8.75	28.77	18.65	7.17
Total	33.48	1.19	9.34	24.22	19.32	12.45

Note: (Tables 2.2 to 2.9) 1–Illiterate; 2–Non-formal; 3–Primary; 4–Middle; 5–Secondary and higher secondary; 6–Graduate and above.

stand out. One is the low levels of schooling and higher education of Muslim respondents, and the other is the large inter-zonal variation on most indicators of educational progress. All in all, the constitutional goal of 8 years of education remains unreachable for a large section of Muslim women.

The enrolment rate of Muslims is 40.66 per cent, which is higher than that of Scheduled Castes (30.28 per cent), but much below the upper castes (63.2 per cent). In other words, nearly 60 per cent of the Muslim respondents never attended school (see Table 2.10). In the rural north (13.52 per cent), a very small proportion and less than a quarter in urban areas (23.15 per cent), report that they have at some stage attended school, while the opposite is evident in the south where over three-quarters in the rural (75 per cent) and urban (77.26 per cent) areas report having attended school. The urban west comes next in terms of proportion of Muslim respondents ever having attended school, while the north zone overall reports lower figures than those for all-India.

TABLE 2.10
Regional Distribution of Women having Ever Attended School (%)
by Community

Community	All India	Rural north	Rural south	Rural east	Rural west	Urban north	Urban south	Urban east	Urban west
SC	30.28	10.95	50.00	54.93	36.36	32.79	80.65	65.62	59.09
ST	28.27	11.11	n.a.	34.15	12.50	14.29	85.71	66.67	57.14
OBC	42.62	17.28	73.97	72.73	40.62	48.86	81.29	80.00	60.29
Others	63.20	41.38	80.00	63.08	62.50	73.68	84.38	77.23	76.06
Muslim	40.66	13.52	75.48	49.18	41.89	23.15	77.26	56.82	63.44

The south on the whole reports a high proportion of women who have ever attended school, and this to be sure has a positive impact on the Muslim educational profile, but only in relative terms. Muslim women still report numbers that are lower than those, for instance, for Scheduled Castes in urban areas. The urban west comes next in terms of respondents ever having attended school, while the north zone generally reports lower figures than those for all-India. Interestingly, the relative position of communities in the urban north is similar to that in the rural north. The major difference in the two zones is that for all communities, the education profile is considerably better for urban areas, and this fits in with the rural–urban disparity in the country as a whole. Broadly speaking, the disparity between upper caste Hindus and Muslims is striking: for the former, all regions except the rural north report proportions higher than the all-India average. Distribution of respondents by socio-economic status reveals the great class divide in schooling. Evidence presented in Table 2.11 shows that the ;ES of households most certainly affects the prospect of school enrolment; that is, the poorer the household, the less likely that they will be able to send their children to school—in contrast to the high SES household where three-quarters have attended school, only 16.11 per cent of low SES households ever attended school. In the urban north, a minuscule percentage of respondents (3.87 rural and 9.17 urban) from the low SES category have attended school. With the exception of the south, the all-India pattern in ever-attended school is repeated in all the three zones. In both the urban and rural south, SES is not a significant factor, but is apparently an important constraint in other parts.

TABLE 2.11
Regional Distribution of Women having Ever Attended School (%) by SES

Community	All India	Rural north	Rural south	Rural east	Rural west	Urban north	Urban south	Urban east	Urban west
Low	16.11	3.87	73.41	28.63	0.57	9.17	82.93	50.22	25.13
Lower middle	27.74	11.91	65.63	35.27	23.58	18.15	66.17	48.78	51.4
Middle	42.86	17.35	65.7	58.58	40.98	30.55	75.5	62.09	70.06
Upper middle	56.83	24.51	71.5	76.95	68.12	58.13	81.18	77.57	59.32
High	70.13	47.93	79.21	90.88	68.12	76.62	87.69	91.1	83.14

Among those who ever-attended school, 98 per cent went to government or private schools, while less than 2 per cent attended a madrassa. By region, slightly more respondents attended a madrassa in the north zone, the majority of them coming from poor households. The same pattern is repeated in the regions, that is mainly poor women go to a madrassas. Fewer respondents go to a madrassa in urban areas, perhaps because of the greater availability and accessibility of schools in towns and cities. In rural areas or semi-urban locations, madrassas are sometimes located in close proximity to residential areas, which makes them an attractive and viable option for women.

The trends reported in Tables 2.2–2.11 underline the relative educational deprivation of Muslims in the more progressive regions and their absolute deprivation in the less developed regions. The best educational outcomes (substantially higher than national averages) are reported in the urban south, followed by the rural south. While Muslims have done comparatively well in the urban south, note that in relation to other groups, they are worse off.

Assessing the status of women by their level of education: classified as illiterate (which we have discussed in the preceding section), primary, middle, higher secondary, and graduate and above, we find that the proportion of *Muslims ever enrolled in school attaining these levels is very low, even lower than the proportion for the OBCs, Scheduled Tribes, and upper castes. Less than 17 per cent Muslim respondents (ever enrolled in schools) completed eight years of schooling and less than 10 per cent completed higher secondary, which is below the national average. There are noticeable zonal variations in the educational attainment of the north and south, even while in the north and the east the rural–urban difference is insignificant; that is, urban location, which has a generally positive association with female education, has no great impact on Muslim women's educational attainment, pointing once again to the poverty of Muslim households as the foremost constraint on access to education, notwithstanding the noticeably greater educational opportunities in urban areas. Not surprisingly, the educational status in the north is abysmal, resulting in substantially smaller numbers in middle school and higher secondary schooling (4.58 per cent and 4.75 per cent, respectively) as opposed to the national average (17.86 per cent and 11.42 per cent, respectively).

Another noteworthy finding is that as we move up the education ladder, there is a significant drop in the proportion of Muslim women in higher education (3.56 per cent), even lower than that of the Scheduled Castes (4.25 per cent), an aspect that has gone unnoticed in the huge body of literature on female education (evidently the Scheduled Castes have managed to gain entry into higher education through reservations). However, in this bleak scenario there are some interesting and surprising facts. As we have seen, Muslims in the urban north have extremely high illiteracy levels (74.36 per cent) and very low proportions in higher secondary level education (6.97 per cent), but the higher education percentage rises to 8.80 per cent, which is only a little less than in the south (9.11 per cent), and indeed exceeding that in the urban east and west. This suggests that despite a small base of literacy in the north, a sizeable proportion manage to go on to higher education.

The rural south reports a substantially lower proportion in the graduate and above category than in the urban north. This is true for all communities, suggesting that here too the rural–urban divide is being reflected. The distribution at the upper end of the spectrum in the urban south is substantially better than in the rural: close to 60 per cent of Muslim respondents are in middle school and above. However, in relation to other groups, the Muslim community reports lower percentages in the higher education spectrum. The distribution in the rural east is better than in the rural north in terms of educational outcomes for respondents of all communities. It is better too in comparison to the all-India distribution, except that the figures for Muslim respondents at the higher end are worse: only 1.33 per cent Muslim respondents are in the graduate and above category, which is even lower than the rural north. The distribution in rural west for Muslims is fairly similar to the all-India average. In the urban west, however, the picture is substantially different. In the graduate and above category, the highest percentages for Muslims are reported in the urban south, followed by the urban west.

Average Years of Schooling

Efforts to address the educational deprivation of women have, in general, focused on improving enrolments at the primary and secondary levels. Yet the constitutional goal of 8 years of schooling remains a distant dream. The average number of years of schooling that women have received is very low: Muslim women 2.7 years and Hindus 3.8 years (see Table 2.12). For Muslims, the average years of schooling is lower than even the Scheduled Castes at the national and regional levels.[3] The differences between zones are considerable, indicating a major gap in schooling achievements and underscoring the huge differences between the north and south, with the north reporting

TABLE 2.12
Average Years of Schooling

Regions	Muslim	Hindu	Total
North	1.6	2.7	2.2
East	2.7	3.7	3.3
South	5.0	5.5	5.4
West	3.3	3.8	3.7
All-India	2.7	3.8	3.4

half the number of years of schooling. Overall, the low average number of years of schooling of Muslim women (2.7 years) indicates a high drop-out rate for them.

Obstacles to Schooling

Women who completed their studies were asked whether they faced any problems, which they had overcome in order to continue their studies. Figure 2.1 documents the affirmative answers to this question. The first point to reiterate, of course, is that this is applicable only to respondents who *continued* their studies. In other words, obstacles that prevented women from continuing their education are not being discussed here. Second, the subsequent charts are based only on the 'yes' responses in Figure 2.1. Thus, 41 per cent of Muslim respondents report themselves to have ever attended school (see Table 2.10); of these, 26 per cent felt that they had to overcome obstacles in order to continue. Further charts are based on their responses (to continue with the same example for Muslim respondents, all-India, this would mean roughly one-tenth of all Muslim respondents). Looking at the all-India picture and regional variations for the 'yes' responses (on the whole), a slightly higher proportion of Muslim respondents than Hindu reported that they had faced obstacles. The two exceptions to

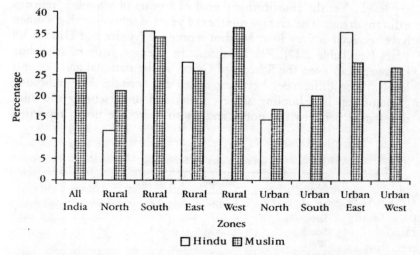

FIGURE 2.1: Percentage of Women who Overcame Obstacles in Education

this are the rural north, where a significantly larger proportion of Muslim respondents faced obstacles, and the urban east, where a significantly larger number of Hindu respondents than Muslim faced obstacles, a pattern contrary to that in the rest of the country.

Those who answered 'yes' to the above question were further asked what obstacles they overcame, and were asked to choose *one* of the following: financial constraints, death of father/mother, and parental opposition. For both Hindus and Muslims (see Figure 2.2), financial constraints seem to outweigh parental opposition as women's chief obstacle to continuing studies; for the country as a whole, the percentages too are very similar for both. In the north zone, financial constraints are much more important for Muslims (proportions similar to all-India) than they are for Hindus, underlining once again the poverty of Muslim households in this part of the country, and this provides the most powerful explanation for the poor levels of Muslim women's education in the north.

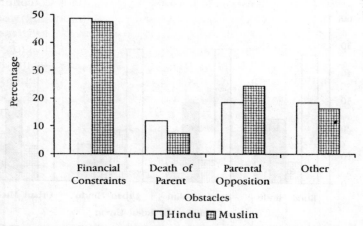

FIGURE 2.2: Obstacles Overcome to Continue Studies

As Figure 2.3 shows, for the rural north, parental opposition is as important as financial constraints for Muslims, but not so in urban areas. Again, for the south zone, financial constraints outweigh parental opposition for Muslims, but this seems to be equally true for Hindus. Note that for the south zone, the percentage of respondents reporting financial constraints is higher for Hindus than for Muslims, and this pattern is replicated in the east. The west (see Figure 2.4),

58 □ *Unequal Citizens*

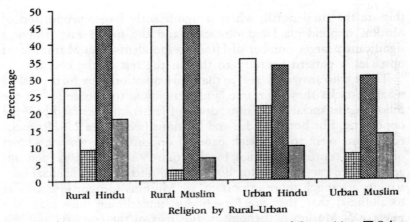

FIGURE 2.3: Obstacles Overcome to Continue Studies: North

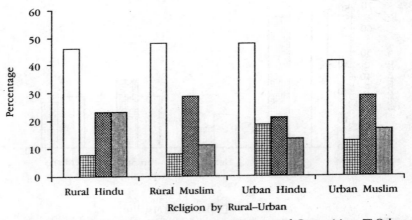

FIGURE 2.4: Obstacles Overcome to Continue Studies: West

in keeping with the all-India pattern, reported that women had to overcome financial constraints rather than parental opposition in both communities in order to continue their studies.

The potential for educational development varies from class to class. As one climbs up the socio-economic ladder, the percentage

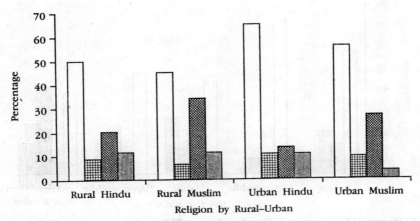

FIGURE 2.5: Obstacles Overcome to Continue Studies: South

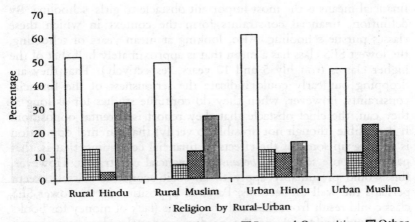

FIGURE 2.6: Obstacles Overcome to Continue Studies: East

of women who face financial constraints declines, while those who report parental opposition increases (see Figure 2.7). For all the regions, low, lower-middle, and middle socio-economic categories overwhelmingly report financial constraints as the principal obstacle to continuing their studies. This clearly indicates that inadequate

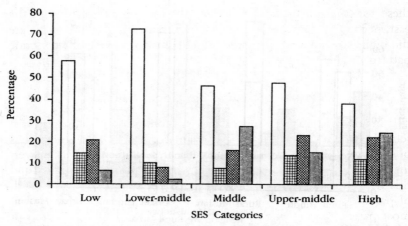

□ Financial Constraints ⊞ Death of Parent ▓ Parental Opposition ▥ Other

FIGURE 2.7: SES Versus Obstacles Overcome to Continue Studies: All-India

financial means is the most important obstacle to girls' schooling. By definition, financial constraints form the context in which these classes pursue schooling. Also, looking at mean years of schooling, the lowest SES class has a mean that is approximately half that of the higher classes (roughly 5 and 10 years, respectively). That they are dropping out early could indicate the seriousness of the financial constraints, however, when they do continue studies for as long as they can, the chief obstacle that they report is parental opposition. It is possible (though not possible to verify) that parental opposition is picking up some of the effects of financial constraint; that is, that parents oppose schooling *because* of financial constraints. However, this would presumably apply to all socio-economic classes, except perhaps the well off sections. Parental opposition in the lower SES class could result from financial constraints (lack of money for books and school uniforms), or the need to undertake domestic chores, or work to support the family. The important question here is whether male children experience the same kind of constraints, whether financial or domestic or socio-cultural, in their pursuit of an education.

Parental opposition is most marked in the north zone, followed by the east. Financial constraints seem to be more important than parental opposition for the south and west for all classes, i.e. *within*

these zones, the percentage reporting the former are greater. For the ·
east, percentages reporting financial constraints in absolute terms are
the highest in the country, which conforms to the overall economic
pattern of the region.

Attitudes to Co-educational Schools

The majority of our respondents have no objection to co-educational
schools, which indicates that they want formal schooling regardless
of the type of school. The all-India percentage of respondents answering in the affirmative varies between 58 and 67 percentage points, and
this rises going up on the SES scale. This finding questions the myth
of parental indifference to schooling and the widespread belief that
most parents prefer single-sex schools and if such schools were not
available they would not send their girls to school. However, there
is no doubt that attitudinally the rural north appears to be the most
conservative, as its percentage of respondents favouring co-education
for all SES categories is lower than the all-India percentages. Moreover,
the trend rising with a rise in SES is not seen in this region; that is,
low, upper middle, and high SES categories have similar percentages,
with lower middle and middle reporting lower percentages, which
means that regardless of class, concerns exist across the board about
co-education schooling for girls. This is an indication of the overall
conservatism of this region, which might point to another important
reason for low schooling levels, that is, a preference for single-
sex schools. This would mean that either the government has to
provide more girls' schools or families would need to invest in private
single-sex schools, as there are very few government girls' schools in
this zone compared to the south zone where there are many more
government or government aided girls' schools. The urban west has
the highest percentage of respondents favouring co-educational schooling. The outlier here is the high SES category, which has the lowest
percentage within the region. This is followed by the urban south and
then by the urban east, both of which have higher than all-India
percentages for all SES categories (see Figure 2.8).

The MWS does, however, reveal a significant generational difference in attitudes towards co-education. The all-India distribution of
respondents by age group and religion is given in Figure 2.9.

The respondents' age plays a major role in the formation of
attitudes with regard to issues such as co-education, indicating an

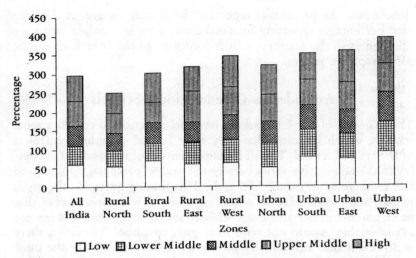

FIGURE 2.8: Attitude about Sending Girls to Co-ed Schools by SES: % of Women Saying Yes

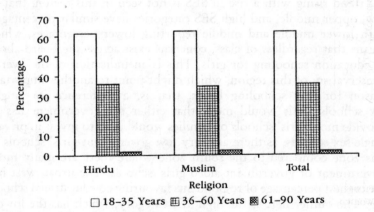

FIGURE 2.9: Distribution of Women by Age-group and Religion

intergenerational shift. For both communities, it is a majority young sample (over 60 per cent of the respondents from both communities are in the 18–35 years age group). Typically, a greater number of younger respondents (aged between 18 and 35 years) favoured sending girls to co-ed schools than the oldest (60 years and above). Given that our data are drawn from one point in time, we cannot accurately .

trace the *change* in attitudes, but even in a static analysis, there is a linear progression across the age-scale of respondents in favour of girls being sent to co-ed schools, as indicated by a gap of over 20 percentage points between the young and the old. The relative conservatism of the rural north is reflected here too: the percentages are lower for all age groups. This again follows the regional pattern discussed earlier, in that liberal attitudes are more common in the south and west, than in the north and east. In keeping with the pattern seen elsewhere, south and west are more open to co-education, generally speaking, than the north and east (see Figure 2.10). The urban–rural interaction is more complicated, in that it varies by region, precluding generalizations that rural India as a whole is less liberal than urban India.

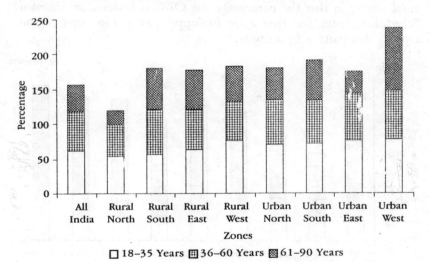

FIGURE 2.10: Attitude about Sending Girls to Co-ed Schools by Age-group: % of Women Saying Yes

The attitudes to co-education vary significantly by community. When asked about whether a girl should be sent to a co-educational school, a significantly greater proportion of Muslims (compared to Hindus) replied in the negative, ranging from a maximum of nearly 60 per cent in the rural north zone to a minimum of 26 per cent in the rural west. At the all-India level, Scheduled Tribes report the lowest percentages in favour of co-ed schools, followed by Muslims, Scheduled Castes, OBC, and then upper castes. In interpreting these results, it should be kept in mind that the sample does not include regions that are predominantly tribal. Also, in the rest of the country, the tribal percentages (except for the rural north) are much higher than the all-India average. For Muslims, the strongest opposition to co-education is in the north, and it is this region that depresses the overall percentage for them in this regard. The highest proportions supporting co-education are reported in the west zone (rural and urban are very close to each other). Surprisingly, the next best responses are from the east, rather than the south (see Figure 2.11). Among Hindus, the Sanskritization hypothesis (belief in greater constraints on women's public visibility as caste status rises) seems to be working in the rural north across the spectrum. There is weaker evidence for this in the rural south, in that the percentage for OBC is lower than that for Scheduled Castes, but rises again for upper castes. No other region reports this pattern in attitudes.

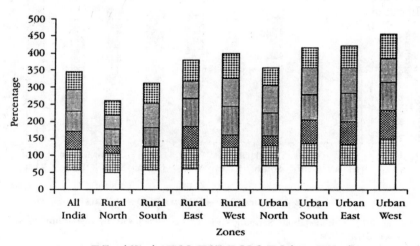

☐ Total Hindu ⊞ SC ▨ ST ▥ OBC ▤ Others ⊞ Muslim

FIGURE 2.11: Attitude about Sending Girls to Co-ed Schools by SES: % of Women Saying Yes

In itself, a preference for sex-segregated education need not necessarily be considered a disadvantage, or a negative community-specific trait. However, given that most girls and boys from poor families go to government schools, which are often co-educational, this simple fact can act as a major constraint. Needless to say, it is also gender specific because it almost never operates in the case of young boys who will be sent to co-educational schools or private schools.

Figure 2.12 captures the differential attitude of Hindus and Muslims on another important aspect of gender difference. The respondents were asked: up to what grade should girls/boys study? The figure reports responses for certain landmark years: Class 8, 10, 12, Bachelor's degree, and Master's degree. Forty-six per cent Muslims and 41 per cent Hindus maintained that girls should be educated up to high school, while another 16 per cent Muslims and 20 per cent Hindus favoured graduation. However, both Hindus and Muslims favour significantly more higher education for boys than for girls. In this respect, gender clearly outweighs community differences. For a given level of education, the gap between those favouring that level for girls and an equivalent proportion for boys seems to be the same across communities. However, there is a significant difference between Hindus and Muslims who want that level of education for girls. Also,

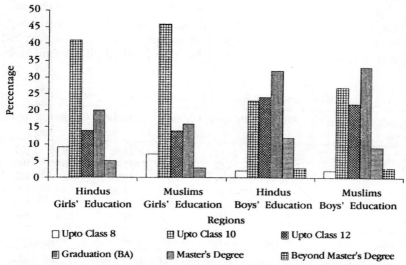

Note: The totals do not add up to 100 per cent as this table reports only selected landmark years in school/college education in India. Thus, for instance, there may be 0.67 per cent respondents who believe that girls should be educated up to Class 4, say, but in order to focus attention on the landmark years, these details are not reported.

FIGURE 2.12: Differences Among Religious Communities in Attitude Towards Girls' and Boys' Education

the proportion for boys is higher, as stated earlier, but the difference in the two proportions (for boys and girls) is similar across communities. This seems to suggest that the gender bias towards boys is independent of religion and parental commitment to female education which is still inadequate in some regions. Attitudes towards female education are strongly influenced by cultural norms and traditions. The low value attached to female education is linked with deep-seated gender relations and the division of labour, which tends to reduce the perceived benefits of such education. The norm of patrilocal exogamy and the practice of dowry have the effect of further discouraging parents from investing in female education.[4] Given these links, which are especially strong in the north, it is hardly surprising that female education has made slow progress in this region.

The education level of their parents and husbands influences educational opportunities for women. However, note the way in which the categories are defined for husband and wife, the option for non-formal education does not exist for husbands. Thus, there are six education categories for the wife and only five for the husband. Also, to reiterate a minor technical point: this is documented only for married women; thus, this chart is not strictly comparable to Table 2.1, which documents the education level of all respondents.

TABLE 2.13
Wife's Education Versus Husband's Education Level

Wife's education level	Illiterate	Primary	Middle	Secondary	Graduate +	Total
1	56.34	15.12	12.16	14.50	1.87	100
2	32.92	14.17	13.85	38.43	0.63	100
3	24.48	35.14	21.21	18.51	0.66	100
4	22.54	16.42	22.50	31.07	7.46	100
5	17.39	7.23	12.90	43.88	18.60	100
6	25.94	0.16	0.89	31.76	41.25	100
Total	41.42	15.10	14.14	22.35	7.00	100

Note: 1–Illiterate; 2–Non-formal; 3–Primary; 4–Middle; 5–Secondary and higher secondary; 6–Graduate and above.

Table 2.13 captures the impact of husband's education: 56 per cent of illiterate women also have illiterate husbands. In general, especially at the two ends of the spectrum, there seems to be a noticeable correspondence between the wife's education level and her husband's.

Notice, *however, that as many as 26 per cent of educated Muslim women have illiterate husbands,* which indicates the high level of school drop-out among Muslim boys and the generally low levels of Muslim male education, which can also act as a hindrance to girls' education. Very often Muslim men limit their education because they are unable to socially leverage it to get jobs. The overall impact of husband's education stands, nevertheless. This is further confirmed by the positive correlation (0.44) between the wife's education level and that of her husband, which is statistically significant. There does not seem to be much regional variation in the correspondence between the husband and wife's education level; what differs is the strength of the correlation between these two variables across the regions. The strongest correlation is found in the rural east (0.54) and the lowest in the urban west (0.28).

Reasons for Dropping Out

The most serious issue affecting basic education of Muslims, other than the significant number who never enrol (more than 60 per cent of respondents in the MWS never enrolled), is the high level of drop-outs. One of the limitations of the MWS data is that it does not report figures or trends on drop-outs. However, the high drop-out rate is obvious from the very small numbers who have completed middle school and higher secondary. Drop-out rates for Muslim respondents are higher, which is why disparities between Muslims and Hindus increase at higher levels of schooling, in contrast to the primary level where the community differences are insignificant.

All those who dropped out of school were asked to specify the reasons for doing so. They were given 15 options and were asked to tick all that were applicable (*not in order of importance*). Thus, most respondents gave multiple responses and, due to the nature of the question, it is not possible to rank the reasons in order of importance for each respondent. However, we can form some idea of relative importance by comparing the frequencies of each response. It is also interesting to test if the difference in frequencies across Hindus and Muslims is statistically significant for a given reason. For example, take the reason that the school is too far away. All those who dropped out of school were asked to specify why this is a problem. The proportion differs between Hindus and Muslims; a chi-square test can be used to ascertain if this difference is statistically significant and thus, to infer whether it would be appropriate to distinguish between the two communities on this basis. The various reasons for dropping out, in terms of their relative importance, are given below.

1. School too far away.
Community difference: insignificant.
Relative importance: insignificant.

2. Transport not available.
Community difference: significant.
Relative importance: marginal.

3. Education not considered necessary.
Community difference: insignificant.
Relative importance: significant.

4. Failed.
Community difference: insignificant.
Relative importance: marginal.

5. Required for household work.
Community difference: significant. This reason seems to be far more important for Hindus than for Muslims.
Relative importance: fairly important.

6. Required for work on farm/family business.
Community difference: insignificant.
Relative importance: marginal.

7. Required for outside work for payment in cash or kind.
Community difference: significant. A significantly greater proportion of Hindus, as against Muslims, cite this as one of the reasons.
Relative importance: marginal.

8. No proper school facilities for girls in the village/locality.
Community difference: insignificant.
Relative importance: fairly important.

9. Financial constraints.
Community difference: insignificant.
Relative importance: very important.

10. Family objected.
Community difference: highly significant. A far greater proportion of Muslims cite this as one of the reasons for dropping out.
Relative importance: less than for financial constraints, but very important.

11. Death of father/mother.
Community difference: insignificant.
Relative importance: fairly significant.

12. Not interested in studies.
Community difference: significant. A higher proportion of Hindus
cite this as one of the reasons.
Relative importance: important, though not particularly.

13. Married off.
Community difference: insignificant.
Relative importance: very important.

14. Attained puberty.
Community difference: insignificant.
Relative importance: minor, but it is possible that 'married off' is
picking up the effect of attaining puberty.

15. Required for care of siblings.
Community difference: insignificant.
Relative importance: insignificant.

On analysis, the three most important reasons cited by respondents
are: financial constraints, followed by family objections and marriage.
A much smaller number cited distance from the school, transport
not available, or required for work. In sum, the most important
reasons for all respondents, in order of decreasing frequencies (ap-
proximate), are: financial constraints (36 per cent); married off (22
per cent); family objected (20 per cent); required for household work
(14 per cent); not interested in studies (10 per cent); death of father/
mother (6 per cent); school too far away (7 per cent); and no proper
school facility in village (5 per cent). If we add up all the gender-
specific reasons in this list (no interest in studies, parents' death,
and no proper school apart) they account for *99 per cent* of the total.
The gender bias is startling. For the most part, the pattern of
responses for Hindus and Muslims was broadly similar, apart from
the following: not interested in studies; required for outside work;
and financial constraints. The latter percentage being much higher for
Muslims is a reflection of their low SES; in other words, economic
reasons combined with family objections account for the low enrolment and high drop-out rates of Muslim women. On the whole,
this reasoning is consistent with the grounds provided by nearly all
studies undertaken on the gap in female education. *PROBE*, for

instance, notes that 'schooling is too expensive' was the first among reasons cited by respondents to explain why a child had never been to school. The cash costs of sending a child to school are not insignificant.[5] It also reported that most parents expressed a much stronger interest in their sons' education than their daughters'. Parents are more likely to invest in their sons' education because, if educated, they will have better employment opportunities. They also have higher expectations from their sons than from their daughters. An additional factor impinging on educational progress is the general level of education, especially male education, in their caste or community. Thus, in a community with high levels of male education, educating a daughter up to the primary or even upper primary level may not raise the costs of her marriage, as there will be plenty of better-educated boys.[6] However, in the Muslim community, which has low levels of male education, parents may not be keen about educating girls for fear of not being able to find suitably educated husbands for their daughters. In addition, if marriage costs rise sharply with education, they may be even less inclined to send them to school.

What then accounts for low schooling? Is it low income and poverty or social and cultural norms, or both? What explains the overall low level of women's education? Taking the highest grade completed as the dependent variable, we did a regression with the following independent (explanatory) variables: standard of living index (SLI), rural dummy, Hindu dummy, three zonal dummies (north, south, and west), husband's education, and respondent's age at first marriage. The results indicate that all these factors are significant. They further suggest that, of all these, SLI and husband's education have the strongest positive effects on the highest grade completed by the respondent. The location of women in terms of rural/urban is also important, in that in relation to urban residence, rural women are substantially worse off. Those in the north and south zones do better than those in the east, but the results are not robust for the west zone. The community difference is significant, that is, Hindus in general do better than Muslims, but this effect is less than both SLI and husband's education—the latter can be seen as another dimension of SES not captured by the SLI index as it is constructed here. Age at first marriage, however, has a strong positive effect on the highest grade completed—that is, the higher her age at marriage, the higher the level of a woman's education.

Conclusion

With all the variations in women's education across different levels and regions, one indisputable fact emerges from the MWS: that there are large and systemic differences between groups in terms of educational attainment. The data confirm the disadvantaged educational status of Muslims, even as it provides a more detailed profile of the variations between groups and regions and the reasons for discontinuation of education.

The general picture emerging is one of modest educational achievements, marked by an appallingly high level of illiteracy and enormous inequalities in schooling between different groups and regions. Overall, 43 per cent Muslim respondents were literate, 59 per cent of them had never attended school, which is a very high proportion indeed. Their presence in higher education is minuscule, even lower than that for Scheduled Caste women. Among the literate, Hindu respondents were better educated than Muslims; and among Hindus, upper castes were better educated. Respondents from households with a higher socio-economic status were more educated than those from poor households. Both Hindus and Muslims favour significantly more higher education for boys than for girls.

Enrolling girls in school is only half the battle, because it is meaningful only if they complete the minimum of 8 years of schooling—which requires that their families be able to resist the pressures of income generation and work in the home. Generally, Muslims lag behind in educational attainment, their prospects of going beyond primary rather lower than that of Hindus and completing school even lower. For Muslim women, not being able to enter the schooling system seems to be the first obstacle. Those that do manage entry do not seem to be able to continue schooling, let alone go on to higher education. Education is an essential means for participation in the economy and society, it can mitigate the impact of social inequality; empirical studies have in fact shown higher returns to education for women than men, but only education beyond the junior/middle level enhances economic activity and participation.[7] For economically disadvantaged groups, such as Muslims, education would be the most promising means of upward mobility. However, the prospects of girls from poor families continuing in schools is quite small in comparison to non-poor families who are almost certain to enter school with a good prospect of reaching middle and even higher secondary levels. The noteworthy exception to this vicious cycle of poverty and low educational attainments is the south zone, where women belonging to low socio-economic classes have as good a prospect of school continuation as girls from high socio-economic classes.

Unlike work and employment patterns, which do not vary greatly from region to region, variations in education levels achieved between regions are a striking feature of the education scenario. Both literacy and schooling levels tend to be higher in the south and west than in the north and east, and are more or less the same for both communities in the south and west. The north and east zones of the country draw attention to the lag in educational enrolment attainment; high levels of deprivation define the educational status in the north, where the majority of women, both Muslim and Hindu, do not attend school. As expected, the north performs worse than others on most indicators of educational progress. This is particularly true of respondents in poor households, which means the prospects of rural and urban Muslim women from poor families in the north ever entering schools is small, with even less chance that they would continue schooling beyond primary stage.

The burden of deprivation falls most on rural women and members of low socio-economic status groups. What is more, inequalities produced by community membership, gender, and residence often have common characteristics, resulting in acute deprivation. In the north, rural Muslim and Scheduled Caste women suffer from deprivation of the worst kind. Add to this the low socio-economic status of the households and the disadvantage is total: an unmistakable expression of the huge burden of economic impoverishment on their educational attainments.

One cause of such gaps is that, in many states, public spending on education is much below requirement. In the north, successive governments have given it a low priority in funding allocations. Even though Kerala is not a prosperous state, it is educationally ahead of other parts of the country, due to the availability and accessibility of schools, signifying that even a less prosperous state with appropriate policies and strong political will can overcome hurdles to women's education. While Kerala is spending 6.3 per cent of its gross domestic product (GDP) on education and Tamil Nadu around 4.4 per cent, Uttar Pradesh's ratio is around 3.7 per cent. Over 60 per cent of teachers in Kerala and over 40 over cent primary school teachers in the south zone are women, in contrast to 18 per cent in Uttar Pradesh.

This is the lowest proportion among all Indian states. Furthermore, road transport is reliable and readily available in Kerala enabling female teachers to travel long distances to teach in rural schools.

Despite a growing demand for school education, the state governments in Uttar Pradesh and Bihar have demonstrated little capacity to ensure schooling,[8] resulting in a dramatic growth of private schools, which are more expensive and cannot be afforded by the majority of the poor.[9] In Uttar Pradesh, the critical problem is non-availability of schools and the poor functioning or non-functioning of the schooling system. Schools are either not available or are inaccessible or of poor quality, a problem aggravated by the paucity of resources and of even simple teaching materials, decrepit school buildings, and even lack of basic facilities such as drinking water and toilets, chronic shortage of teachers, lack of accountability of teachers leading to teacher absenteeism, and negligence as politically influential teachers have been more interested in their own financial betterment than the improvement of school facilities.[10] The problem is compounded by the reluctance of parents to send their girls to schools that are far away for fear of their safety. In addition, lack of female teachers, and absence of basic amenities combined are the key factors that hold back women's education in the north.[11]

Two issues follow from these findings. One, there do exist a set of common problems that determine educational progress of women regardless of religion. Second, and more significantly, there are community specific problems: financial constraints, low standard of living, parental objection, and low returns on education that make education less attractive for Muslims. The MWS findings demonstrate that the low socio-economic status of Muslims adversely affects women's education and conversely a higher standard of living and husband's education have the strongest positive effects on the highest grade completed by the respondent.

Specifically, low socio-economic status and financial constraints appear to be the most important factors in hampering access to Muslim women's education, although this invariably constrains women more than men. Many girl children cannot go to school because their parents are too poor to afford the costs of schooling. That they drop out as early as the primary school level could indicate the seriousness of financial constraints; however, when they do continue studies for as long as they can, the chief obstacle is parental opposition. Financial constraints outweigh parental opposition as the principal obstacle to schooling because a high proportion of households lacks the financial means to send children to school and finds it even more difficult to support them through schooling. However, the burden of financial constraints clearly works more against girls' schooling than that of boys, since the opportunity costs of girls' schooling is high—girls perform a larger share of family labour, and therefore its benefits are seen to be negligible compared to the investment made. Not only is education for girls unlinked to future employment, but for the most part it can actually be detrimental to a girl's marriage prospects: parents may thus have to spend twice, first to educate her, and then to marry her off by incurring extra costs. This gap in education and employment opportunities is an important aspect of gender inequality and is also a powerful instrument of perpetuating it. Withdrawing her from school, moreover, enables her time and labour to be utilized within the home, in a way that is never the case with boys. Thus, gender, class inequality, and community biases persist across the board and combine and reinforce one another to put a brake on Muslim women's education, and, consequently, on their overall development and inclusion in the social mainstream.

Endnotes

1. Female literacy rates varied from 20 per cent in Rajasthan and 25 per cent in Uttar Pradesh to 86 per cent in Kerala, reflecting very uneven efforts to expand educational achievements. These literacy rates refer to the age group of 7 years and above and are based on 1991 Census data presented in *Selected Educational Statistics 1998–99*, Ministry of Human Resources and Development, New Delhi, 2000. For a discussion of Census data on female literacy, see Jean Drèze and Amartya Sen, 'Basic Education as a Political Issue', in *idem, India: Development and Participation*, Oxford University Press, New Delhi, 2002.

2. James Massey, *Studies in Educational and Socio-economic Problems of Minorities in India*, Report of the National Commission for Minorities, 1998. Massey notes that the literacy level among Muslims is, on an average, 10 per cent below the national level.

3. The higher average years of schooling reported by MWS compared to PROBE (1.8 years) and *Human Development in South Asia India Human Development Report, A Profile of Indian States in the 1990s*, Abusaleh Shariff, National Council of Applied Economic Research, New Delhi: Oxford University Press, 1999. (1.2 years) could be due to the sampling bias of the MWS which was a 60:40 urban–rural sample. See *Probe Report on Basic Education in India* (PROBE), Oxford University Press, New Delhi, 1999.

4. These cultural norms are discussed in Jean Drèze and Amartya Sen, 'Basic Education as a Political Issue', pp. 161–2.

5. *PROBE*, p. 20. According to *PROBE*, the average cost of sending a child to school works out to Rs 318 per year.

6. *PROBE*, p. 20.

7. Geeta Kingdon and Jeenmol Unni, 'How Much does Education Affect Women's Labour Market Outcomes in India? An Analysis Using NSS Household Data', Working Paper No. 92, Gujarat Institute of Development Research, Ahmedabad, 1997; D. Malathy and P. Duraiswamy, 'Returns to Scientific and Technical Education in India', *Margin*, 21(5), September 1998.

8. See Jean Drèze and Amartya Sen, 'Fa ic Education as a Political Issue'.

9. In Tamil Nadu, 88 per cent of habitations have a government primary school within a distance of one kilometre, which has helped in producing a significantly better schooling rate there.

10. Geeta Kingdon and Mohammed Muzammil, 'A Political Economy of Education in India-I: The Case of UP,' *Economic and Political Weekly*, 36(32), 11 August 2001, pp. 3052–63.

11. Piyali Sengupta and Jaba Guha, 'Enrolment, Dropout and Grade Completion of Girl Children in West Bengal', *Economic and Political Weekly*, 37(17), 27 April 2002, pp. 1621–37.

3

Marriage

Marriage in India is near-universal. The Muslim Women's Survey reports that the overwhelming majority (85–90 per cent) of women across all social groups are currently married, with the next biggest categories being widowed and never-married; at the all-India level, these are the three most significant categories.

Respondents were asked to give information on their current marital status; number of marriages; age at first marriage; age at which first marriage was dissolved, if divorced; last age at marriage; their opinion on the ideal age at marriage for boys and girls, and reasons for their preference; whether aware of the legal minimum age at marriage for boys and girls; whether this legal norm is followed in their community, and if not, why. Finally, respondents were asked whether they had noted an increase in the age at marriage for girls in their community in the recent past.

Age at Marriage

The MWS shows that 88 per cent of Indian women are currently married (see Table 3.1), with slightly more Muslim women (86 per cent) than upper caste Hindus (84 per cent), in this category. It further shows that 60 per cent Muslim and 55 per cent Hindu women are married by the age of 17 years,[1] and that women with low education levels—illiterate or up to primary—across region and religion, are more likely to be married below the legal age than women with medium or high levels of education.

The Survey reports that the all-India mean age at first marriage is 15.6 years (see Table 3.2), i.e., *almost a whole year lower* than that reported in the National Family Health Survey (NFHS). Our data also indicate that age at first marriage fluctuates between 14 and 18

TABLE 3.1
Current Marital Status by Community

All-India groups	Current marital status								Total
	1	2	3	4	5	6	7	9	
SC	90.29	0.06	4.70	0.00	0.25	0.00	4.69	0.00	100
ST	85.50	0.00	8.61	0.00	0.00	0.36	5.52	0.00	100
OBC	88.35	0.45	6.35	0.29	0.04	0.00	4.52	0.00	100
Others	83.87	0.22	8.45	0.41	0.41	0.15	6.48	0.00	100
Muslim	85.94	0.33	6.70	0.47	0.43	0.34	5.77	0.02	100
Total	87.64	0.25	6.41	0.23	0.22	0.09	5.15	0.00	100

Note: 1–Currently married; 2–married but *gauna* not performed; 3–widowed; 4–divorced; 5–separated; 6–deserted; 7–never married; 9–others.

TABLE 3.2
Mean Age at First Marriage: All-India

Religion–caste groups	Summary of age at first marriage	
	Mean	No. of observations
SC	15.3	618
ST	15.5	93
OBC	15.7	829
Others	15.8	553
Muslim	15.5	7192
Total	15.6	9285

years, but reveal some interesting urban–rural and regional differences. The mean age at marriage for upper caste Hindu women across rural India (see Tables 3.3–3.6) is *lower* than that for Muslim women, except in the rural east, where it is 15.1 years for Muslims and 16.9— or 17—years for upper caste Hindus. The figure is the lowest for rural north (13.9 years), followed by rural west (14.2 years) and rural south (14.3 years), for upper caste Hindus.

The picture for urban India is only marginally better, especially for Hindu women, who report a mean age at marriage of 17 years (see Tables 3.7 and 3.8) except, surprisingly, in the west, where the age drops to 15.9 years, marginally lower than the Muslim figure of 16.0 years. Urban and rural east report the lowest figures for Muslim women, at 15.1 and 14.7 years respectively. Hence, rural north for Hindu women and urban east for Muslims are the outliers.

78 □ *Unequal Citizens*

TABLE 3.3
Mean Age at First Marriage: Rural North

Religion–caste groups	Summary of age at first marriage	
	Mean	No. of observations
SC	14.7	201
ST	14.8	9
OBC	14.9	191
Others	13.9	58
Muslim	15.3	895
Total	14.8	1354

TABLE 3.4
Mean Age at First Marriage: Rural South

Religion–caste groups	Summary of age at first marriage	
	Mean	No. of observations
SC	17.3	32
OBC	16.3	73
Others	14.3	20
Muslim	16.0	571
Total	16.2	696

TABLE 3.5
Mean Age at First Marriage: Rural West

Religion–caste groups	Summary of age at first marriage	
	Mean	No. of observations
SC	15.9	22
ST	14.4	16
OBC	18.4	32
Others	14.2	16
Muslim	16.2	413
Total	16.2	499

TABLE 3.6
Mean Age at First Marriage: Rural East

Religion–caste groups	Summary of age at first marriage	
	Mean	No. of observations
SC	16.0	71
ST	16.0	41
OBC	16.9	22
Others	16.9	65
Muslim	15.1	974
Total	16.1	1173

TABLE 3.7
Mean Age at First Marriage: Urban South

Religion–caste groups	Summary of age at first marriage	
	Mean	No. of observations
SC	16.0	62
ST	18.1	7
OBC	16.2	139
Others	18.1	32
Muslim	16.5	1152
Total	16.5	1392

TABLE 3.8
Mean Age at First Marriage: Urban East

Religion–caste groups	Summary of age at first marriage	
	Mean	No. of observations
SC	15.0	64
ST	17.1	6
OBC	15.9	40
Others	17.3	101
Muslim	14.7	1033
Total	16.1	1244

Figures for never-married Hindu women in the rural north and rural south are 6.9 per cent and 25 per cent, respectively—that is, *one-fourth of caste Hindu women in the rural south have never married.* Corresponding figures for never-married Muslim women are: 5.8 per cent in the rural north and 5.6 per cent in the rural south. In the rural north, 5.48 per cent of Muslim women are widowed, with the corresponding figure in the rural south being 9.1 per cent. The exceptional figure here is for Muslim widows in the rural south (9.1 per cent), higher even than the poorer rural east, where it is 6.9 per cent; *urban east,* however, *reports the highest percentage for Muslim widows* (9.6 per cent). The MWS is not able to offer an explanation for this finding, but large age differences between spouses may be a factor. However, the truly startling finding for rural south is the extremely high figure for caste Hindu widows—20 per cent.

Other exceptional findings are: a very high percentage of *both* widowed and never-married—i.e., single—upper caste Hindu women in the rural north and south, the former being as high as 20 per cent in the south and 13.7 per cent in the north.

80 □ *Unequal Citizens*

Rural south has some other surprises for upper caste Hindu
women, who simultaneously report a significantly lower number of
currently married women (55 per cent); and a correspondingly *high*
number of those who are widowed (20 per cent) and never-married
(25 per cent). This is so unusual in the all-India context that it needs
some explanation through further probing or analysis. Rural west,
by contrast, reports no incidence of widowhood among upper caste
Hindus, unlike the urban west, where the percentage is higher than
that for Muslim women—7.04 as against 6.43 per cent.

North India has generally been seen as backward, socially and
economically, yet the urban north reports the highest percentage of
never-married Muslim women (10.04), higher than the all-India proportion; there seems to be a departure here from the general pattern
of early marriage as a consequence of poverty and conservatism. The
urban south, meanwhile, (Tables 3.9 and 3.10) reports the highest
percentage of never-married Scheduled Caste and Other Backward
Castes, followed by a significant proportion of the same in the urban
east (see Tables 3.10 and 3.11).

TABLE 3.9
Current Marital Status: Urban North

Religion–caste groups	Current marital status								Total
	1	2	3	4	5	6	7	9	
SC	90.16	0.00	7.38	0.00	0.00	0.00	2.46	0.00	100
ST	100.00	0.00	0.00	0.00	0.00	0.00	0.00	0.00	100
OBC	87.12	0.38	6.82	0.00	0.00	0.00	5.68	0.00	100
Others	89.47	1.05	4.21	0.00	0.00	1.05	4.21	0.00	100
Muslim	82.41	0.33	5.73	0.50	0.83	0.00	10.04	0.17	100
Total	87.96	0.49	5.97	0.06	0.10	0.30	5.10	0.02	100

TABLE 3.10
Current Marital Status: Urban South

Religion–caste groups	Current marital status							Total
	1	2	3	4	5	6	7	
SC	80.65	1.61	3.23	0.00	0.00	0.00	14 52	100
ST	85.71	0.00	14.29	0.00	0.00	0.00	0.00	100
OBC	75.54	2.16	9.35	0.72	0.00	0.00	12.23	100
Others	84.38	0.00	9.38	0.00	0.00	0.00	6.25	100
Muslim	83.68	0.87	8.42	0.35	1.04	0.17	5.47	100
Total	79.40	1.51	8.02	0.40	0.21	0.03	10.43	100

TABLE 3.11
Current Marital Status: Urban East

Religion–caste groups	Current marital status							Total
	1	2	3	4	5	6	7	
SC	79.69	0.00	9.38	0.00	0.00	0.00	10.94	100
ST	100.00	0.00	0.00	0.00	0.00	0.00	0.00	100
OBC	87.50	0.00	2.50	0.00	2.50	0.00	7.50	100
Others	86.14	0.99	7.92	0.00	0.00	0.00	4.95	100
Muslim	80.45	0.00	9.68	0.39	0.29	0.68	8.52	100
Total	84.24	0.41	7.46	0.05	0.45	0.09	7.30	100

TABLE 3.12
Current Marital Status: Urban West

Religion–caste groups	Current marital status								Total
	1	2	3	4	5	6	7	9	
SC	72.73	0.00	0.09	0.00	0.00	0.00	18.18	0.00	100
ST	85.71	0.00	0.00	0.00	0.00	14.29	0.00	0.00	100
OBC	85.29	0.00	2.94	0.00	0.00	0.00	11.76	0.00	100
Others	84.51	0.00	7.04	0.00	0.00	0.00	8.45	0.00	100
Muslim	81.14	0.84	6.43	1.48	0.63	0.32	9.06	0.11	100
Total	81.92	0.16	5.91	0.28	0.12	0.49	11.10	0.02	100

Note: (Tables 3.9 to 3.12) 1–Currently married; 2–married but gauna not performed; 3–widowed; 4–divorced; 5–separated; 6–deserted; 7–never married; 9–others

Muslim women, the next comparable group to Scheduled Castes in terms of socio-economic status (SES) in the urban east (Tables 3.11 and 3.12), are fairly close as far as both widowhood and never-married status are concerned, at 9.68 and 8.52 per cent, respectively.

An analysis by economic status shows that the overwhelming majority of women from all socio-economic classes are currently married (see Table 3.13), indicating that gender and customary practice, rather than class, are the determining factors as far as women's marital status is concerned. What is noteworthy, however, is that the percentage of women who never marry rises steadily in direct proportion to a higher socio-economic status. This may be a consequence of a combination of factors: higher educational status and job opportunities; a measure of economic security; even, perhaps, over-qualification *vis-à-vis* prospective grooms, an important consideration especially for Muslim girls. The incidence of widowhood, however, is largely unaffected by economic factors, with the proportion of widows among the poorest sections being almost the same as that among the richest, except for the urban west, which reports a very high percentage of widows among Scheduled Castes and Tribes; and the incidence of desertion which is markedly higher than for all other classes of communities. Here again, gender seems to be the critical factor.

The significant regional variation as far as Muslim women are concerned is rural south, which reports the highest percentage of those never-married (20.36), accounted for, perhaps, by a higher incidence of male out-migration to the Gulf countries or a better educational status.

Divorce and Remarriage

Not only are the majority of Indian women currently married, they are also married only once. At an all-India level, the MWS indicates that only a very small percentage (2.85) of the poorest women report a second marriage (see Table 3.14), with the rural north and south reporting the highest percentages—4.26 and 4.69 per cent, respectively (see Tables 3.15 and 3.16).

TABLE 3.13
Current Marital Status by SES

Five-fold classi-fication of SLI	Current marital status								Total
	1	2	3	4	5	6	7	9	
1	92.26	0.16	4.78	0.52	0.76	0.17	1.35	0.00	100
2	89.23	0.18	6.62	0.02	0.16	0.21	3.57	0.00	100
3	83.55	0.17	7.95	0.58	0.39	0.10	7.20	0.05	100
4	88.01	0.52	6.85	0.23	0.06	0.00	4.33	0.00	100
·5	85.34	0.33	4.92	0.06	0.04	0.02	9.28	0.00	100
Total	87.39	0.27	6.36	0.32	0.30	0.10	5.25	0.02	100

TABLE 3.14
Number of Times Married by SES: All-India

Five-fold classi-fication of SLI	No. of times married				Total
	1	2	3	9	
1	96.20	2.85	0.02	0.93	100
2	97.75	0.35	0.01	1.88	100
3	98.04	0.85	0.02	1.09	100
4	99.44	0.24	0.10	0.22	100
5	99.14	0.24	0.00	0.61	100
Total	98.10	0.95	0.03	0.92	100

TABLE 3.15
Number of Times Married by SES: Rural North

Five-fold classi-	No. of times married				Total
fication of SLI	1	2	3	9	
1	95.66	4.26	0.04	0.04	100
2	97.38	0.28	0.00	2.34	100
3	97.84	0.39	0.00	1.77	100
4	99.92	0.08	0.00	0.00	100
5	100.00	0.00	0.00	0.00	100
Total	97.80	1.34	0.01	0.85	100

TABLE 3.16
Number of Times Married by SES: Rural South

Five-fold classi-	No. of times married				Total
fication of SLI	1	2	3	9	
1	95.31	4.69	0.00	0.00	100
2	99.65	0.24	0.12	0.00	100
3	94.39	2.72	0.11	2.78	100
4	99.58	0.28	0.07	0.07	100
5	94.88	0.11	0.00	5.01	100
Total	96.53	1.79	0.06	1.61	100

Note: (Tables 3.13 to 3.16) 1–Lowest socio-economic index; 2–Lower-Middle SLI; 3–Middle SLI; 4–Upper Middle SLI; 5–High SLI.

Given that the incidence of divorce, desertion, and separation is also very low, this may not be an altogether unexpected finding; we should note, however, that this is contrary to the general assumption that Muslim women are commonly divorced or deserted on account of polygamy and unilateral divorce. (Indeed, a survey of 15,000 Muslim women carried out by the Women's Research and Action Group (WRAG) in 46 districts of India in 1993–5, reported that a total of only 5 per cent of the total sample had been either divorced, separated, or remarried.)[2] It is, however, possible that women may not admit to or report being divorced because of the social stigma attached to it. In the MWS, although Muslim women reported the highest incidence of remarriage at 2 per cent, the figure is too small to be significant. Here again, the rural south (see Table 3.17) is noteworthy for having the highest proportion of second marriages— 3.40 per cent among Muslim women—accounted for, perhaps, by the high incidence of widowhood noted earlier. Urban east, which also reported a high percentage of widows—almost 10 per cent—indicates the highest number of second marriages for Muslim women. Notwithstanding this finding, the proportions are small.

TABLE 3.17
Number of Times Married by Community: Rural South

Religion–caste groups	No. of times married				Total
	1	2	3	9	
SC	96.77	0.00	0.00	3.23	100
OBC	97.01	2.99	0.00	0.00	100
Others	93.33	0.00	0.00	6.67	100
Muslim	94.52	3.40	0.76	1.32	100
Total	96.28	1.92	0.07	1.73	100

TABLE 3.18
Current Marital Status: Rural East

Religion–caste groups	Current marital status							Total
	1	2	3	4	5	6	7	
SC	91.55	0.00	4.23	0.00	1.41	0.00	2.82	100
ST	80.49	0.00	12.20	0.00	0.00	0.00	7.32	100
OBC	86.36	0.00	9.09	0.00	0.00	0.00	4.55	100
Others	90.77	0.00	4.62	1.54	1.54	0.00	1.54	100
Muslim	87.89	0.31	6.98	0.10	0.31	0.62	3.80	100
Total	88.32	0.07	6.63	0.41	0.85	0.14	3.58	100

Note: 1–Currently married; 2–married but gauna not performed; 3–widowed; 4–divorced; 5–separated; 6–deserted; 7–never married.

All-India figures for divorce are even more startling: 0.41 per cent for upper caste Hindu women and 0.47 for Muslims. Again, contrary to the prevailing impressions, the exception to this figure is the rural east, where divorced upper caste Hindu women report a high 1.54 per cent (see Table 3.18); a corresponding high rate for Muslim women is found in the urban west (1.48 per cent). We might assume that this low figure for divorce conceals high rates of desertion and separation, but this is not borne out by our data—all-India percentages for both are 0.09 and 0.22, respectively.

Ideal Age at Marriage

Notwithstanding the fact that early marriage is the norm for women across class and community, our question on what, in the respondents' view, is the ideal age at marriage for boys and girls elicited some interesting responses. By far the largest percentage of Hindu and

Muslim women—26.32 and 33.70, respectively—thought that 25 years was the ideal age for boys (see Figure 3.1); and 31.42 per cent of Hindu and 35.31 per cent of Muslim women thought 18 years was the ideal age for girls (see Figure 3.2).

Community differences are insignificant; but what is significant is that the majority of women, over 70 per cent, believe that the *ideal* age

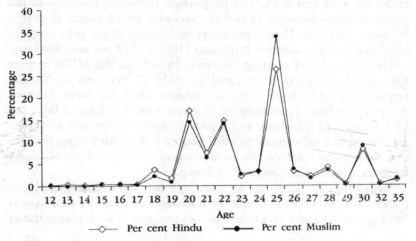

FIGURE 3.1: Ideal Age at Marriage for Boys

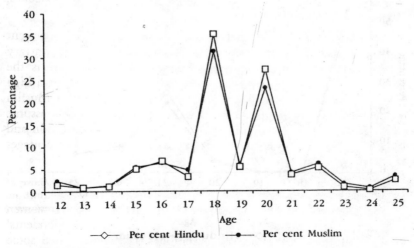

FIGURE 3.2: Ideal Age at Marriage for Girls

for girls corresponds to the *legal minimum* age or above. In other words, the *desire* for later marriage manifests itself attitudinally, but not in actual practice because, as we have seen, the overwhelming majority of women are married before they reach the legal minimum age.

The landmark years, thus, are 18, 20–1, 25, and 30; but attitudinal differences based on gender become apparent when we compare the tables for girls and boys. The proportion favouring marriage in the pubertal years—between 12 and 18 years—for girls is higher than that for boys: Muslims: 18 per cent for girls; Hindus: 21 per cent for girls; Muslims: 1.34 per cent for boys; and Hindus: 2.14 per cent for boys.

Later or delayed marriage for girls (which, in the MWS, is after the age of 20 years) is favoured by only 10 per cent of Muslim respondents and 14 per cent of Hindus; while for boys, later or delayed marriage (after the age of 25 years in our break-up) is favoured by 17 per cent Muslims and Hindus. Both figures are not very significant, nor are community differences; it is worth noting, though, that across the country, *the occurrence of later or delayed marriage increases with higher standards of living.*

Regarding the legal age of marriage for boys, half the Hindu respondents, and a little over that of Muslims, had no awareness of it (see Figures 3.3 and 3.4). Only about 25 per cent in both communities

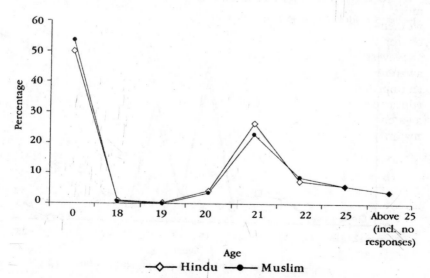

FIGURE 3.3: Awareness of Minimum Legal Age at Marriage for Boys

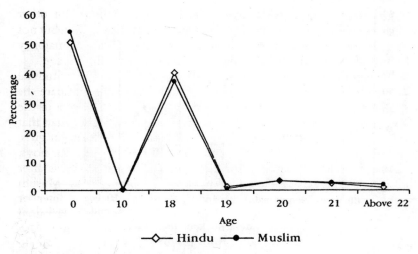

FIGURE 3.4: Awareness of Minimum Legal Age at Marriage for Girls

correctly reported the legal age, indicating not community differences so much as widespread ignorance, further reinforcing the view that marriage is one of those critical events in people's lives that is regulated more by customary practice—especially with regard to Muslim women—and gender than it is by either class, community, or religion—or, for that matter, by the law.

Nevertheless, one finding from our data is notable, and this is that awareness of the legal age of marriage for girls rises dramatically with an improvement in women's educational status—81 per cent of highly educated women are aware of the correct age (see Table 3.19). Overall, awareness for girls is higher than that for boys, possibly because the majority of boys are married after the legal age, in any case.

TABLE 3.19
Awareness of Legal Age at Marriage for Girls by Women's Education

Women's education	Girls	Boys
Illiterate	23.26	14.01
Non-formal	26.43	15.33
Primary	40.62	22.00
Middle	55.81	38.11
Secondary +	73.69	48.15
Graduate and above	80.58	68.82

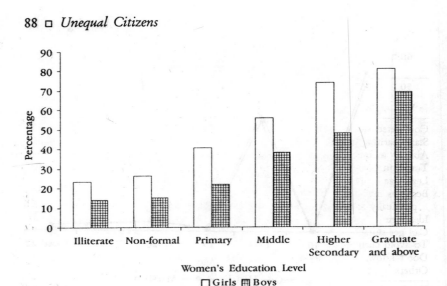

FIGURE 3.5: Proportion that is Correctly Aware of Legal Age at Marriage

The MWS did not specifically ask respondents about the circumstances of their marriage—that is, choice of partner, age preference, and so on—but it is generally accepted that the question of choice with regard to marriage is practically non-existent for the vast majority of women. Decisions on when, to whom, at what age, and in what manner to get married are seldom in their control. In such a social and cultural context, where marriage and motherhood are seen to be the primary objectives of a woman's life—her 'career', if you like— it is almost inconceivable that she will oppose either the option itself, the partner chosen for her, or the circumstances in which her marriage takes place. It might seem an indulgence, then, to seek answers to attitudinal questions on the subject; nevertheless, we did put some questions to our respondents on their reasons for preferring to follow the legal age norm, or a 'delayed' marriage, and our findings are presented below.

Across the country, roughly half (46 per cent)—and 47 per cent for Muslims—our respondents favoured late (21+ years) marriages for boys (see Table 3.20) so that they could earn and support families adequately; followed by 11 per cent who said it was the ideal age; and 9 per cent who believed that they would, by then, also be 'mentally and physically mature'. These reasons were given priority over other considerations such as education, tradition, etc. Inter-community

TABLE 3.20
Reasons for Ideal Age at Marriage for Boys

| | Religion-caste groups | | | | | |
	SC	ST	OBC	Others	Muslim	Total
Completed studies	4.98	9.96	6.61	8.54	5.51	6.61
Starts earning	44.95	53.51	42.90	49.42	47.12	45.85
Able to maintain family	7.59	2.74	7.54	7.47	6.00	7.07
Tradition	3.73	7.11	3.27	0.81	2.72	3.10
Legal age	2.97	4.48	2.10	3.99	4.57	3.17
Becomes mentally and physically mature	8.46	7.58	8.85	11.31	8.18	9.02
Ideal age	13.60	1.19	13.73	6.34	9.01	11.03
Can get suitable match	5.56	7.78	5.73	8.47	8.87	6.71
To avoid chance of love affairs	1.70	1.37	0.66	0.66	1.15	0.99
Don't know/Can't say	0.05	0.00	0.00	0.00	0.12	0.03
Others	1.28	0.35	0.64	0.15	0.45	0.70
Total	100.00	100.00	100.00	100.00	100.00	100.00

differences were negligible; while regional variations indicated that respondents in the south were marginally less concerned about earning capacity.

Reasons for preferring later—read legal—marriage for girls (see Table 3.21) had a more mixed response, with the greater percentage of women, 23 per cent—and notably, 22 per cent Muslim women—citing 'no problem during childbirth' as the main reason, followed closely by 'becomes mentally mature'. These two predominant factors are supported by chances of a better education (10.3 per cent); 'tradition' (7.5 per cent); followed by a clear endorsement of 18 years and above as being the 'ideal' age (7.4 per cent). The exception to this is west India, where the distribution is more even, as evident in Table 3.25.

An unambiguous gender bias is evident in these attitudes, with an implicit and explicit recognition that husbanding, householding, and breadwinning are male responsibilities; and reproduction, domestic activities, and caring for the family are women's jobs, for which physical maturity is desirable but not necessarily anything else. The most cited reasons—making up 6 per cent of the responses—for girls' early marriage are: to reduce burden on parents; lack of education; and availability of a good match. Of the three, reducing the burden (most probably financial) on parents is the most pressing. A subset of responses is equally revealing; reasons such as 'can get a good match', 'reduce burden on family', 'avoid chances of a love affair', and 'less

TABLE 3.21
Reasons for Ideal Age at Marriage for Girls All-India

	SC	ST	OBC	Others	Muslim	Total
			Religion–caste groups			
Can get good education	7.72	11.70	10.62	14.82	9.19	10.39
Can get good match	4.14	1.78	4.38	2.88	4.90	3.95
Can manage family	6.64	4.80	3.75	8.13	7.72	6.03
Tradition	7.72	13.41	9.26	3.61	5.62	7.49
Legal age	3.55	2.93	2.45	7.72	4.68	4.09
Becomes mentally mature	9.58	18.77	14.98	12.58	13.06	12.85
No problem during childbirth	27.26	14.29	22.52	20.20	22.01	23.00
Ideal age	5.02	13.89	5.28	12.47	8.41	7.44
Problem in getting good match	4.87	0.50	7.56	3.20	3.50	5.00
Good match at early age	0.62	0 26	2.95	0.60	1.33	1.44
Right age at marriage	1.27	2.78	1.98	2.50	2.66	2.00
Reduce burden on parents	3.70	4.26	1.71	2.44	3.13	2.78
Life enjoyment	0.00	0.00	0.06	0.08	0.17	0.06
Less dowry at early age	1.11	0.00	0.37	0.00	0.49	0.52
To avoid chance of a love affair	5.63	7.34	2.60	2.85	3.29	3.92
Can take care of family responsibilities	7.04	1.46	4.63	3.13	5.64	5.04
Came to know from TV	0.00	0.00	0.00	0.00	0.02	0.00
Total	100.00	100.00	100.00	100.00	100.00	100.00

TABLE 3.22
Reasons for Ideal Age at Marriage for Girls: North Zone

	SC	ST	OBC	Others	Muslim	Total
			Religion–caste groups			
Can get good education	4.79	0.00	7.44	17.57	6.18	7.73
Can get good match	4.41	0.00	5.34	2.42	6.33	4.59
Can manage family	5.50	3.26	0.82	3.92	4.24	3.37
Tradition	12.00	0.00	11.36	3.94	6.18	9.73
Legal age	1.86	9.84	1.65	7.13	2.00	2.71
Becomes mentally mature	10.13	21.32	15.42	20.79	17.45	14.64
No problem during childbirth	25.31	19.69	24.59	17.61	19.93	23.22
Ideal age	1.55	22.95	2.10	8.43	5.68	3.58
Problem in getting good match	5.34	3.26	9.48	4.88	4.81	6.70
Good match at early age	0.93	0.00	2.78	0.00	1.12	1.48
Right age at marriage	0.93	0.00	0.60	1.13	2.56	1.00
Reduce burden on parents	3.79	0.00	2.41	0.93	2.69	2.67
Life enjoyment	0.00	0.00	0.00	0.00	0.09	0.01
Less dowry at early age	1.86	0.00	0.52	0.00	0.83	0.95
To avoid chance of a love affair	7.51	19.69	3.61	3.18	4.18	5.28
Can take care of family responsibilities	7.82	0.00	5.18	3.75	7.39	6.07
Came to know from TV	0.00	0.00	0.00	0.00	0.02	0.00
Total	100.00	100.00	100.00	100.00	100.00	100.00

TABLE 3.23
Reasons for Ideal Age at Marriage for Girls: South Zone

	Religion–caste groups					
	SC	ST	OBC	Others	Muslim	Total
Can get good education	22.02	0.00	17.64	8.66	10.90	16.45
Can get good match	5.55	16.67	1.31	1.08	3.02	2.57
Can manage family	5.49	0.00	6.34	10.61	5.25	6.50
Tradition	4.87	16.67	7.39	8.44	8.27	7.16
Legal age	1.25	0.00	2.36	5.30	4.48	2.74
Becomes mentally mature	15.28	0.00	13.95	6.39	13.18	13.06
No problem during childbirth	19.71	16.67	20.53	28.79	19.34	21.21
Ideal age	9.23	16.67	8.94	9.52	10.70	9.37
Problem in getting good match	5.49	0.00	3.93	1.08	5.68	4.11
Good match at early age	0.62	0.00	4.71	0.00	2.78	2.92
Right age at marriage	5.55	33.33	4.74	6.39	3.70	5.23
Reduce burden on parents	0.62	0.00	0.80	9.52	5.27	2.44
Life enjoyment	0.00	0.00	0.27	0.00	0.29	0.18
Less dowry at early age	0.00	0.00	0.00	0.00	0.34	0.04
To avoid chance of a love affair	0.00	0.00	0.27	4.22	2.57	1.01
Can take care of family responsibilities	3.68	0.00	2.62	0.00	2.64	2.50
Total	100.00	100.00	100.00	100.00	100.00	100.00

TABLE 3.24
Reasons for Ideal Age at Marriage for Girls: East Zone

	Religion–caste groups					
	SC	ST	OBC	Others	Muslim	Total
Can get good education	10.03	15.42	11.08	13.25	11.81	12.18
Can get good match	2.70	2.49	7.04	5.15	3.51	3.92
Can manage family	11.73	4.99	15.12	13.80	14.11	12.15
Tradition	0.00	22.90	8.08	2.69	4.10	5.58
Legal age	8.85	2.49	1.50	11.70	7.89	7.93
Becomes mentally mature	5.35	12.47	8.83	3.37	6.03	6.23
No problem during childbirth	37.51	13.39	36.83	17.76	26.83	26.14
Ideal age	8.14	12.47	6.29	18.72	9.00	11.82
Problem in getting good match	1.28	0.00	0.00	0.00	0.52	0.46
Good match at early age	0.00	0.46	2.25	0.46	0.98	0.59
Right age at marriage	0.24	2.95	0.00	3.69	2.51	2.06
Reduce burden on parents	5.58	7.48	0.75	3.14	3.26	4.25
Life enjoyment	0.00	0.00	0.00	0.23	0.25	0.12
Less dowry at early age	0.00	0.00	0.00	0.00	0.13	0.03
To avoid chance of a love affair	2.79	2.49	0.75	1.68	2.84	2.26
Can take care of family responsibilities	5.58	0.00	1.50	2.69	5.62	3.60
Total	100.00	100.00	100.00	100.00	100.00	100.00

TABLE 3.25

Reasons for Ideal Age at Marriage for Girls: West Zone

	Religion–caste groups					
	SC	ST	OBC	Others	Muslim	Total
Can get good education	4.69	11.40	12.00	15.21	10.41	10.87
Can get good match	3.89	0.00	4.40	0.00	6.44	2.95
Can manage family	3.89	5.70	7.05	4.55	3.43	5.23
Tradition	0.00	0.00	3.28	1.55	4.65	1.89
Legal age	5.49	0.00	7.12	1.55	5.19	4.40
Becomes mentally mature	8.68	32.90	18.07	16.18	19.27	17.46
No problem during childbirth	25.75	12.87	8.79	27.23	17.56	18.24
Ideal age	16.37	11.40	13.12	10.75	15.08	13.30
Problem in getting good match	9.38	0.00	9.28	7.65	5.33	7.39
Good match at early age	0.00	0.00	0.56	3.00	1.33	1.01
Right age at marriage	0.80	1.47	4.33	0.78	2.05	2.13
Reduce burden on parents	2.39	0.00	0.56	0.00	1.34	0.85
Life enjoyment	0.00	0.00	0.00	0.00	0.08	0.01
Less dowry at early age	0.00	0.00	0.56	0.00	0.47	0.23
To avoid chance of a love affair	6.29	11.40	3.28	3.78	2.04	4.93
Can take care of family responsibilities	9.28	5.70	7.61	4.65	2.43	6.53
Came to know from TV	0.00	0.00	0.00	0.00	0.16	0.02
Total	100.00	100.00	100.00	100.00	100.00	100.00

dowry at an early age' were offered by respondents *only* with reference to girls, and while indicating a preference for marrying them off before the age of 18 years. Conversely, the importance of earning and being able to support a family is desirable *only* for boys, and this is generally borne out by the real-life experience of men: pubertal marriages are rare among them (we are not considering child-marriages here), and under-age marriages are most uncommon.

The relative unimportance of higher education and paid work for women would seem to be self-evident to most of our respondents, regardless of community, because of their relative unimportance in accomplishing the task of reproduction, mothering, and looking after the family. On the contrary, obviating the possibility of an undesirable love affair—which would almost certainly jeopardize marriage prospects for the girl herself, and might also bring social opprobrium in its wake—and guarding against 'over-qualification' (and consequently 'disqualification')—in the marriage market are very important. This becomes clearer when we note that, for those women who expressed a preference for marriage at 18 years or later, an important reason is being able to get a better education. This is especially so for upper caste

Hindu women (who reported a much higher percentage) especially in the north and south.

If we relate this to our earlier finding that between 60–70 per cent of our sample indicated the desirability of later (above 18 years) marriage for girls, _especially_ among Muslims across all four regions, its significance becomes obvious; that is, women seem to understand the link between later marriage and greater opportunities for educating themselves, with at least the potential for working outside the home, should the need arise, even if they cannot actually act upon this realization. One should not overstate the case, however, because the most important reasons for preferring marriage at 18 years still remain tied to motherhood and domesticity—a reduced risk of problems during childbirth, and being able to discharge household responsibilities satisfactorily.

A somewhat minor, but nevertheless quite significant, finding is that 75 per cent of all the women in our sample replied that the legal age norm is followed in their communities, a response that is belied by their actual ages at marriage. This inconsistency could have two possible explanations: either that respondents are referring to boys in their community (who are generally married above the legal age), or that _they would like to follow this norm_, as expressed in their preference for delayed marriages, noted earlier.

Reasons for _not_ observing the legal age norm are important, and are primarily the following: reducing the burden on parents; lack of education; and availability of a good match (see Figure 3.6). Economic reasons appear to be more important for Muslims than Hindus but

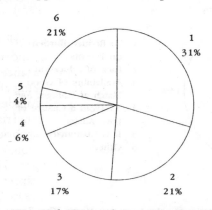

1 To Reduce Burden on Parents
2 Lack of Education
3 Availability of Good Match at Younger Age
4 To Avoid a Chance of Love Affairs
5 It is Customary
6 Others

FIGURE 3.6: Reasons for not Observing the Legal Age Norm

both are equally concerned about avoiding chances of love relationships (see Figure 3.7).

The significant regional difference here is in the west zone, for which the importance of the availability of a good match outweighs all other reasons (see Figure 3.8).

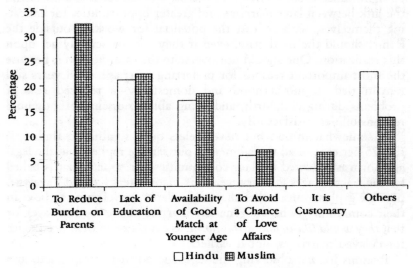

FIGURE 3.7: Reasons for not Following the Norm by Religion

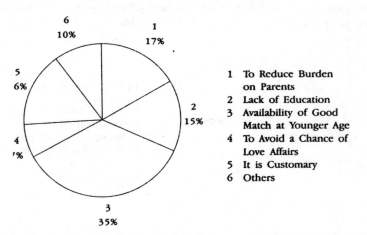

1 To Reduce Burden on Parents
2 Lack of Education
3 Availability of Good Match at Younger Age
4 To Avoid a Chance of Love Affairs
5 It is Customary
6 Others

FIGURE 3.8: Reasons for not Following the Legal Age Norm: West Zone

Notwithstanding all the above, it should be noted that recent surveys, including the MWS, have all reported a rising age at marriage for girls in the country. The NFHS (1998–9) reports that in rural India, the proportion of women married by the age of 15 years declined from 29 per cent for the age-group 20–4 years, to 18 per cent for the age group 15–19 years. In urban areas, the corresponding decline is from 9 per cent to 5 per cent. Tables 3.26 and Figure 3.9 give the breakdown in the MWS by community.

TABLE 3.26
Increase in Age at Marriage, by Community

Religion–caste groups	Yes	No	Don't know/ can't say	Others	Total
SC	57.92	26.36	15.47	0.25	100
ST	51.14	34.78	14.09	0.00	100
OBC	60.63	25.58	13.52	0.28	100
Others	68.05	18.67	13.10	0.19	100
Muslim	63.09	25.07	11.55	0.29	100
Total	60.97	24.99	13.80	0.24	100

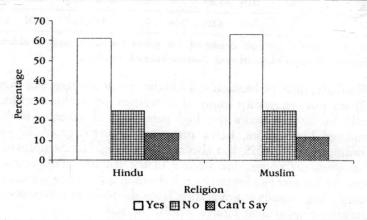

FIGURE 3.9: Have You Found any Increase in Age at Marriage for girls?

Marriage, SES, and Education

Does the respondent's standard of living or socio-economic status have a bearing on her never-married status? Our data seem to indicate as much, with the proportion of never-married women rising steadily as one moves up the scale. Regional variations are more or less consistent with the all-India picture—the significant exception, as noted earlier, being the rural south, where the proportion of never-married women is higher for all SES classes (except the poorest) than the all-India average; and in the high SES category it is 20.3 per cent, corresponding almost exactly with that in the urban south, but in reverse, where the highest proportion of single women, 19.5 per cent, belong to the poorest section. Another notable difference is found in the urban west (see Table 3.27), where there is a dramatic rise in the number of deserted women (13.5 per cent) and widows in the two poorest categories (15.4 and 16 per cent, respectively).[3]

TABLE 3.27
Current Marital Status by SES: Urban West

	1	2	3	4	5	6	7	9	Total
Low	78.9	0.00	15.41	4.86	0.21	0.21	0.41	0.00	100
Lower middle	68.47	0.00	16.08	1.26	0.00	13.55	0.63	0.00	100
Middle	83.13	2.19	4.83	0.18	0.36	0.18	9.13	0.00	100
Upper middle	80.79	0.17	7.38	0.09	0.04	0.00	11.54	0.00	100
High	83.35	0.05	1.85	0.32	0.00	0.00	14.37	0.05	100
Total	81.55	0.49	6.05	0.59	0.1	0.41	10.79	0.02	100

Notes: 1–Currently married; 2–married but gauna not performed; 3–widowed; 4–divorced; 5–separated; 6–deserted; 7–never married; 9–others.

Similarly, higher education and a higher age at marriage (see Figure 3.10) do not necessarily imply that women enter the workforce; Kerala, for instance, has a very high percentage of women who have completed high school, has a mean age at marriage of 20 years according to the NFHS, but also one of the highest unemployed or not-at-work percentages for women in the country. This could, of course, be because employment opportunities for women are limited, forcing a huge female out-migration from the state, and consequently depressing employment figures within the state.

Conclusion

What is evident from our discussion is that the one more or less constant feature in the lives of Indian women, regardless of class, caste, community, and region, is marriage. As noted earlier, 95 per cent of all women are married by the age of 25 years, and motherhood

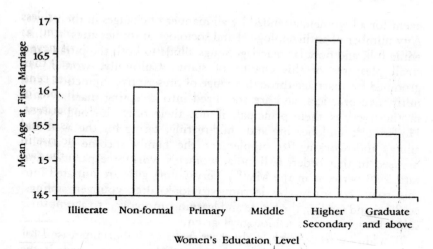

□ Mean age at first marriage

FIGURE 3.10: Mean Age at First Marriage by Women's Education Level

follows soon after marriage.[4] (In the MWS, more than 65 per cent
women reported that they were unable to access government health
centres, either because they were too far or because the facilities
were inadequate. The implications of all this even for women's
reproductive health status are self-evident.) According to the Census
of India, 1991, the average number of children Indian women bear
is 3.7; the MWS reports that Muslim women, on average, have more
living children (3.5) than Hindu women (2.8). Of those who are
married, over 85 per cent remain married till they are widowed; and
less than one per cent of all women, urban and rural, are divorced,
according to both the NFHS and the MWS. It would be correct then
to say that, for the better part of their lives (45 years on average),
the unvarying norm for the majority of women is their marital
status. They may be working, self-employed or unemployed;
students or otherwise, at different stages of their lives; they might
conceivably change their regional location and even their class status;
but only a minuscule proportion is likely to see a change in their
marital status.

It can be argued, then, that the significance and impact of this single
fact is much greater for women than it is for men, in general.
Marriage—and exogamous marriage, in particular—is a watershed

event for all women, attended by all manner of changes in their lives. Any number of anthropological and sociological studies attest to this, while folk and popular marriage songs allude to both the pitfalls and small pleasures of this change of status. Culturally, women are groomed for marriage through a range of prescriptive injunctions and normative practices, and are socialized into accepting marriage and motherhood as their principal, if not their only, lifelong career. Housework, childbearing and child-rearing, caring for the aged and ailing, and working to supplement the family income generally proceed in that order. (All-India, women's workforce participation rate is 20 per cent in the MWS.) Very young girls are initiated into this role very early, by learning to look after younger siblings, cooking and tending the house and learning, moreover, to accept their subordinate status as a biological given.

In addition to poverty, early marriage is an important reason for discontinuing education as far as young girls are concerned. If the mean age at marriage for Indian women is 15.6 years, chances that they will complete their high school education are slim. The MWS data indicate that financial constraints (36 per cent), married off (22 per cent), and parental objection (20 per cent) accounted for Muslim girls in our sample dropping out of school. We have already noted a correlation between early marriage and a low socio-economic status, and the percentage of Muslims in this category, all-India, is higher than that of Hindus. The rising graph for later age at marriage for Muslim girls, however, is to be welcomed, because it indicates a gradual improvement in both their socio-economic, as well as educational, status. Though the increase is slight (varying between one and three years, according to the NFHS), it is significant, and the likelihood that it will continue to increase is an indication of positive change.

Endnotes

1. The 1998–9 investigation conducted by the NFHS on a sample of 90,000 women in India reported that 94 per cent of *all* Indian women are married by the age of 25 years, and that the median age at first marriage is 16.4 years, i.e. 18 months below the legal minimum age at marriage. Even more revealing, it reports that 61 per cent of *all* women (70 per cent rural, 40 per cent urban) are married before the age of 18 years.

2. Vahida Nainar, *Muslim Women's Views on Personal Laws: The Influence of Socio-economic Factors*, Women's Research and Action Group, Mumbai, 2000.

3. We may recall that in the early and mid-1980s in Maharashtra, women's and peasants' organizations mobilized a Parityakta movement focusing on the high incidence and plight of separated and deserted women in the state, lending credence to this finding.

4. According to the *South Asia Human Development Report*, 60 per cent of Indian women are stunted and underweight in their childbearing years, and 8 out of 10 are seriously anaemic during pregnancy; moreover, on an average, 50 per cent of lactating mothers in South Asia have a caloric intake that is 70 per cent less than the recommended *minimum*. *Human Development in South Asia 2000: The Gender Question*, Mahbub ul Haq Human Development Centre, Oxford University Press, Karachi, 2000.

4

Women's Work

This chapter explores the work status of respondents and related issues of type of work done, reasons for working or not working, decision-making about work, and the nature of control over their earned income. While dealing with women's work status, two sets of issues arise: the first relates to invisibility or under-reporting and under-measurement, which is a common phenomena and has been widely critiqued and commented upon by feminist scholarship;[1] the second relates to the noticeably low work participation of Muslim women even after taking into account the invisibility and under-reporting. We focus mainly on low work participation because under-reporting should apply to Hindus and Muslims alike.

Work Status of Women

The majority of Indian women work throughout their lives, yet official statistics recognize only certain types of work measured in terms of wage-earning economic activity as productive and that are counted in the measurement of national income. Not surprisingly, statistics on work participation rates continue to show low figures for women workers because a considerable amount of work done by women does not find mention in this.

Traditionally, work has been defined as activities for 'pay or profit', though now, in keeping with the suggestion of the system of *National Accounts 1993*, the term 'economic activity' rather than 'work' is used in official statistics.[2] The definition of economic activity has been broadened to include several domestic activities carried out by women[3] but the underlying emphasis on paid work remains unchanged. This income-oriented approach to the definition of work can capture only those who are in wage and salaried employment, self-employment

outside the household, and self-employment in cultivation and
household industry for profit. Many activities, which are for self-
consumption, are not counted as work. The invisibility of women's
work in economic accounting systems is thus due to the flawed
definition of economic activity.[4]

In order to ascertain the work status of women, respondents were
asked: do you work?; with the following options for responses: 1=self-
employed; 2=wage worker/employee; 3=salaried; 4=unpaid family
worker; 5=none of these. Table 4.1 indicates that for the country as
a whole, the overwhelming majority of respondents self-report themselves to be not working. More important, the low work participatio 1
pattern holds for all regions. Among social groups, Muslims and upper
caste women participate the least in comparison to the Scheduled
Castes (30 per cent) and OBCs (22 per cent). The average rate of
participation for Muslim respondents is 14 per cent, which in itself
is lower than that for Hindus (18 per cent), and significantly lower
than that of Scheduled Castes (37 per cent), and OBC (22 per cent).

TABLE 4.1
Work Status of Women by Community

Community	1	2	3	4	5	Total
SC	3.97	21.02	2.11	2.57	70.33	100
ST	0.71	23.77	2.08	10.22	63.22	100
OBC	4.03	11.22	1.10	4.79	78.86	100
Others	4.13	6.12	2.81	1.02	85.92	100
Muslims	2.70	7.58	1.83	2.05	85.74	100
Total	3.67	13.44	1.87	3.37	77.65	100

Note: 1–Self employed; 2–Wage worker/employee; 3–Salaried; 4–Unpaid family worker;
5–None of these.

Among Muslim who report work participation, the largest proportion is in the wage worker/employee category followed by the self-
employed. For example, the work participation rate for urban
Muslim respondents is 11.4 per cent, while it is 16 per cent for Hindus,
and the rural work participation is only 20 per cent for Muslims
and 37 per cent for Hindus. Like their male counterparts the majority
of urban Muslim women (60 per cent) are in the self-employed
category. In general, the differences between Muslims and Hindus are
pronounced and most Muslim women are self-employed, with only
a very few in formal employment. *Muslims appear to have a distinct*

employment profile, marked by the preponderance of self-employment, of both men and women.

There is no significant regional variation in work participation, even though varied cultural norms that govern women's work across regions are recognized and ought to result in variations in work participation. A wide variation in the work participation of groups in rural areas than urban is a noteworthy feature of work participation. The Scheduled Castes report higher levels of work in rural areas, ranging from 36 per cent in the north to 16 per cent in the east zone, than in urban areas But significantly, Scheduled Castes, despite poverty and lower restric ions on mobility, are much closer to the national figures of low work participation in all the urban zones, except the west.

The low level of work participation nationally and regionally reported in the MWS echoes a larger problem that all survey data/ quantitative analyses on women's work run into in the Indian context. The aggregate numbers in the MWS, as indeed in other surveys, are also counter-intuitive at another level: with widespread low standard of living index (SLI), indicative of high levels of poverty, simple economic survival of the family would compel women to take up productive economic activity and work. Also, given the high level of landlessness in the rural sample, the prospects of women not working seem slight. Women at home undertake a wide range of agricultural work and it is likely that respondents have discounted their own contribution as part of daily household chores.[5] These women, as part of household enterprise, may not be paid for their own labour and, therefore, feel that their contribution is unproductive.

One of the reasons for the discrepancy between recorded data and the facts of everyday lives of women is the way data is collected. This is usually limited to monetized work. Secondly, surveys often speak to the head of the household whose habitual response to the question: 'Does your wife work?' would be 'No, she's just a house-wife'. However, our survey was canvassing information directly from women respondents and was not confined to monetized work, that is, work that results in earning or wage. Yet, respondents deny any involvement in any kind of economically productive activity. Even though many of these women are in all probability doing home-based work or agricultural work, during surveys many of them refer to themselves as housewives, even though they may well spend 14–16 hours a day working and earning an income for the household.[6]

Keenly aware of this background, the MWS tried to probe deeper into the work status of the respondents, even those whose first response was that they did not work. At the all-India level, when asked if they were either self-employed, wage workers/employees, salaried, unpaid family workers, or none of these, 85 per cent of Muslim respondents again opted for 'none of these'. The only other category that had numbers of some significance is the second category: wage worker/employee, with 7.58 per cent of Muslim respondents reporting themselves to be in this category.

Work and Socio-economic Status

For reasons mentioned above, we asked more questions in order to assess the work status of the respondents. While the overall numbers did not change significantly, we did get a few interesting insights into the relationship between reporting of work, decision-making, reasons for working or not working, and how this differs by community. Significantly, the proportions of not working women are high across all SES categories. However, the percentage of not working increases with a rise in SES status, ranging from 86 per cent for the highest SES categories to 64 per cent for the lowest SES categories (see Table 4.2). High status is often associated with both higher education and low work participation. The regional distribution matches the all-India pattern, except the urban west zone, in which, surprisingly, the low SES category reports a significantly lower proportion not working (68 per cent). The large variation in work participation of the highest and lowest SES categories indicates that poor women are working because they cannot afford to remain unemployed, and as

TABLE 4.2
Work Status of Women by SES

	1	2	3	4	5	Total
Low	2.21	31.49	0.33	1.69	64.24	100
Lower middle	2.56	16.06	2.22	4.89	74.27	100
Middle	2.79	12.04	1.94	4.09	79.13	100
Upper middle	4.39	5.80	3.09	1.96	84.77	100
High	5.99	1.29	2.20	4.24	86.24	100
Total	3.54	13.32	1.95	3.32	77.86	100

Note: 1–Self employed; 2–Wage worker/employee; 3–Salaried; 4–Unpaid family worker; 5–None of these.

66 per cent of households belong to the low and middle SES categories, many more women should be working, and yet the majority report that they do not work.

Work Status and Type of Family

Table 4.3 indicates that the vast majority of respondents (between 77 and 85 per cent) replied that they did not work, and further, that this does not change significantly by type of family. We can see that the difference in responses between the nuclear and joint family is not significant though the proportion not working goes up to 84 per cent for those in extended families as against 76 per cent for those in nuclear families.

TABLE 4.3
Work Status of Women by Family Type

	1	2	3	4	5	Total
Nuclear	3.69	14.26	1.92	3.26	76.86	100
Joint	3.64	11.68	2.04	3.88	78.76	100
Extended	0.84	12.71	1.74	0.17	84.54	100

Note: 1–Self employed; 2–Wage worker/employee; 3–Salaried; 4–Unpaid family worker; 5–None of these.

The correlation between type of family and reported work status is very weak (0.0434), and that between husband's work and the reported work status of respondent is even weaker (0.0234). Thus, not working is unrelated to the type of family that the respondent belongs to and to her husband's work status. Table 4.4 shows the distribution of husband's work versus work status of the respondent. The majority of the respondents report that they do not work and that the correlation between the husband's work and respondent's self-reported work status is very weak. The regional picture is analogous.

All those who opted for 'none of these' were then asked: 'Have you ever worked for cash or kind in the past?' Overwhelmingly huge proportions of 98 per cent replied 'no'. This question further confirmed the responses that were given to the preceding question. The community differences are not very significant here; in reality, there are no differences between the proportions of Scheduled Castes, OBC, upper caste Hindus; and Muslims reporting no work. They are indeed in close proximity to one another (in the range of 96 to 98 per cent); the proportion of Scheduled Tribes respondents that replied

TABLE 4.4
Work Status of Women by Husband's Work Status

	1	2	3	4	5	Total
Agriculture	1.85	6.46	1.02	7.62	83.05	100
Agricultural labour	1.56	30.66	0.58	3.15	64.02	100
Unskilled labour	3.05	19.56	0.55	2.03	74.76	100
Skilled labour	2.98	7.93	1.31	0.96	86.83	100
Doctor/engineer/lawyer	2.59	2.24	5.31	0.49	89.38	100
Small business	3.80	5.01	2.99	7.81	80.39	100
Large business	6.52	1.39	0.91	0.00	91.18	100
Driver	5.48	8.16	1.95	0.24	84.17	100
Teacher	0.95	11.71	17.84	0.14	69.36	100
Clerical jobs	6.70	0.65	4.16	2.39	86.10	100
Class IV services	3.05	14.87	1.30	0.16	80.63	100
Others	1.75	14.32	1.14	2.05	80.73	100

Note: 1–Self employed; 2–Wage worker/employee; 3–Salaried; 4–Unpaid family worker; 5–None of these

'no' was 90 per cent, also very high, but lower than that for other social groups (see Figure 4.1).

Recognizing this tendency of women to under-report their own productive work, a series of further probing questions was asked. All those who answered 'no' to the above question were queried further about their involvement in economically productive work. They were asked the following question: 'Sometimes we do not

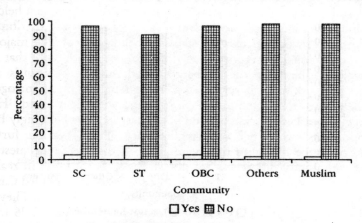

FIGURE 4.1: Have You Ever Worked for Cash or Kind in the Past?

consider such activities like working on our own farm, sitting in our own shop, participating in our own family business, or selling products like ghee, milk, flowers, fruits or vegetables, *papad*, etc. as gainful employment as there may not be direct cash earning or it may not be a regular job. Please recall whether you have ever engaged in such activities?' These questions did not, however, yield answers to alter the picture substantially. Again, the dominant response to this was 'no', and with only minuscule proportions reporting economic activity, these figures are almost similar to those reported in the previous paragraph. The responses to that question are summarized in Figure 4.2.

It appears that the respondents were not differentiating between the two questions. The reason for this could lie in the nature of the decision-making authority within the household. In order to assess that, they were asked: 'Who decides whether a female member in the house should work outside or not?' Several options were offered: the two most important proved to be husband and self, in that order. At the all-India level, the highest proportion of women who replied husband was Muslim (72 per cent), compared to 67 per cent of upper caste Hindu women. The responses for self proved to be the highest for upper caste Hindu women (22 per cent), followed by OBC and Scheduled Tribes (19 per cent), Scheduled Castes (17 per cent), and Muslims (14 per cent).

Thus, Tables 4.1–4.4 and Figures 4.1–4.2 very strongly underscore women's low economic activity. Despite very detailed probing, the

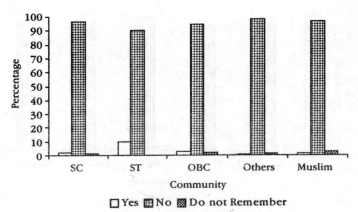

FIGURE 4.2: Women's Involvement in Any Productive Work

MWS finds extremely low women's work participation rates, even when the stress is not on direct earning or gainful employment or regular job. This is somewhat surprising in the face of the poverty faced by large numbers of women that ought to drive them into work. The work picture does not square with rampant poverty and deprivation which is a defining characteristic of this sample of households. One obvious explanation could be under-reporting, as mentioned earlier. But despite a series of probing questions addressed to women themselves, a majority of them say they are not involved in productive work, which suggests under-reporting, but also the need to explore the reasons for not working. That impoverishment should drive women to wage work or any kind of gainful employment seems quite rational, and many women engaged in home-based work are not counting their own home-based work, which they probably see as an extension of domestic work. The other reasons could be the gender stratification system and fewer opportunities for work. In short, cultural and structural factors combine to explain low work participation. The low work participation may point to low industrial and economic growth and therefore lower availability of jobs in the north and east zones.

The only exception in this bleak picture of women's work participation is the west zone with relatively better rates of work participation. Indeed this may be due to greater employment opportunities coming from higher industrial growth in the west zone, particularly in and around Mumbai, Vadodara, and Ahmedabad. Also there may be fewer barriers to female participation in economic activities, as compared to that in the north zone with a relatively smaller number of households having working women, which is explained in part by cultural factors: women in the north, known for low female status, have less control over their mobility and are subject to seclusion norms, and hence are likely to be out of the labour force.

Types and Patterns of Work

Respondents who had reported working were asked a range of questions on the kind of work they did and whether it was full-time or part-time, and whether they were paid in cash or kind. Figure 4.3 shows the distribution of those who did report themselves to be working as salaried and wage workers.

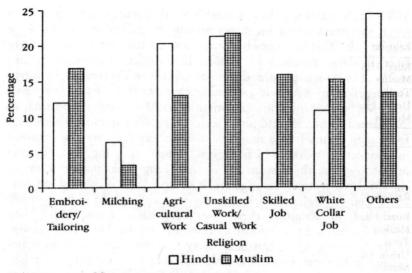

FIGURE 4.3: Salaried/Wage Workers by Religion

As to the type of work reported in Figure 4.3, the important feature of this distribution is that the largest proportion of respondents from both communities are in the unskilled category. However, the differ-ence between the two communities is significant in the skilled job category where Muslims report a significantly higher proportion. This is also true for white-collar jobs, although the difference is smaller. Muslims are also significantly lower in terms of agricultural work. For Hindus, agricultural work is the next important category after un-skilled work.

In the rural north, the pattern for agricultural work is the opposite of the all-India pattern, here Muslim women's participation being higher, while in the other three zones it is the opposite. There is also an appreciably higher proportion of Muslims in white-collar jobs. Muslim respondents, except in the rural east, report a higher than the all-India rate of participation in agricultural work in all regions. The rural south follows the all-India pattern for skilled jobs, although the proportions are lower. In contrast to the all-India trend, the propor-tion of Muslims in unskilled jobs is much higher. In the rural north, Muslims seem to be more evenly distributed across occupations, with skilled jobs, agricultural work and unskilled work/casual work being the most important categories.

TABLE 4.5
Salaried/Wage Worker by Religion: North Zone

Religion	1	2	3	4	5	6	7	Total
Rural Hindu	14.29	14.29	14.29	14.29	0.00	7.14	35.71	100
Muslim	12.00	4.00	20.00	20.00	24.00	16.00	0.00	100
Total	14.06	13.26	14.86	14.86	2.39	8.03	32.15	100
Urban Hindu	0.00	4.76	4.76	19.05	0.00	30.95	38.10	100
Muslim	30.99	0.00	1.41	23.94	15.49	18.31	8.45	100
Total	2.96	4.31	4.44	19.52	1.48	29.74	32.26	100

TABLE 4.6
Salaried/Wage Worker by Religion: South Zone

Religion	1	2	3	4	5	6	7	Total
Rural Hindu	11.11	11.11	44.44	11.11	0.00	0.00	22.22	100
Muslim	11.11	0.00	22.22	27.78	5.56	5.56	27.78	100
Total	11.11	10.65	43.53	11.80	0.23	0.23	22.45	100
Urban Hindu	13.33	0.00	6.67	33.33	0.00	26.67	20.00	100
Muslim	12.28	5.26	0.00	28.07	8.77	17.54	26.32	100
Total	13.16	0.87	5.57	32.47	1.44	25.17	21.04	100

TABLE 4.7
Salaried/Wage Worker by Religion: East Zone

Religion	1	2	3	4	5	6	7	Total
Rural Hindu	12.5	0.00	0.00	50.00	25.00	12.50	0.00	100
Muslim	12.12	6.06	18.18	18.18	18.18	18.18	9.09	100
Total	12.43	1.16	3.48	43.91	23.69	13.59	1.74	100
Urban Hindu	22.22		0.00	0.00	22.22	33.33	22.22	100
Muslim	29.73		2.70	35.14	8.11	13.51	10.81	100
Total	23.1		0.31	4.08	20.58	31.03	20.90	100

TABLE 4.8
Salaried/Wage Worker by Religion: West Zone

Religion	1	2	3	4	5	6	7	Total
Rural Hindu	20.00		80.00	0.00	0.00	0.00	0.00	100
Muslim	12.00		32.00	12.00	20.00	4.00	20.00	100
Total	19.57		77.40	0.65	1.08	0.22	1.08	100
Urban Hindu	10.53		5.26	36.84	5.26	0.00	42.11	100
Muslim	27.63		2.63	21.05	6.58	10.53	30.26	100
Total	13.22		4.85	34.36	5.47	1.66	40.24	100

Note: (Tables 4.5 to 4.8) 1–Embroidery/tailoring; 2–Milching; 3–Agricultural work; 4–Unskilled work/casual work; 5–Skilled job; 6–White-collar job; 7–Others.

In the urban north (see Table 4.8), the largest numbers of Muslim respondents are engaged in embroidery/tailoring, unskilled work/ casual work, white-collar jobs, and skilled jobs, in that order. Over half the Hindu respondents are engaged in white-collar jobs. For Muslims in the south zone (see Table 4.9), the largest category is unskilled work, followed by 'others', white-collar jobs, and embroidery/tailoring. The gap between the two communities is the starkest in the skilled job category. For Muslims in the urban east (see Table 4.10), the single largest category is unskilled jobs, and here the gap between the two communities is sharpest in the skilled jobs category. There is a significantly lower proportion of Muslims in the white-collar job category. In the urban west, the largest category for Muslims is 'white collar jobs', followed by embroidery/tailoring. In the latter category, the proportion of Hindus is significantly lower than that of Muslims. Also, in the white-collar jobs, the proportion of Muslim is significantly higher than that of Hindus.

Self-employed Women

All the respondents who replied self-employed[7] to the first question were further asked what exactly they were engaged in. The options were: 1 = professional (doctor/lawyer/architect/teacher); 2 = vocational (tailor, beautician, etc.); 3 = petty business (fruit vendor, vegetable vendor, milk ghee, etc.); 4 = large business (runs her own school or company); 5 = small business (papad, *agarbatti*, craft/artisan); 6 = social work; 7 = others.

The all-India pattern suggests that among the self-employed, the largest category for Muslim respondents comprises small business, which is essentially an artisanal category, followed very closely by the vocational category (see Figure 4.4). This confirms the view that the self-employed essentially operate small family-owned businesses. This is indeed the only category in which Muslims score above the national average, thus substantiating the trend that they are mainly engaged in self-employment. A very small proportion of Muslim women, much below the national average, occupy the professional category, whereas significantly greater proportion of Hindu women, slightly above the national average, are professionals (see Figure 4.5). Not surprisingly, both communities have very small proportions in the large business category, but again Hindus have a slightly larger presence here, approximating the national average.

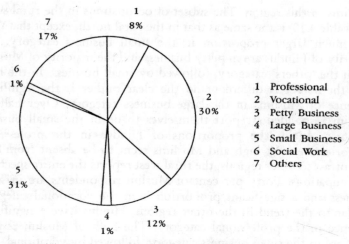

FIGURE 4.4: Division of Self-employed Women: Muslim

1 Professional
2 Vocational
3 Petty Business
4 Large Business
5 Small Business
6 Social Work
7 Others

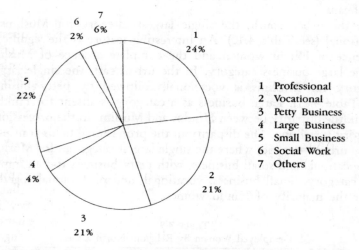

FIGURE 4.5: Division of Self-employed Women: Hindu

1 Professional
2 Vocational
3 Petty Business
4 Large Business
5 Small Business
6 Social Work
7 Others

A smaller subset of occupations is prevalent in the rural north (see Table 4.9). The single largest category is vocational, though again the proportions for Hindus are higher. Both in the professional and small business categories, there are larger proportions of Hindus than Muslims, an indication of the overall low economic status of

Muslims in this region. The subset of occupations in the rural south (see Table 4.10) is the same as that in the rural north, except that there is a much larger proportion in the small business category. The majority of Hindus are in petty business and the majority of Muslims are in the 'others' category, followed by small business. In the rural east, the subset is different and the clear outlier is the significant presence of Muslims in the large business category. Over half the Muslim responden s report themselves to be in the small business category. Again, the proportions of Hindus in the professional categories are very high and Muslims seem to be absent from this. In contrast to other regio: s, the rural west reports the entire spectrum of occupations. Forty per cent of Muslim respondents are in small business and a significant proportion is in the vocational category. Similar to the trend in the other regions, Hindus have a significant presence in the professional category. The bulk of Muslim respondents are in the small business category, followed by vocational. The proportions of Muslim respondents in other occupations are not significant.

In the urban south, the single largest category for Muslims is vocational (see Table 4.10). An interesting feature is the significant presence of Hindu women and the complete absence of Muslims in the large business category. In the urban east, the single largest category for Muslims is vocational, followed by petty business (see Table 4.11). Large business as a category is absent for Hindus. Again, the disparity between Hindus and Muslims in the professional category is striking. The disparity in the professional fields continues in the urban west too, where the single largest categories for Muslims are vocational and small business, with petty business too an important category. Small business, vocational, and professional together cover the majority of Hindu women.

TABLE 4.9
Self-employed Women by Religion: North Zone

Religion	1	2	3	4	5	6	7	Total
Rural Hindu	22.22	44.44	0.00		22.22		11.11	100
Muslim	16.67	33.33	8.33		16.67		25.00	100
Total	21.43	42.87	1.18		21.43		13.08	100
Urban Hindu	6.90	20.69	24.14	6.90	41.38	0.00	0.00	100
Muslim	6.45	24.19	8.06	0.00	53.23	1.61	6.45	100
Total	6.84	21.10	22.24	6.08	42.78	0.19	0.76	100

TABLE 4.10
Self-employed Women by Religion: South Zone

Religion	1	2	3	4	5	6	7	Total
Rural Hindu	10.00	20.00	60.00		0.00		10.00	100
Muslim	0.00	13.33	13.33		33.33		40.00	100
Total	9.69	19.79	58.54		1.04		10.94	100
Urban Hindu	15.38	30.77	15.38	15.38	7.69		15.38	100
Muslim	2.44	29.27	21.95	0.00	17.07		26.83	100
Total	13.57	30.56	16.31	13.23	9.01		16.99	100

Note: (Tables 4.9 and 4.10) 1–Professional (doctor/lawyer/architect/teacher); 2–Vocational (tailor, beautician, etc); 3–Petty business (fruit/vegetable vendor, milk, ghee, etc.); 4–Large business (runs her own school or company); 5–Small business (papad, agarbatti, crafts/artisan); 6–Social work; 7–Others.

TABLE 4.11
Self-employed Women by Religion: East Zone

Religion	1	2	3	4	5	6	7	Total
Rural Hindu	33.33	16.67	16.67	0.00	33.33			100
Muslim	0.00	33.33	0.00	11.11	55.56			100
Total	30.69	17.99	15.35	0.88	35.10			100
Urban Hindu	37.50	25.00	12.50		0.00		12.50	100
Muslim	7.14	35.71	21.43		17.86		14.29	100
Total	34.44	26.08	13.40		1.80		12.68	100

TABLE 4.12
Self-employed Women by Religion: West Zone

Religion	1	2	3	4	5	6	7	Total
Rural Hindu	40.00	0.00	10.00	10.00	30.00	10.00	0.00	100
Muslim	3.33	23.33	20.00	3.33	40.00	6.67	3.33	100
Total	38.78	0.77	10.33	9.78	30.33	9.89	0.11	100
Urban Hindu	21.43	21.43	7.14		35.71	0.00	7.14	100
Muslim	4.69	31.25	17.79		28.13	3.13	14.06	100
Total	18.49	23.16	8.91		34.38	0.55	8.35	100

Note: (Tables 4.11 and 4.12) 1–Professional (doctor/lawyer/architect/teacher); 2–Vocational (tailor, beautician, etc); 3–Petty business (fruit/vegetable vendor, milk, ghee, etc.); 4–Large business (runs her own school or company); 5–Small business (papad, agarbatti, crafts/artisan); 6–Social work; 7–Others.

Reasons for Not Working

This particular variable is perplexing, but on closer examination draws attention to the conundrum of women's lives. Respondents were asked why they did not work: the range of options offered was varied, and included several reasons not commonly listed in surveys. This enumeration of reasons, moreover, followed equally detailed enquiries regarding type, nature, and duration of work that women engage in, wages earned, and the like, thus offering respondents an opportunity to express their constraints with regard to economic activities. This notwithstanding, a very high 65 per cent chose not to answer this question at all, with Hindu respondents reporting a somewhat higher percentage than Muslims: 66 per cent as against 59 per cent (see Table 4.13). It is very likely that the 65 per cent women who did not respond were reluctant to articulate their reasons for not working, for all the usual reasons that women remain silent. As we know, factors like marriage and motherhood, restrictions on mobility, an interrupted education, and strict regulation of women's activities can be major constraints on their ability to work outside the home but they may be reluctant to articulate these constraints. Of the remaining 35 per cent, 11 per cent said they felt no need to work (read no financial need); 8 per cent claimed family responsibilities as the reason; 4 per cent said they lacked the education; and about 5 per cent laid the blame on a lack of employment opportunities that would enable them to work. Significantly, however, marriage, childbearing, no permission, purdah, and constraints on mobility (generally considered to be obstacles to women's working options) total up to a mere 6 or 7 per cent at most. A mere 1.59 per cent respondents indicated a disinclination to work.

As Table 4.14 indicates, a few respondents (1026 to be precise) gave secondary reasons for not working. As a secondary reason, lack of skills, no permission from husband/parents, lack of employment opportunities, and among the gender-specific reasons, marriage, lack of mobility, and family responsibilities assume considerable importance. But, it is noteworthy that for the respondents, purdah continues to be an unimportant obstacle to working. For our respondents, purdah is neither a primary nor secondary reason for not taking up employment outside the home. This implies that too much should not be made of cultural norms in explaining the exclusion of Muslim women from work participation considering that social and cultural obstacles to women's work constitute a very small percentage of reasons for not working.

TABLE 4.13
Primary Reasons for not Working

	Hindu	Muslim	Total
No need to work	10.53	11.02	10.59
Disinclination	1.55	1.82	1.59
Family responsibilities	7.23	11.04	7.75
Childbearing/rearing	17.00	0.95	1.14
Lack of education	3.98	4.10	3.99
Lack of skills	0.98	0.55	0.92
No permission from husband/parents	1.84	2.42	1.92
Lack of employment opportunities	4.25	5.19	4.38
Got married	0.84	1.24	0.89
Lack of mobility	0.69	2.07	0.88
Purdah	0.14	0.14	0.14
Other reasons	0.62	0.49	0.60
No response	66.20	58.97	65.21
Total	1891	6096	(7987)100

TABLE 4.14
Secondary Reasons for not Working

	Hindu	Muslim	Total
Disinclination	5.70	2.28	5.15
Family responsibilities	9.15	7.52	8.89
Childbearing/rearing	8.20	4.02	7.52
Lack of education	9.99	9.24	9.87
Lack of skills	12.91	15.02	13.25
No permission from husband/parents	17.16	13.74	16.61
Lack of employment opportunities	16.60	16.06	16.51
Got married	9.77	15.68	10.72
Lack of mobility	10.06	14.41	10.76
Purdah	0.00	1.07	0.17
Total			1026

Reasons for Working

Respondents were asked what prompted them to work. For all economic classes, the single most cited reason for working is to support the family, rather than to supplement family income. However, expectedly, utilizing time as a reason for working increases as we go up the SES spectrum. This picture is fairly uniform, with regional variations being minimal, as indicated by Table 4.15.

Table 4.16 follows the predictable pattern, given the close relationship between low SES and the Muslim community and between high SES and reasons for not working. Muslims are close to the Scheduled Castes and Tribes groups in terms of SES, and this is reflected in similar proportions of these two groups working to support the family. The next important reason seems to be supplementing the family income. Upper caste Hindus and OBCs have the largest proportions among women who work to utilize their time, obviously reflecting their higher SES. The only variation of some interest is in the switch between the upper castes and OBC in terms of which of these two groups constitutes the highest proportion of women who work to utilize their time. The urban south is the only region that has a high proportion of Muslim respondents who report that they work to utilize their time, which, given the relatively better position of Muslim women in this region, is not surprising.

TABLE 4.15
Reasons for Working by SES

	1	2	3	7	9
Low	69.15	26.59	0.93	1.07	2.25
Lower middle	81.19	16.57	0.31	0.02	1.91
Middle	72.99	19.31	7.20	0.44	0.05
Upper middle	73.39	14.33	10.07	0.03	0.19
High	62.15	11.75	22.30	3.78	0.03
Total	72.54	19.46	6.06	0.86	1.09

TABLE 4.16
Reasons for Working by Community

	1	2	3	7	9	Total
1 SC	80.10	14.85	4.26	0.79	0.00	100
2 ST	75.49	20.46	4.05	0.00	0.00	100
3 OBC	63.51	25.20	6.87	1.20	3.22	100
4 Others	61.88	25.38	11.60	1.14	0.00	100
5 Muslims	77.50	14.94	5.34	1.21	1.02	100
Total	72.06	19.89	6.01	0.92	1.11	100

Note: (Tables 4.15 and 4.16) 1–To support the family; 2–To supplement income; 3–Utilize time; 7–Others; 9–No response.

Decision-making about Work

To gauge women's autonomy in decision-making about their own work, the respondents were asked: 'Who decides whether a female member in the house should work outside or not?' The majority of women sa:d that their husbands play the central role in deciding whether tley should work outside the home or not (see Table 4.17). The proportion of Muslim women who so responded is slightly higher than that for upper caste respondents, but not significantly. Note that the role of parents-in-law in this decision is not very important. A slightly higher proportion of respondents answer 'yes' to fathers-in-law, in comparison to mothers-in-law, but again the difference here is not significant. Next to the husband, the most important person to decide about working outside the home is the woman herself.

TABLE 4.17
Decision-making about Women's Work by Community

	1	2	3	4	5	6	7
Hindu	18.73	69.06	4.29	1.24	2.55	1.54	1.95
SC	16.75	70.02	4.00	1.22	3.74	2.40	1.27
ST	18.50	75.98	1.41	2.74	0.00	0.00	1.37
OBC	19.24	68.52	3.66	1.27	1.77	1.44	3.15
Others	21.98	67.33	5.45	0.75	1.99	0.85	1.57
Muslim	14.41	71.78	4.53	1.73	1.81	1.33	3.97

Note: 1–Self; 2–Husband; 3–Father; 4–Mother; 5–Father-in-law; 6–Mother-in-law; 7–Others.

Regional variations reveal that across social groups, the proportion of respondents citing husbands is larger in the north and east than in the south and west zones. This is hardly surprising as regional cultures and development patterns influence women's employment. In the north zone (Uttar Pradesh and Bihar), which is generally more conservative and patriarchal, cultural norms govern women's work outside, and often work is treated as a mark of low status, and therefore only women from either poor households or high-income groups go out to work. The same family responsibilities that drive men to seek employment serve to keep women at home. In the south zone, rural proportions are higher than urban, but this is not so for the west zone. Looking at the regional variation, women among all social groups from the rural west had higher than the all-India proportions for deciding for themselves and lower than the all-India proportions for husbands taking the decision; the rural east, however, presented the opposite tendency, i.e. lower than all-India percentages for self and higher than all-India percentages for husbands. Taking the self-responses to be a measure of autonomy, the urban west zone reports the most favourable outcomes: here 24 per cent of Muslim respondents said they themselves decided, while 62 per cent cited their husbands to be the decision maker.

Another indicator of women's autonomy is the extent of control they exercise over their earnings, and of course this is relevant only for those who self-report themselves to be working for cash or kind, which, as we have already seen, is a minority. Analysing the responses to the question about who decides what to do with income, it transpires that the three most important are 'self', 'jointly with husband', and 'husband'. Very interestingly, and contrary to the general impression, 'self' is the most frequent response for all social groups, whereas proportions for the latter two responses vary by social group. For instance, 45 per cent Muslim respondents say they decide (in comparison to 52 per cent upper caste Hindu respondents); 21 per cent say their husbands do (in comparison to 18 per cent upper caste Hindu respondents); and 19 per cent decide jointly with them (17 per cent for upper caste Hindu respondents). For Scheduled Caste respondents, the pattern is different: the proportions are 36 per cent for 'self', 35 per cent for 'jointly with husband', and 15 per cent for 'husband'. The regional variation in the responses of Muslim women indicates that significantly greater proportions of urban women report 'self', compared to rural women, and this is true for all four zones. Interestingly, and this is a deviation from earlier patterns, the urban north reports the most favourable outcome in terms of women's control over their own income. As many as 63 per cent here answer 'self', followed by 13 per cent who decide 'jointly', with husbands deciding only for 9 per cent. While interpreting these results, however, it is useful to bear in mind that 85 per cent of Muslim women in the urban north self-report themselves to be not working.

Decision-making and SES

As before, across socio-economic classes, the majority of respondents reported that their husbands decide whether a female member of their family should work outside the home or not (see Table 4.18). Significantly, the proportions reporting 'self' are higher in the lower SES classes than in the upper ones, suggesting that poverty may drive women to decide on their own that there is no alternative to their working, and this pattern is replicated in all the regions. Interestingly, there does not seem to be a consistently significant difference between the urban and rural areas.

TABLE 4.18
Decision-making about Women's Work by SES

	1	2	3	4	5	6	7
Low	26.47	63.80	2.04	1.42	1.63	0.79	3.04
Lower middle	18.55	73.63	2.91	0.30	2.36	0.28	0.83
Middle	16.07	68.58	5.56	1.94	2.35	1.38	3.24
Upper middle	14.24	75.12	3.26	0.99	1.68	2.43	2.16
High	16.45	66.49	7.51	1.45	4.56	2.53	0.90

Decision-making and Education

Contrary to received wisdom, a woman's education level, according to the MWS, has an insignificant impact on whether she can decide to work outside the home (see Table 4.19). Surprisingly, women who are more educated do not necessarily have a greater capacity to decide, and so higher proportions are not self in this category; more educated women do, however, report higher percentages for fathers and less for husbands. This difference may not, however, mean much; what is significant is that the respondent herself is not deciding in the majority of cases.

TABLE 4.19
Decision-making about Women's Work by Women's Education Level

	1	2	3	4	5	6	7
Illiterate	20.06	69.63	1.42	0.95	2.48	1.69	3.19
Non-formal	49.92	43.73	1.20	0.00	0.61	0.46	4.03
Primary	18.68	76.05	2.97	0.99	0.93	0.10	0.15
Middle	15.76	70.95	6.77	1.06	2.92	1.19	0.78
Higher secondary	13.22	70.37	8.93	2.31	2.18	1.66	0.25
Graduate and above	12.16	55.72	17.83	4.1	3.68	2.61	1.18

Note: (Tables 4.18 and 4.19) 1–Self; 2–Husband; 3–Father; 4–Mother; 5–Father-in-law; 6–Mother-in-law; 7–Others.

There is, however, a positive relationship between age and the capacity to decide, progressing linearly across age groups. Over half the oldest respondents in our sample claim that they themselves decide whether a female member will work outside the home or not (see Table 4.20).

TABLE 4.20
Decision-making about Women's Work by Age Group

	1	2	3	4	5	6	7
18–35 years	11.93	70.87	6.35	1.98	3.93	2.35	1.67
36–60 years	27.01	68.56	1.11	0.22	0.07	0.17	2.80
61–90 years	51.03	41.87	0.04	0.00	0.04	0.00	6.96

Note: 1–Self; 2–Husband; 3–Father; 4–Mother; 5–Father-in-law; 6–Mother-in-law; 7–Others.

Earnings

Data on earnings in the MWS illustrate the same problem of unreliability suffered by other data sets in India. The problem is that earnings are seldom accurately reported in survey data. Economists have written about these issues: when part of the earnings are in kind, they are often not considered to be income; when households are both production and consumption units, there may be no conceptual separation of income and expenditure; in addition, women's earnings are quite often taken over by the husband or other family members and are thus not reported by the women themselves as 'theirs'. Moreover, a lot of unpaid work is undertaken, so data on earnings are frequently not satisfactory indicators either of women's involvement in productive work or of their economic status. This may explain why a very high proportion of respondents (77 per cent) in the MWS replied zero to the question: 'What is your average monthly earning?' Remember that this question was asked only of those respondents who reported doing paid work. Another 13 per cent replied that they earned between Re 1 and Rs 500, while the remaining 10 per cent gave answers ranging from Rs 516 to Rs 20,000. This pattern of responses is the same across communities, indicating that gender rather than class or community is the determinant here.

More useful are responses on how income is to be spent. The following question was posed: 'Who decides about how money earned by the respondent will be used?' Thus, in this set, among Muslims,

the highest proportions reported are respondents who decide themselves: a high 45 per cent (see Table 4.21). Less than half of them (21
per cent) say that their husbands decide exclusively, followed by 19
per cent who decide jointly with their husbands. The only community that has a larger percentage of respondents deciding themselves
is the upper caste. Besides, both for Scheduled Castes and OBCs, the
proportions of respondents deciding themselves and jointly with
husband are larger than those for whom the husband decides.

TABLE 4.21
Decision-making About Use of Women's Earning by Community

	1	2	3	4	5	6	7
SC	36.32	14.70	34.90	6.45	0.21	3.26	3.36
ST	34.80	18.05	16.87	0.00	0.00	4.02	16.27
OBC	29.38	18.41	30.98	5.32	1.29	2.15	7.15
Others	52.21	17.49	17.28	3.58	0.00	2.65	6.80
Muslim	45.12	21.01	18.96	3.55	1.44	0.75	6.75

Note: 1–Respondent; 2–Husband; 3–Jointly with husband; 4–Parents/in-laws;
5–Elders; 6–Jointly with someone else; 7–Family's joint decision.

The rural north follows the all-India pattern, except that among
upper caste Hindus, a very high proportion (50 per cent) report that
the family decides jointly. It is possible that this is an outlier. Among
Muslims, the combined proportion of husband alone and jointly
with husband exceeds that of the respondent alone. For upper caste
Hindus, it appears to be a neat three-way division. Here the deviation
from the all-India pattern comes from the very high proportion of
Scheduled Castes that decide on their own (close to 67 per cent).
Among OBCs, those who decide with someone else are substantial
(20 per cent). It is not clear what this means. An overwhelming
proportion of upper caste Hindu women in the rural west claim that
their husbands exclusively decide what to do with their earnings.
For the other groups, the pattern is similar to that prevalent at the
all-India level. The proportions for 'respondent alone decides' are very
high—reflecting perhaps the urban–rural dichotomy. All the social
groups are very close to one another in terms of this response.
Somewhat surprisingly, the proportions for respondent alone decides
in the urban south, though higher than the all-India averages, are
lower than those of the urban north. The proportions for jointly
with husband are substantial for all social groups, except for the

Scheduled Tribes who are not a substantial presence in the region. The urban east mirrors the urban north pattern. Muslims report a small proportion of husband alone decides and relatively speaking, a much larger percentage for jointly with husband. The urban west has a distribution similar to that of the urban south.

Contribution of Earnings to the Family Income by Community

Overall, 65 per cent respondents report that all their earnings contributed to the family income. Given the unreliability of earnings data, it is not clear what these figures indicate, but they do point to the poverty of the households and the dependence of the family on their income. It corresponds to the National Institute of Urban Affairs (NIUA) studies on the status of working women in low-income households and their contribution to the family and household income. Similarly, the MWS shows that women's earnings are extremely significant and without their earnings, the family would plunge deep into poverty.[8]

The correlation between the SES, average monthly income, and how much the respondents' earnings contributed to the latter is significant; the insignificant *negative* correlation between the SES and women's earnings, however, reinforces the point about the unreliability of earnings data. Nevertheless, the majority of respondents say that they contributed their entire earnings to the family. The proportions are greatest among respondents in the lower middle and middle SES categories: 77 and 70 per cent, respectively (see Table 4.23). Those in the highest socio-economic class have the lowest proportions, suggesting that among the better-off sections of the people, families are less dependent on women's earnings than others. This further corroborates the earlier findings.

TABLE 4.22
Contribution of Women's Earning to Family Income

	1	2	3	4	5
SC	6.29	12.49	7.81	2.15	70.46
ST	3.29	0.00	1.67	4.02	81.03
OBC	17.67	20.27	4.86	4.81	47.15
Others	10.20	6.88	4.40	5.42	73.10
Muslims	8.64	9.44	3.37	4.49	72.29
Total	10.29	12.87	5.51	3.75	64.50

TABLE 4.23
Contribution of Women's Earning to Family Income by SES

	1	2	3	4	5	Total
Low	10.68	19.50	7.04	0.29	62.27	100
Lower middle	5.86	10.47	3.89	0.97	76.87	100
Middle	4.93	10.65	3.76	2.75	69.51	100
Upper middle	11.68	8.85	3.81	9.41	63.66	100
High	24.44	6.46	7.56	11.65	49.80	100
Total	10.02	12.59	5.22	3.63	65.61	100

Note: (Tables 4.22 and 4.23) 1–Almost nothing; 2–less than half; 3–about half; 4–more than half; 5–all.

For many women, the basic purpose of work is enhancement of income and alleviation of poverty, and therefore, gainful employment is essential for survival. Employment of women has greater impact on poverty than that of men because, as the preceding discussion shows, women tend to deploy their earnings more on basic needs of the households, and particularly on improving the well-being of their children, which can have a greater economic impact than the employment of men.

Conclusion

The MWS presents a picture of very low women's work participation. It reports particularly low levels of Muslim women's work participation (14 per cent), and this is also true of the upper caste respondents in the sample studied. More respondents from Scheduled Castes and low socio-economic classes are engaged in work. The differential pattern can be partly explained by the higher landownership of Hindus reported by the MWS and by the fact that more Hindu women are engaged in farm work whereas Muslim women are less likely to work in agriculture.

Notwithstanding extended definitions of work and detailed probing of the many possible permutations and combinations of what is classified as work, reporting does not yield better results. Much has been written about the existing social accounting, official classification systems, and the gender-biased definitions of work and employment, contributing to a 'statistical veil' over women's work. Often the male bias in data collection is blamed for a gross underestimation of women's work and why it is undervalued, invisible, and unrecognized. However, as the MWS indicates, the fault does not lie solely with policy-makers and male investigators, but also with ordinary men and women motivated by the prevalent attitudes and status codes that restrain them from providing accurate descriptions of women's productive activities.[9]

A number of micro case studies[10] confirm the suspicion that certainly in rural areas, a far greater number of women work than the figures indicate.[11] Though the MWS findings are, in all probability, an underestimation of women's actual work participation rates, on the other hand, they do reflect inter-group disparity, with Muslim and upper caste Hindu women showing lower rates of work participation. The results indicate significant inter-caste differences in work participation rates, occupations, and earnings. Due to fewer restrictions on public visibility and mobility, a less restrictive social regime, Scheduled Caste women have a higher work participation rate, especially in rural areas, than all other women. Thus, overall, Scheduled Caste women have a slight advantage and reservations would appear to enhance that advantage. By contrast, the social norms that influence the involvement of non-Scheduled Caste women in work are related to their position in the social stratification system and marked by an associated withdrawal from the labour force. Even though few poor families can afford the luxury of keeping women at home, working for wages is seen to be an indicator of low status and work outside the home is considered secondary for women. Muslim women are likely to be engaged in self-employment or family-based concerns or home-based work, and it is quite possible that their involvement in family business might at times go unnoticed and unmeasured.[12]

Whatever the case may be, the proportions of non-working women are huge irrespective of socio-economic status, community, place of residence, or region. The main issue in the MWS regarding Muslim women's employment has to do with the low work participation of Muslim respondents despite the preponderance of poor women in this sample. With an overwhelmingly large proportion of Muslim respondents from a low socio-economic background, for whom remaining unemployed is not an option, we would expect poverty to drive them into work as much as it does Hindu women from a comparable economic status—the Scheduled Castes, for instance. But the MWS data does not support this option: 85 per cent Muslim women report that they are not working, a figure which is much higher than that for Scheduled Castes, and the rest are concentrated in low-end jobs.

The regional picture, with the exception of higher economic activity in the west zone, is similar to the national trend. Several recent studies on women's work have argued that region plays a more determining role in work participation than religion.[13] Though South Indian Muslim women have comparatively greater mobility and are not subject to seclusion this does not translate into increased work participation in the south zone in our sample. In fact, the lack of regional variation in work participation in the MWS underlines the low employment of Muslim women. Regular salaried jobs constitute a minuscule proportion of the work category in the MWS.

In sum, four points are worth noting. The first is the under-reporting of work; second, the generally low work participation of women in this sample, i.e. below the national average for the country reported in the Census of 1991; the third, the low levels of work participation across all regions and very low proportions in skilled jobs. The fourth feature that distinguishes Muslim women's work profile is that two-thirds of Muslim women, like their male counterparts, are self-employed and least likely to be employed in regular salaried jobs in urban areas.

Shram Shakti, the Report of the National Commission on Self-Employed Women and Women in the Informal Sector (Government of India 1988), provided the earliest description of self-employed women, as small producers and home-based workers, who either supply their produce to middlemen through informal contractual arrangements or have their own small vending businesses. The work pattern reported in the MWS corresponds to this description, indicating that women who work do so in petty trade, retailing establishments, small business, and home-based work such as tailoring, embroidery, etc. In short, Muslim women have a higher probability of being self-employed in home-based work. They are concentrated in domestic and low-paid or unpaid work. They often undertake piece-rate work in the home, arguably the lowest paid or unpaid and low-skilled work of all.

The key issue that needs to be addressed is the noticeably low work participation of Muslim women. It has been usually explained in terms of restrictions imposed on them in the public domain. Contrary to the popular idea that Islam imposes cultural restrictions, such as purdah, and therefore greater gender inequality, the MWS findings point out that these restrictions on women's physical mobility are not limited to Muslim women since other communities share them in more or less the same degrees. Given that the levels of autonomy and mobility of Muslim and Hindu women are also not very different,

Muslim women's work participation may be impeded by several other factors. A crucial issue for women is whether they are employed at all, and patterns of decision-making in Muslim households may well influence the issue of work outside the home. But again the MWS does not indicate a significant difference in decision-making patterns: nearly 72 per cent Muslim and 67 per cent Hindu respondents identified husbands as the authority that decides whether female members should work outside or not. This implies that lack of autonomy is not a constraint for Muslim women only and that such restrictions cannot be depressing Muslim women's employment alone.

Two major reasons for the low work participation of Muslim women are their restricted engagement in agriculture owing to differential patterns of landownership in rural areas and their exclusion from low-level jobs in urban areas. The second reason, that is, the limited access to low-level jobs is particularly important in view of the large proportions of Muslims residing in urban areas who would be potentially interested in such jobs. As Muslims and as women, they are twice as disadvantaged in access to jobs generally and possibly even low-level jobs in the informal sector and casual labour. This is borne out by the NSS data which show that of the uneducated Muslim women, only about 8 per cent find employment as casual labour in public works, when compared to over 21 per cent of Hindu uneducated women. Though the 1990s have seen a substantial increase in regular work for women, including regular salaried employment, even as the share of self-employment has declined, the opportunities for Muslim women seem to have not improved at all. Perhaps because urban employment often requires skills that most Muslim women in this sample would not possess. Most Muslim women are simply not in competition with males or other women, are absent from the subsectors of manufacturing, and if they happen to be working at all they would be concentrated in low-paying and low-skill jobs that are really extensions of the domestic domain, and this type of work could easily be the most disadvantaged. This may heighten discrimination against women at various levels evident in low work participation rates, small proportion of women in better paid jobs, and low earnings of Muslim women in the unprotected wage sector, and it gets further aggravated by an overall social discrimination within families, which discourages women from acquiring the skills and education needed to enter the labour market.

Further research, among other things, will clarify these arguments and observations.

In any event, special interventions are required to ensure economic participation of women, because even special programmes meant for women's development and employment often bypass them, as the chapter on access to social welfare so vividly reveals. This point comes through clearly from the nationwide study undertaken by the National Commission on Self-Employed Women and Women in the Informal Sector, which shows that given the right opportunities, women from the lower strata of society would benefit immensely. From the experience of organizations such as Self-Employed Women's Association (SEWA), as well as numerous examples of successful cooperative and micro-credit experiments, it would appear that a combination of social, economic, and catalytic factors, including assistance for productive activities and enhancement in organizations providing bargaining strength, make for both greater incidence and visibility of women's work. We cannot assume that in the above cases, the usual gender and class specific constraints were absent, or that compelling economic reasons alone enabled women to break free of them. Rather, a range of strategic interventions, policy as well as developmental, empowered them to successfully enter into organized economic activity where they had not been earlier, to improve their conditions and terms of labour, and, despite all manner of odds, negotiate complicated financial and social obstacles. These experiments show that women, especially poor women, are both bankable and reliable as workers if a modicum of economic and community support is made available to them. When this becomes more widespread, it is likely that many more women will be working and a much more accurate picture of women's work status will emerge.

Endnotes

1. Lourdes Beneria (ed.), *Women and Development: The Sexual Division of Labour in Rural Societies*, Praeger, New York, 1982.

2. Saraswati Raju and Deepica Bagchi (eds), *Women and Work in South Asia: Regional Patterns and Perspectives*, Routledge, London, New York, 1993, p. 2.

3. N. Lalitha, 'Women in the Unorganized Manufacturing Sector in India: A Sectoral Analysis', *Indian Journal of Labour Economics*, 42(4), 1999.

4. *Human Development in South Asia 2000: The Gender Question*, Mahbubul Haq Human Development Centre, Oxford University Press, Karachi, 2000, p. 52.

128 □ *Unequal Citizens*

5. It is important to note that in rural India, household enterprise is the predominant form of organizing economic activity that is defined as the following: 'working members of the household act as a collective unit in the household asset base for generating gross income, which, after intermediate costs are netted out, is shared among members of the household, including non-workers'. Ashwini Deshpande, 'Casting Off Servitude: Caste and Gender Inequality in India', in Kathleen Blee and France Winddance Twine (eds), *Feminism and Anti-racism: International Struggles*, New York University Press, New York, 2001, pp. 328–48.

6. Kalyani Menon-Sen and A. K. Shiva Kumar, p. 55.

7. According to the National Sample Survey (NSS), the self-employed are either own-account workers, self-employed employers, or unpaid family helpers.

8. Om Prakash Mathur, 'Women, Urban Poverty and Economic Development', in Noeleen Heyzer and Gita Sen (eds), *Gender, Economic Growth and Poverty*, Kali for Women, New Delhi, 1994, p. 172.

9. See Ashwini Deshpande, 'Casting Off Servitude: Caste and Gender Inequality in India'.

10. Ibid.

11. Joan Mencher, 'South Indian Female Cultivators: Who are They and What They Do?' in A. M. Shah, B. S. Baviskar, and E. A. Ramaswamy (eds), *Social Structure and Change Vol. 2: Women in Indian Society*, Sage Publications, New Delhi, 1996, pp. 56–78.

12. According to the NSS, the lowest participation rates are recorded for Muslim women: 11 per cent for urban and 19.6 per cent for rural areas.

13. Bina Agarwal, *A Field of One's Own: Gender and Land Rights in South Asia*, Cambridge University Press, Cambridge, UK, 1994; Lynn Bennet, *Women, Poverty and Productivity in India*, EDI Seminar, Paper No. 43, The World Bank, Washington, D.C., 1992; Saraswati Raju and Deepica Bagchi, *Women and Work in South Asia*.

5

Decision-making

Women's decision-making capacity and their presence and participation in decision-making—within the family, in public, at work, and in decision-making bodies, whether institutional or political—are an important gauge of their autonomy and empowerment. Increasing both the level and quality of their participation, especially at the political and policy levels, has been a major plank of the international women's movement, which has consistently drawn attention to it and lobbied for it at national and international forums. The United Nations (UN) system recognizes it as a major policy initiative, and most international donor and lending agencies require a gender component—whose primary objective is women's empowerment—to be included in all the programmes, activities, and organizations they support.

Some data on women in decision-making have been compiled by the United Nations Development Programme (UNDP) in their Human Development Reports, and a more detailed analysis is available in *Human Development in South Asia: The Gender Question*,[1] from which we get a broad idea of comparative trends by country. As with most such data, however, the true picture remains elusive, mainly because women's everyday experiences are not accounted for. Their primary arena remains the domestic, not the public, where few enumerators have ventured in order to capture the complicated, and sometimes contradictory, circumstances in which women negotiate, bargain, concede, manipulate, and otherwise express agency.

The questions posed by the Muslim Women's Survey represent a very modest attempt at trying to understand the dynamics of decision-making among Muslim and Hindu women in our sample. The issues we wished to address fall into three broad clusters: work-related; household- and family-related; and expenditure- and income-related.

In the first, questions were asked about who makes decisions regarding women's work outside the home; about their income; about how that income is disposed of and by whom; and about when and where a woman is allowed to enter the workforce, and when she must withdraw from it. The second cluster deals with household matters; children's education; marriage, birth, and death ceremonies; major illnesses. The third cluster deals with major purchases and/or investments; and travel. Responses to the work cluster have been dealt with in the chapter on work, a very important aspect of women's autonomy, but one which remains marginal, as we have already discussed. The remaining two clusters, located in the private domain, yield the following, somewhat unexpected, results.

About 35 per cent, or roughly one-third, of respondents from both communities maintain that decisions regarding household expenditure are made by them jointly with their husbands, with another one-third—32 per cent Hindu, and 34 per cent Muslim—reporting that only their husbands decide (see Table 5.1). Roughly the same proportions report similarly on decisions regarding children's education (see Table 5.2). Only 10 per cent report taking decisions by themselves alone, and community differences are negligible.

A slightly greater involvement by the rest of the family is noticed in decisions relating to marriage, with correspondingly lower percentages for 'self' and 'husbands alone' (see Table 5.3). The same is true for birth and death ceremonies (see Tables 5.4 and 5.5), again reflecting the fact that these are essentially family-oriented decisions and activities.

Women's decision-making *on their own* declines with regard to major purchases and major investments (see Tables 5.6 and 5.7), whereas husbands deciding on these, alone, remains consistent with other decisions—i.e. on household expenditure, children's education, and marriage—suggesting that women's reduced participation may be taken over by the 'whole family' here, which reports a slightly higher degree of involvement. Or it could be otherwise, as discussed later.

Over 50 per cent of our respondents said that they were consulted on all decisions regarding household and consumption expenditure, marriage, and birth and death ceremonies, but this consultation declines noticeably with regard to major illness, major purchases and investments, and travel (see Figures 5.1–5.9). The significant community difference here is that *Muslim women report greater consultation than Hindus for all categories*, and especially for major purchases and investment, although the reasons for this are not readily apparent.

TABLE 5.1
Who Decides about Household Expenditure?

Religion	1	2	3	4	5	6	7	8	9
Hindu	5.23	3.08	5.60	31.91	10.49	35.49	1.09	6.89	0.22
Muslim	5.61	2.87	3.21	34.05	9.75	35.17	0.57	8.50	0.26
Total	5.28	3.05	5.30	32.17	10.40	35.45	1.03	7.08	0.23

TABLE 5.2
Who Decides about Children's Education?

Religion	1	2	3	4	5	6	7	8	9
Hindu	4.78	2.17	5.42	34.25	8.49	36.41	1.15	7.04	0.28
Muslim	5.08	2.18	3.29	34.02	8.33	37.38	0.50	8.83	0.38
Total	4.82	2.17	5.16	34.22	8.47	36.53	1.07	7.26	0.29

TABLE 5.3
Who Decides about Marriage?

Religion	1	2	3	4	5	6	7	8	9
Hindu	4.99	2.43	5.78	30.46	6.38	38.4	1.05	10.16	0.34
Muslim	5.07	2.52	3.77	31.29	6.77	38.21	0.43	11.60	0.33
Total	5.00	2.44	5.53	30.56	6.43	38.38	0.97	10.34	0.34

TABLE 5.4
Who Decides about Birth Ceremonies?

Religion	1	2	3	4	5	6	7	8	9
Hindu	5.08	2.03	5.68	31.88	7.09	38.08	1.05	7.82	1.29
Muslim	4.83	2.24	3.47	31.84	7.54	37.69	0.50	9.69	2.20
Total	5.05	2.06	5.41	31.88	7.14	38.03	0.98	8.05	1.40

TABLE 5.5
Who Decides about Death Ceremonies?

Religion	1	2	3	4	5	6	7	8	9
Hindu	4.80	2.39	5.65	32.04	7.43	35.28	1.02	10.49	0.90
Muslim	5.08	2.57	3.53	32.03	7.24	36.48	0.47	11.81	0.79
Total	4.84	2.42	5.39	32.04	7.40	35.43	0.95	10.65	0.89

TABLE 5.6
Who Decides about Major Purchases?

Religion	1	2	3	4	5	6	7	8	9
Hindu	4.74	2.20	5.41	31.22	6.17	36.75	1.02	11.46	1.02
Muslim	5.27	2.00	3.46	33.17	6.56	36.10	0.49	11.80	1.14
Total	4.80	2.18	5.17	31.46	6.22	36.67	0.96	11.51	1.03

132 □ Unequal Citizens

TABLE 5.7
Who Decides about Major Investments?

Religion	1	2	3	4	5	6	7	8	9
Hindu	4.81	2.18	5.31	32.82	5.37	34.86	1.02	11.81	1.81
Muslim	5.31	2.02	3.44	34.67	6.09	34.22	0.50	11.64	2.11
Total	4.87	2.16	5.08	33.05	5.46	34.79	0.96	11.79	1.85

Note: (Tables 5.1 to 5.7) 1–Father/father-in-law; 2–Mother/mother-in-law; 3–Jointly with parents/parents-in-law; 4–Husband; 5–Self; 6–Husband and self jointly; 7–Brother; 8–Whole family; 9–No response.

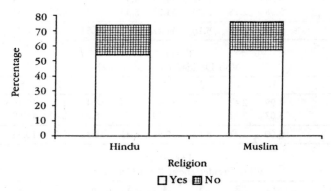

FIGURE 5.1: Consultation of Women with Regard to Household Expenditure

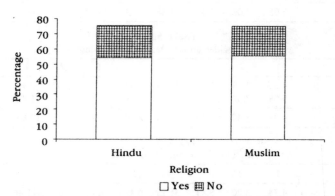

FIGURE 5.2: Consultation of Women with Regard to Consumption Expenditure

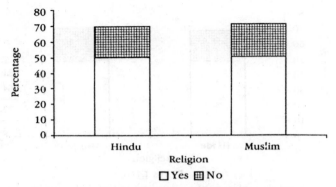

FIGURE 5.3: Consultation of Women with Regard to Marriage

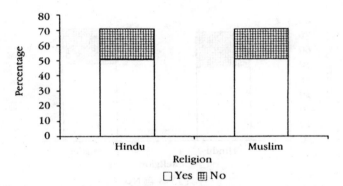

FIGURE 5.4: Consultation of Women with Regard to Birth Ceremonies

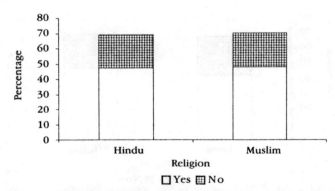

FIGURE 5.5: Consultation of Women with Regard to Death Ceremonies

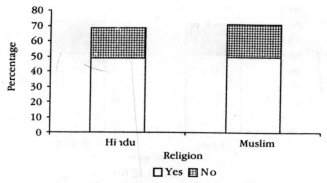

FIGURE 5.6: Consultation of Women with Regard to Treatment of Major Illness

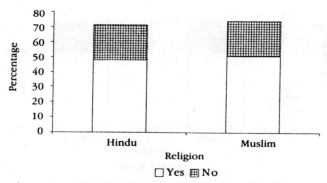

FIGURE 5.7: Consultation of Women with Regard to Travel

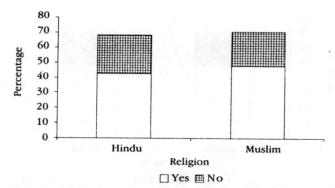

FIGURE 5.8: Consultation of Women with Regard to Major Purchases

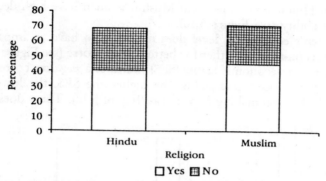

FIGURE 5.9: Consultation of Women with Regard to Major Investment

Autonomy in Decision-making

Let us now look at the findings of the MWS on those decisions that women take by themselves, and the percentage who do so. (We should mention here that the MWS deliberately avoided asking questions about decisions regarding cooking, purchasing jewellery, and other purely 'womanly' preoccupations.) No more than 10 per cent of respondents, Muslim or Hindu, report taking decisions by themselves, across all classes, and in all the areas identified; but even this proportion drops to almost half when it comes to deciding about marriage, and major purchases and investments. Interestingly, however, Muslim women report marginally greater decision-making capacity than Hindus, but the difference is not significant. It is possible (a) that this 10 per cent represents female-headed households (we may recall that the number of Muslim women who are divorced, separated, deserted, widowed, and never-married totals 13.6 per cent) or households with no male members; and (b) that the percentage deciding purchases and investments is very small because surplus funds are unavailable—i.e., no decision is possible. As far as marriage is concerned, it is likely that, even in the absence of male members, decisions are taken in consultation with other family members.

A working decision-making index (DMI),[2] constructed from the responses to our categories/clusters, indicates that the majority of women—a high 62 per cent—from both communities has no role at all in decision-making in the family/household. Fifteen per cent Hindu and 11 per cent Muslim women have a moderate role; while 24 per cent Hindu, and 26 per cent Muslim women have high decision-making ability (see Figure 5.10).

Women's educational level does not seem to have an impact on their decision-making, either for better or for worse (see Figure 5.11), but their socio-economic status (SES) indicates a *negative* correlation with a rise in economic status: the higher the SES, the lower are women's decision-making powers (see Figure 5.12). There does seem

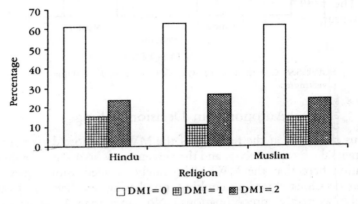

FIGURE 5.10: Decision-making Index (DMI) by Religion

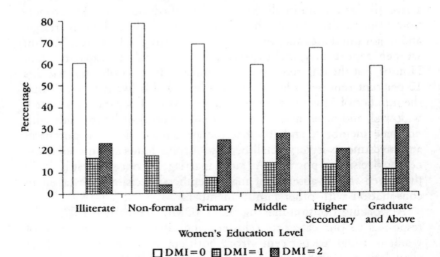

FIGURE 5.11: DMI by Women's Education Level

to be a generational shift, though, with younger women reporting greater decision-making (see Figure 5.13) and this, together with the fact that this is a predominantly Muslim sample, may account for their slightly better situation *vis-à-vis* joint decision-making. Rural women report the lowest proportions, as do women from the east zone, and the west zone reports the highest levels, urban and rural, for high decision-making ability (see Figures 5.14 and 5.15).

The most significant finding with regard to regional variations, however, is that women's decision-making ability is largely unaffected

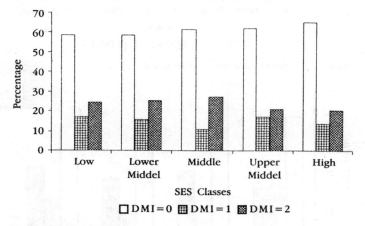

FIGURE 5.12: DMI by SES

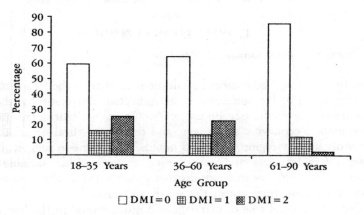

FIGURE 5.13: DMI by Age Group

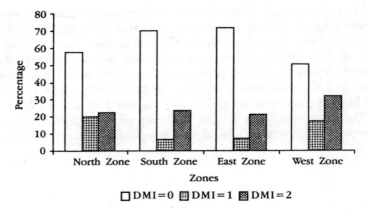

FIGURE 5.14: Zonal Variation in DMI: Rural

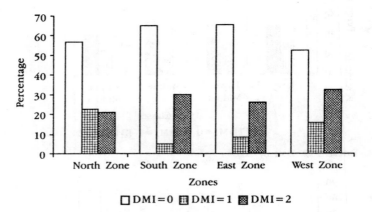

FIGURE 5.15: Zonal Variation in DMI: Urban

either by their own educational attainment or that of their husbands (see Figure 5.16); by community, as indicated above; or by their exposure to the media (see Figure 5.17). We see a slight correlation between socio-economic status, age, and residence—rural or urban— but hardly any by region, except as noted. This seems to suggest that gender overrides class and community as far as this variable is concerned, but that women are distinctly better off in the west and north zones than they are in the south and east.

Given the central role of marriage and motherhood in the lives of Indian women, the question of how decisions regarding family size

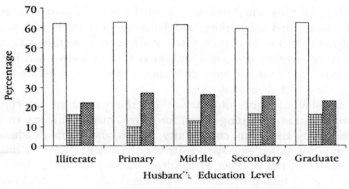

FIGURE 5.16: DMI by Husband's Education Level

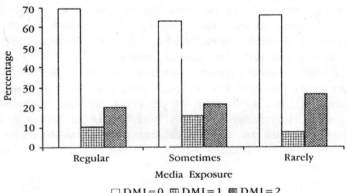

FIGURE 5.17: DMI and Media Exposure

are made is naturally quite important. We may, understandably, assume that childbearing for Indian women does not necessarily entail any discussion or conscious 'decision-making', that children get born as a natural and desirable consequence of marriage; but the MWS elicited some rather interesting information on the subject, which we present as an important component of decision-making.

The MWS reports that Muslim women had more living children (3.5) than Hindus (2.8); and the National Family Health Survey (Second Round) reported that the median age at first birth for women, all-India, is 19 years, with age at last birth being 29 years. Across the

140 □ *Unequal Citizens*

country, Hindus and Muslims reported lower median ages at first birth than Christians, Sikhs, and Jains, ranging from 17.7 years in Andhra Pradesh to 23 years in Goa.[3] It also noted a significant positive correlation between education and age at first birth—women who had completed high school were *five years* older than illiterate women when they had their first child.

The MWS sought information on the nature of inter-spousal communication regarding when and how many children to have, correlated by age group, community, region, and women's education. The question posed to respondents was: have you and your husband ever discussed the number of children you would like to have? All-India, a rather high proportion (56 per cent) said they had; 43 per cent said they had not done so. A clear generational shift is evident in the responses, as Figure 5.18 indicates. Sixty-two per cent women in the 18–35 year age group said yes, as did 46 per cent in the 35–60 year age group, but only 14 per cent among the 60–90 year-olds did so. Conforming to the usual pattern, urban women report more discussion than rural women, at 64 and 53 per cent respectively, but it is the regional variations that are intriguing.

The highest number reporting such discussions are in the east zone (69 per cent), followed by the south zone (61 per cent), west zone (57 per cent), and north zone (48 per cent), predictably the lowest. The generational change is reflected here, too, in the same way as age at first birth, with one startling difference for the south zone—only

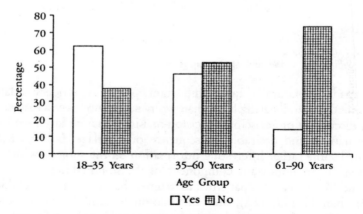

FIGURE 5.18: Have You and Your Husband Discussed the Number of Children You would Like to Have?

one per cent women in the 60 years and above age group said that they had discussed the issue with their husbands, far lower than the low north zone, which reported 12 per cent for this group (see Figures 5.19–5.22).

Muslim women reported the least discussion at 51 per cent, Scheduled Tribes the most at 59 per cent. Rural Muslims report even less, at 49 per cent, but the sharpest urban–rural divide is among Hindus, at 67 and 52 per cent respectively and, of course, Muslim

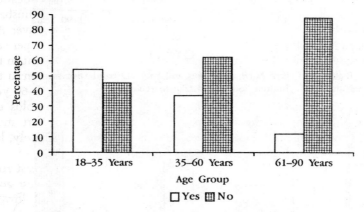

FIGURE 5.19: North Zone: Have You and Your Husband Discussed the Number of Children You would Like to Have?

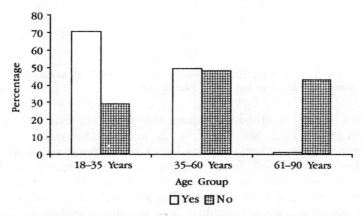

FIGURE 5.20: South Zone: Have You and Your Husband Discussed the Number of Children You would Like to Have?

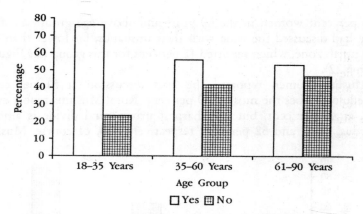

FIGURE 5.21: East Zone: Have You and Your Husband Discussed the Number of Children You would Like to Have?

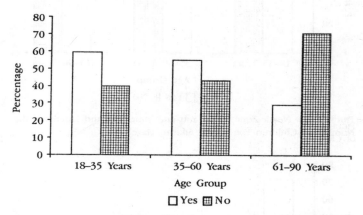

FIGURE 5.22: West Zone: Have You and Your Husband Discussed the Number of Children You would Like to Have?

women in the north zone report the lowest proportion—only 36 per cent replied yes. But here, as indicated by our findings, *regional location* rather than gender or community seems to be the determining factor, because 65 per cent Muslim women in the east zone responded in the affirmative. Here's the conundrum: the east zone, an outlier with regard to almost all other indicators— SES, education, work, mobility, and so on—nevertheless scores the highest on interspousal communication! Why this should be so certainly requires more probing than the MWS attempted, especially because the east zone reports high total fertility rates, overall.[4]

The MWS found a positive correlation between women's education and interspousal communication, even in rural India, where the figures are usually lower—75 per cent women with a high school education, compared to 47 per cent who were illiterate, said they had discussed family size with their husbands. Rural–urban differences

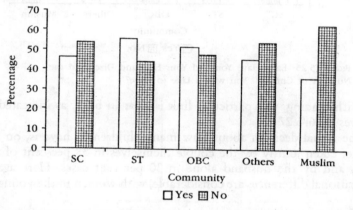

FIGURE 5.23: North: Have You and Your Husband Discussed the Number of Children You would Like to Have?

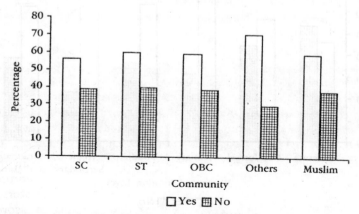

FIGURE 5.24: South: Have You and Your Husband Discussed the Number of Children You would Like to Have?

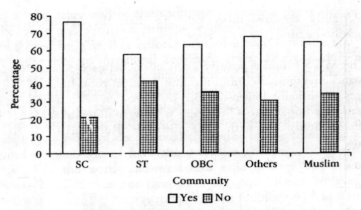

FIGURE 5.25: East: Have You and Your Husband Discussed the Number of Children You would Like to Have?

notwithstanding, this particular link is clear in both, as indicated in Figures 5.26–5.27

The actual decision about how many children to have is, on the whole, taken jointly by the couple themselves in 38 per cent of the cases, and by the husband alone in 30 per cent cases. Here again, generational differences are considerable, with women in the youngest

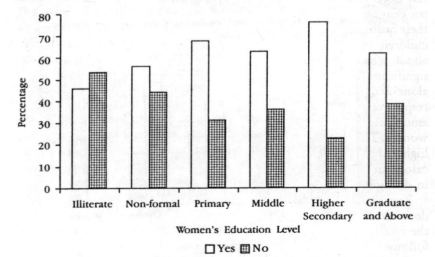

FIGURE 5.26: Rural: Have You and Your Husband Discussed the Number of Children You would Like to Have?

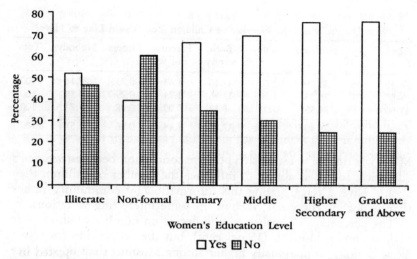

FIGURE 5.27: Urban: Have You and Your Husband Discussed the Number of Children You would Like to Have?

age group, 18–35 years, reporting proportions that are *five times* higher (41.6 per cent) than women in the oldest age group, 60 and above. This last is corroborated by the finding that among 60–90 year-olds, 58 per cent urban and 65 per cent rural women replied that neither they, their husbands, their in-laws, nor anybody else decided on how many children to have, suggesting that childbearing was not something about which decisions needed to be taken. The really sharp and significant difference, of course, is in the proportions for 'husbands alone' and 'wives alone' deciding—30 per cent, compared to 2.5 per cent, respectively. The gender imbalance is clear and dramatic, especially among older women, but the situation is not much better for younger women. The fact that the incidence of joint decision-making is slightly higher than unilateral decisions taken by husbands is a positive indicator, but it does not necessarily follow that women are equal partners in decision-making or that they have any real choice in the matter.

Regionally, the north zone presents the lowest figure for joint decisions on this issue, at 27 per cent, roughly half the national average; the south and west zones the highest at 50 and 49 per cent, respectively, followed closely by the east zone at 47 per cent.

A widely-held perception is that if only women were better educated this would have a positive effect on their family-size, but the

TABLE 5.8

Who Decides about the Number of Children You Would Like to Have?

Age	Husband	Wife	Both jointly	Parents-in-law	Others	Nobody	Total
18–35	31.29	2.70	41.16	1.63	0.73	22.14	100
35–60	26.23	2.06	32.96	1.24	0.29	36.38	100
60–90	21.55	0.00	8.15	0.00	0.08	57.71	100
Total	29.40	2.44	37.87	1.48	0.56	27.57	100

MWS was unable to establish a positive connection between women's education and their ability to influence the number of children they should have. Disaggregating this information by community rather than education, however, throws up some interesting variations.

The percentage of husbands who decide on number of children is highest among Muslims (35 per cent), but the proportion for wives alone deciding is marginally higher among Muslims than upper caste Hindus—2.04 and 1.82 per cent, respectively; the highest figure in this category is reported by Scheduled Castes (3 per cent); while joint decision-making is greatest among Scheduled Tribes (46 per cent). In urban India, however, this percentage is the highest for Scheduled Castes, at 53 per cent. A comparatively better position, thus, seems to be a factor of *socio-economic status* rather than education, community, or location in this case. This is indicated most clearly in the south zone, where the figure for *wives deciding by themselves* is a remarkably high 33 per cent among Scheduled Tribes—who, incidentally, also report a high 50 per cent for joint decision-making. Seventy-two per cent upper caste Hindus in the south zone also decide family-size jointly, but this figure drops to 18 per cent in the north zone (see Tables 5.9 and 5.10).

TABLE 5.9

Who Decides about the Number of Children by Community: North Zone

Caste	Husband	Wife	Both jointly	Parents-in-law	Others	Nobody	Total
SC	25.53	2.13	28.89	0.99	1.97	40.49	100
ST	45.89	0.00	50.85	0.00	0.00	03.26	100
OBC	23.50	2.29	30.53	3.74	0.00	39.71	100
Others	33.48	0.45	17.94	0.67	0.45	47.01	100
Muslim	32.74	1.27	15.90	0.56	2.80	46.66	100
Total	26.91	1.84	27.13	1.95	01.06	41.02	100

TABLE 5.10
Who Decides about the Number of Children by Community: South Zone

Caste	Husband	Wife	Both jointly	Parents-in-law	Others	No-body	No Response	Total
SC	35.56	4.84	43.35	1.23	0.00	9.63	5.40	100
ST	0.00	33.33	50.00	0.00	0.00	16.67	0.00	100
OBC	32.70	3.59	48.88	1.78	0.60	10.93	1.51	100
Others	4.29	7.01	71.82	0.00	0.00	16.88	0.00	100
Muslim	36.28	2.86	46.64	1.51	0.35	9.86	2.51	100
Total	30.58	4.44	49.65	1.40	0.35	11.15	2.43	100

Conclusion

Low decision-making capacity is the general condition of women in India, and it is not significantly affected by either their own educational attainment or that of their husbands; by community; or by their wage-earning capability. Three other factors, however, do seem to indicate a positive impact—age, with younger women reporting greater joint decision-making; residence, urban women being better-off than rural; and socio-economic status. The last-mentioned, though, actually reports *lower* decision-making capacity with a higher SES, thus indicating a negative correlation. Again, the regional variation shows the south zone in a lower ranking than even the north zone, which is also unexpected.

The MWS consciously avoided asking questions on purely domestic activities—i.e., what to cook, etc.—focusing instead on those common familial and household concerns that involve decisions on household expenditure; number of children; children's education; marriage; birth and death ceremonies; major illnesses; travel; major purchases; and major investments. Given this shift in focus, the finding that roughly 35 per cent of Muslim women are part of joint decision-making in the family is quite encouraging; the fact that this percentage increases with the younger age group indicates a positive trend, and is to be welcomed.

But interpreting or analysing data, whether empirical or statistical, on women's decision-making presents several problems, as other analysts have observed. Naila Kabeer's summary of a few empirical studies carried out in India, Bangladesh, Nigeria, Egypt, Zimbabwe, Nepal, Iran, and Pakistan is instructive.[5] Almost all these studies used roughly the same variables as the NFHS and MWS to measure women's decision-making as an indicator of their agency but, Kabeer cautions, 'not all of them are equally persuasive...because not all have the same *consequential significance* in women's lives'. (An obvious example would be the greater consequential significance of a decision regarding a suitable match for her daughter than, say, purchasing a utility item for the house.) Second, very few cultures have sharply divided power distribution, with men making all the decisions and women making none: it is much more common to find a hierarchy of decision-making with some areas predominantly male and others—such as those related to food—primarily female. Third, formal decision-making by men may well conceal informal power exercised by women in influencing those decisions, a dynamic that is practically impossible to measure statistically. Just as there is a hierarchy of decisions, so too, there is a hierarchy of the significance of decisions, and women can—and do—exercise the option *not* to decide, selectively. By this strategy they may, simultaneously, maintain a public image of submissiveness while actually gradually increasing their influence and participation in the home. In other words, agency may not be an unvarying, constant feature in their decision-making; rather, as Val Daniels has suggested elsewhere, it may be useful to think of women's 'agentive moments', and at what points these moments occur. Finally, as Srilatha Batliwala notes in her discussion of empowerment, there is a certain implicit, but widely-held, value placed in our cultures on *abdicating* decision-making in favour of adults, older family members, and male heads.[6] If this operates in the case of younger males in the household, it is certainly true of women, young and old, depending on the significance of the decision to be taken.

There is a further distinction that we might make in terms of what can be called 'control' decisions—such as those regarding mobility, education, health, major purchases and investments, and work; 'management' decisions—such as what and how much to cook, and how household expenditure is to be managed; and 'family life' decisions—such as those regarding marriage, illness, birth and death ceremonies, and travel. It is interesting to note that although approximately 35 per cent of women in the MWS take decisions *jointly* with their husbands in all three categories in this cluster, the findings from our Survey on women's mobility indicate strong control exercised by men, primarily husbands, in practically every aspect of women's lives; this corroborates the finding that 60 per cent of all respondents were not involved in any decision-making at all, as reported by themselves.

Decision-making in families, as Bina Agarwal points out, is itself a complex process, allowing for differences in individual preference, in budget constraints, and control over resources.[7] At the same time, decisions also involve very complex gender and generational relations within the household. This may be seen, for instance, in both the MWS and NFHS in the finding that older women have greater decision-making powers. Hierarchies *between* women in the household are also important and so, as Agarwal notes, assertiveness (as a factor in household decision-making) is more acceptable in older women; from mothers-in-law than from younger daughters-in-law; from daughters-in-law with sons than from those without; and from daughters rather than daughters-in-law.

The finding in the MWS that 35 per cent women take decisions jointly with their husbands, and approximately 50 per cent are consulted on them, does not enable us to determine whether decision-making itself is conflictual, co-operative, or collective. For instance, it may be collective with regard to birth and death ceremonies or marriage, or co-operative as far as household expenditure is concerned, but conflictual when it comes to major investments and purchases, or children's education—or even women's desire to visit their natal families. That is, just as women may well *influence* decisions without actually making them, so too may they comply or concede without actually agreeing or approving.

Both Naila Kabeer and Bina Agarwal mention men's and women's 'separate spheres' of decision-making based on socially recognized gender roles, while sharing some common responsibilities and some resources and activities. Generally speaking, one might say that the purely household-specific decisions—as far as what to cook and the daily care of children and other dependants is concerned—are made by women in the family; while those with greater consequences for the family as a whole—and one might add, for gender relations—are made by men. Moreover, social norms mediated by gender, age, and marital status exert a powerful influence on women's own self-perceptions regarding their role in decision-making—taking decisions that are likely to disturb the household's economic or emotional equilibrium or, for that matter, its gender relations is an option few women are willing to exercise. Doing so may come perilously close to what Bina Agarwal calls the 'threat point'—a breakdown of relations, which most women will avoid.[8] Naila Kabeer notes a similar recognition by women of the merits of *not* exercising agency, strategically, arguing that 'agency has both positive and negative meanings in relation to power,' especially in societies and cultures where social norms or 'traditions' are powerfully present.[9]

Important to note for our purposes, however, is that, by and large, women exercise very little agency in making those critical-choice decisions that affect their own lives: whether and how much to study; whether, where, and when to work; when and whom to marry; how many children to have; whether or not to practise contraception; and whether or not they may be able to avail of health care. It is true that all of the above are mediated by class, community, and customary practice on the one hand, and state-supplied support and services on the other; but it also appears to be the case that patriarchal control overrides other material constraints, so that even if the latter were absent or minimal, one could not say with confidence that women would be more autonomous.

This is reinforced by our findings on the severe constraints placed on women's mobility, whereby the extent of control is both wide-ranging and near-total. We may recall that an astounding *86 per cent of women*, Hindu and Muslim, said that they needed permission from their husbands for *any and all* of the activities listed in our question-naire. The culture or practice of seclusion, or curtailed mobility, is thus much less a community-specific than a gender-specific condition, regardless of purdah although, as noted earlier, there are interesting class and regional variations.

In conclusion then, the combination of extreme material depriva-tion, state neglect, and patriarchal control make for an intensification of women's subordination, so much so that, as Srilatha Batliwala says, 'Men's traditional power over the women in their households is reinforced by control over her body and physical mobility; by the right to abdicate from all responsibility for housework and care of the children; the right to physically abuse or violate her; the right to spend family income on personal pleasures (and vices); the right to abandon her to take other wives; the right to take unilateral decisions which affect the whole family; and the countless other ways in which poor men—and indeed men of every class—have unjustly confined women.'[9]

Endnotes

1. *Human Development in South Asia: The Gender Question*, Mahbubul Haq Human Development Centre, Oxford University Press, Karachi, 2000.

2. The DMI has been constructed as follows: all the 'yes' responses to the questions asked were added up for each respondent (1 point for each 'yes' response). This new variable was termed 'Consult', and takes values from 0 to 9. DMI is thus determined as follows:

Consult 0 means DMI=0, which implies that women have no role in decision-making in their families.

Consult between 1 and 5 means DMI=1, which implies that women have a moderate role in decision-making.

Consult between 5 and 9 means DMI=2, which implies that women have a high role in decision-making.

3. NFHS, op. cit., p. 57.

4. NFHS, op. cit., p. 87.

5. Naila Kabeer, 'Resources, Agency, Achievements: Reflections on the Measurement of Women's Empowerment', *Development and Change*, vol. 30, 1999, pp. 435-64, Institute of Social Studies, The Hague.

6. Srilatha Batliwala, 'Empowerment of Women in South Asia: Concepts and Practices', FAO-FFHC/AD, Delhi, 1993.

7. Bina Agarwal, 'Bargaining' and Gender Relations: Within and Beyond the Household', *Feminist Economics*, 3(1), Spring 1997.

8. Bina Agarwal, 'Bargaining and Gender Relations', op. cit.

9. Naila Kabeer, 'Resources, Agency, Achievements', op. cit.

10. Srilatha Batliwala, 'Empowerment of Women in South Asia', op. cit.

6

Mobility

The Muslim Women's Survey (MWS) did not attempt an exhaustive
assessment of autonomy among Muslim women, but it did undertake
a fairly detailed survey of two of its important components, mobility
and decision-making (for the latter, see Chapter 5), to present at least
the contours of their status in this regard.

Freedom of movement and of association are fundamental rights
in all parts of the world, and in India are guaranteed and safeguarded
by the Constitution. As with other rights and guarantees, however,
there is a wide gap between precept and practice, and in the case of
women, a yawning gap. Empirically, experientially, and impression-
istically, we know that, in India, women's mobility is severely
curtailed in practically every part of the country, and across community and class. The chimera of a liberated, autonomous, independent,
and freely choosing modern Indian woman, is largely that: a chimera.
The reality is quite the opposite; yet few serious attempts have been
made to gauge women's freedom of movement in a systematic and
comprehensive manner. The National Family Health Survey (NFHS)
was the first large-scale survey to include the question of mobility in
its discussion on autonomy, as an essential element in empowerment,
and its findings are instructive. The MWS goes much further than
the NFHS by extending the scope of the discussion, as well as by
desegregating the data by community, class, and region to highlight
both inter-regional and inter-community differences.

The questions posed to our respondents on the extent of mobility
they enjoyed encompassed a combination of activities that are
personal, social, familial, political, economic, or work- and health-
related. They range from the necessary—for example, marketing or
going to the doctor—to the purely pleasurable—visiting family and
friends, going to the cinema, etc.—and include questions regarding

permission to work, to attend election meetings, religious or cultural events, and political demonstrations; whether or not permission is required for any of them; and who it is sought from. Our questions on decision-making were as detailed, as seen in the previous chapter.

A very high proportion (70 per cent) of respondents—Hindu and Muslim—all-India, across classes, reported that they needed permission from their husbands to go to work, and a staggering 86 per cent said they needed it for *all* the activities enumerated.

After husbands, the next highest percentage is reported for fathers—4.51 per cent for Hindus, 5.45 per cent for Muslims—followed by mothers-in-law—2.25 and 1.54 per cent, respectively. For Muslim women, mothers report a marginally higher percentage. Never-married girls would seek permission from their fathers, married women from husbands and in-laws, and older women may even need permission from sons for some activities. Community differences, as we can see, are negligible, suggesting again that gender, rather than religion or even class, is the determining factor; although a higher percentage (75 per cent) of Muslim women reported needing permission than Hindu women (69 per cent) for going to work.

The NFHS both corroborates and details the MWS as far as two areas of activity/mobility are concerned—going to the market, and visiting friends and relatives, by age. The significant finding is that the percentage of respondents who do not require permission to visit friends and relatives is far *lower* than that for going to the market; and older women—45–9 years—are the most mobile. The degree of mobility declines in direct relationship to age: younger women are more restricted, and the least mobile belong to the age group 15–19 years. Here, only 10 per cent do not require permission to visit friends and relatives, while 13 per cent do not require permission to go to the market. Again, rural women are more constrained than urban; illiterate more than literate and high school graduates; and Muslim women more than Hindu.

Taking the full range of activities and permission required for undertaking them, we have devised a freedom of movement index (FMI)—analogous to the decision-making index presented in Chapter 5—which measures mobility on a scale of 0–3. If no permission is required, the FMI takes a high value of 2; if permission falls in the range 1–5 (on a range of 0–11), i.e., if women need permission for less than half the categories, FMI takes a medium value of 1, and if permission is in the range 5–11, i.e., if women need permission for

TABLE 6.1
Whose Permission is Required to Go to Work: Hindu

Religion	Father	Husband	Brother	Mother	Father-in-law	Mother-in-law	Other family member	Others
Hindu	4.51	86.03	0.88	1.43	1.7	2.25	1.11	1.86

TABLE 6.2
Whose Permission is Required to Go to Work: Muslims

Religion	Father	Husband	Brother	Mother	Father-in-law	Mother-in-law	Other family member	Others
Muslim	5.45	86.35	0.59	1.94	1.46	1.54	0.92	1.13

more than half the categories, then FMI takes the lowest value, 0. Based on this, the all-India distribution of FMI is given in Table 6.3.

TABLE 6.3
Freedom of Movement Index

FMI	Per cent
0	75.57
1	14.16
2	10.27
Total	100.00

As noted earlier, the majority of women have a low FMI; disaggregated by community, the picture is much the same, except with regard to upper middle and upper socio-economic groups, where a greater proportion of Muslim women in the former category (80 per cent) has a lower FMI score than Hindus (73 per cent) (see Tables 6.4 and 6.5).

TABLE 6.4
Freedom of Movement by Community and SES: Hindus

Five-fold classification of SLI	FMI			
	0	1	2	Total
1	75.51	12.02	12.48	100
2	79.25	11.19	9.56	100
3	75.44	14.70	9.86	100
4	73.21	15.74	11.05	100
5	74.24	16.64	9.12	100
Total	75.34	14.20	10.46	100

TABLE 6.5
Freedom of Movement by Community and SES: Muslims

Five fold classification of SLI	FMI			
	0	1	2	Total
1	77.23	12.14	10.63	100
2	78.84	11.38	9.78	100
3	75.21	15.88	8.90	100
4	79.61	13.70	6.69	100
5	76.23	14.93	8.84	100
Total	77.23	13.91	8.86	100

Note: (Tables 6.4 and 6.5) 1–Lowest SLI; 2–Lower-Middle SLI; 3–Middle SLI; 4–Upper-Middle SLI; 5–Upper SLI.

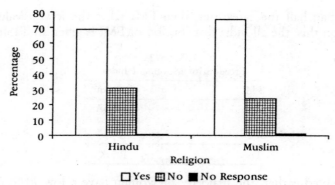

FIGURE 6.1: Permission Required for Going to Work

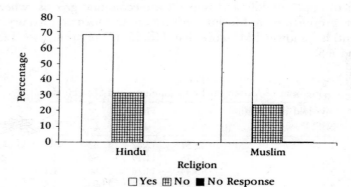

FIGURE 6.2: Permission Required for Going to the Market

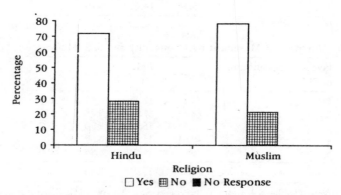

FIGURE 6.3: Permission Required for Going to Doctor/Health Centre

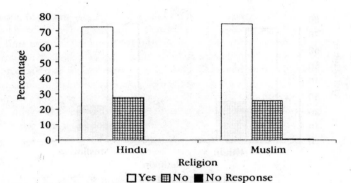

FIGURE 6.4: Permission Required for Going to Election Meetings

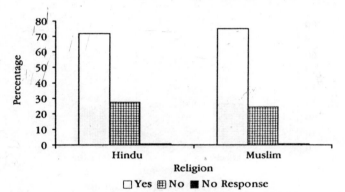

FIGURE 6.5: Permission Required for Going to Religious Meetings

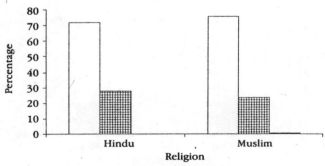

FIGURE 6.6: Permission Required for Social or Cultural Gatherings

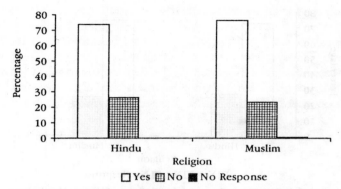

FIGURE 6.7: Permission Required for Work-related Activities

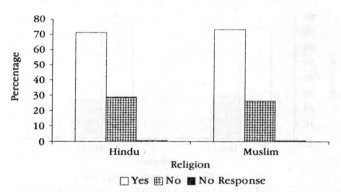

FIGURE 6.8: Permission Required for Demonstrations

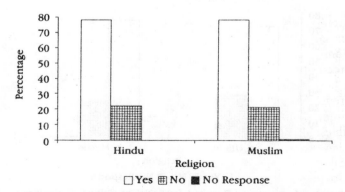

FIGURE 6.9: Permission Required for Going to the Cinema/Theatre

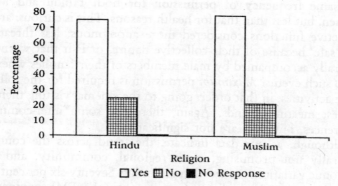

FIGURE 6.10: Permission Required for Natal Home Visit

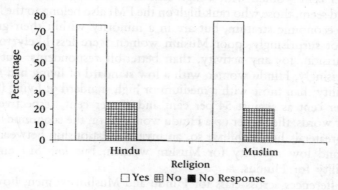

FIGURE 6.11: Permission Required to Meet Friends

Attending to personal health needs requires more permission than either going to work or to the market, both of which have an economic or domestic function. Women's health needs are generally accorded low-priority, as is well-known from innumerable studies on their health status, but what is notable in our data is the community difference—Muslim respondents report a significantly higher need for obtaining permission for this than Hindus. It is possible that primary health-care centres are less readily accessible to Muslim women who may have to travel a longer distance, or that they are generally manned by male doctors; or that only private medical care is readily available and so permission is required to pay for it. For an economically depressed community, this would be an important consideration.

Attending religious, cultural, social, or election meetings requires the same frequency of permission for both Hindu and Muslim women, but less than that for health reasons. This is curious: are such collective functions considered more anonymous, less threatening, and 'safe' because of their collective nature, or is it that women are generally accompanied by male members of their families when they go to such events? *Maximum* permission is required for the following three activities, in that order: going to the cinema; visiting their natal homes; meeting friends. Again, there are some inter-community differences, but they are not significant.

Although, as our data indicate, the trend across the country is generally not promising, some regional, community, and socio-economic variations are worth mentioning. Seventy-six per cent of the poorest women have the lowest score on the FMI, compared to 74 per cent women with a high standard of living. Paradoxically, it would seem, those who rank high on the FMI also belong to the lowest socio-economic stratum, but are in a minority within their group.

Not surprisingly, poor Muslim women were less likely to need permission, for any activity, than better-off respondents, but quite surprisingly, Hindu women with a low standard of living had *far less* mobility than those with a medium or high standard of living (SLI)— 62 per cent as against 54 per cent and 48 per cent, respectively. In other words, the higher up a Hindu woman is on the economic ladder, the greater is her mobility; so, an inverse relationship between high SLI and low mobility for Muslim women, but *low* SLI and *low* mobility for Hindus.

Differences across class for Hindu and Muslim women, however, are significant: among Muslims, rural women with a high SLI are much more curtailed than their urban sisters, but this gap almost vanishes for urban Muslim women from *any* class. For both Hindus and Muslims, the percentage of urban women who needed *no* permission to leave the house belonged to the low SES category, and were double the percentage of those in a high SES category.

Is the difference to be explained in terms of class or community? It is not clear; but what appears to be the case from our data (as distinct from the NFHS findings) is that while women's educational status does not seem to make a very great difference to their freedom of movement, either for Muslims or Hindus. It does have *some* impact, though. North India is generally considered to be much more purdah-oriented than any other part of the country, and this is borne out by our data as well, but a correlation between educational levels and mobility suggests a *downward trend with higher education* among both Muslim and Hindu respondents. This is true of the east zone as well, which is surprising, as is the finding that Hindu women seem to be far more constrained than their Muslim sisters, the more highly educated they are. Women in the west and south zones are predictably better-off, with higher mobility and much less inter-community difference, overall; the south zone has the lowest number of respondents ranked low on the FMI, especially in the middle, upper middle, and high socio-economic categories, and a correspondingly higher proportion of women (42 per cent) who rank 1 and 2 on the scale. The south zone has the highest percentage in the medium (1) category, a correspondingly lower percentage in the lowest rank, and a higher average at 15 per cent, than the national average, 10 per cent, in the high rank. Contrary to received wisdom, however, women in the south zone have the lowest decision-making capacity in the country, even though they are generally better educated and relatively more mobile. By and large, then, the picture is depressingly similar, overall.

TABLE 6.6
Distribution of Respondents by Permission Required
to Go Outside for Various Purposes: North Zone

Five-fold classification	FMI			Total
of SLI	0	1	2	
1	74.63	12.71	12.67	100
2	88.52	5.23	6.25	100
3	84.98	7.47	7.55	100
4	86.28	6.80	6.92	100
5	86.09	7.68	6.23	100
Total	83.44	8.31	8.25	100

TABLE 6.7
Distribution of Respondents by Permission Required
to Go Outside for Various Purposes: South Zone

Five-fold classification	FMI			Total
of SLI	0	1	2	
1	73.79	10.95	15.26	100
2	76.51	15.61	7.88	100
3	47.87	34.03	18.11	100
4	53.72	30.51	15.78	100
5	54.62	30.37	15.02	100
Total	57.12	27.51	15.37	100

162 □ *Unequal Citizens*

TABLE 6.8
Distribution of Respondents by Permission Required
to Go Outside for Various Purposes: East Zone

Five-fold classification of SLI	FMI			Total
	0	1	2	
1	76.50	11.34	12.15	100
2	68.52	15.75	15.72	100
3	81.37	10.19	8.43	100
4	80.73	8.51	10.76	100
5	79.94	12.58	7.48	100
Total	77.59	11.53	10.89	100

TABLE 6.9
Distribution of Respondents by Permission Required
to Go Outside for Various Purposes: West Zone

Five-fold classification of SLI	FMI			Total
	0	1	2	
1	80.73	10.77	8.50	100
2	68.57	23.81	7.62	100
3	64.79	27.92	7.29	100
4	60.86	26.55	12.59	100
5	59.40	28.68	11.92	100
Total	65.83	23.93	10.24	100

Note: (Tables 6.6 to 6.9) 1–Lowest SLI; 2–Lower-Middle SLI;
3–Middle SLI; 4–Upper Middle SLI; 5–Upper SLI.

Across class and community, however, the one category of women
who need no permission for any activity are single (as distinct from
never-married) women, i.e., those who are divorced, separated/
deserted, or widowed, but here the zonal variations are surprising
(see Tables 6.10–6.13). The north *and* south zones indicate the greatest
mobility for deserted women, followed by those who are widowed
and divorced; by contrast, the east zone reports maximum freedom
of movement for widows, followed by those who are separated or
deserted, but not for divorcees (who, in fact, are as constrained as
those who have never been married); and the west zone repeats similar
high percentages for widows' mobility, but a very low ranking for
deserted women.

TABLE 6.10
Current Marital Status: North

Current marital status	FMI			
	0	1	2	Total
Currently married	86.32	8.46	5.21	100
Gauna not performed	100.00	0.00	0.00	100
Widowed	26.45	10.26	63.29	100
Divorced	80.95	2.38	16.67	100
Separated	94.99	1.67	3.34	100
Deserted	15.78	0.00	84.22	100
Never married	95.73	2.40	1.87	100
Others	100.00	0.00	0.00	100
Total	83.44	8.32	8.25	100

TABLE 6.11
Current Marital Status: South

Current marital status	FMI			
	0	1	2	Total
Currently married	59.58	29.66	10.76	100
Gauna not performed	72.14	26.72	1.15	100
Widowed	23.37	14.43	62.20	100
Divorced	0.51	39.35	60.14	100
Separated	58.75	26.56	14.69	100
Deserted	0.00	0.00	100.00	100
Never married	75.41	21.96	2.63	100
Total	57.12	27.51	15.37	100

TABLE 6.12
Current Marital Status: East

Current marital status	FMI			
	0	1	2	Total
Currently married	82.56	12.86	4.57	100
Gauna not performed	100.00	0.00	0.00	100
Widowed	9.57	2.47	87.96	100
Divorced	93.05	0.00	6.95	100
Separated	59.26	0.00	40.74	100
Deserted	43.51	0.00	56.49	100
Never married	93.83	3.04	3.13	100
Others	100.00	0.00	0.00	100
Total	77.59	11.53	10.89	100

164 □ *Unequal Citizens*

TABLE 6.13
Current Marital Status: West

Current marital status	FMI			
	0	1	2	Total
Currently married	69.01	23.81	7.18	100
Gauna not performed	76.12	5.75	18.13	100
Widowed	31.16	4.22	64.62	100
Divorced	15.94	62.76	21.30	100
Separated	42.45	43.17	14.39	100
Deserted	88.18	7.88	3.94	100
Never married	52.37	38.27	9.36	100
Others	100.00	0.00	0.00	100
Total	65.83	23.93	10.24	100

It is possible that this greater freedom is because this group of women is without husbands; but, in fact, young, never-married women, who also have no husbands, are the most constrained because they *will* have husbands and so must be supervised: only 4 per cent Muslim and Hindu never-married respondents had no constraints on their mobility. Urban poor women, Hindu and Muslim, report the highest mobility, at 13.1 and 14.4 per cent respectively, which again confirms the norm: higher status entails far less mobility.

TABLE 6.14
Current Marital Status: All-India

Current marital status	FMI			
	0	1	2	Total
Currently married	79.37	14.50	6.12	100
Gauna not performed	83.07	9.91	7.02	100
Widowed	21.80	8.68	69.52	100
Divorced	31.86	28.74	39.39	100
Separated	64.37	2.23	33.40	100
Deserted	41.79	1.75	56.46	100
Never married	80.81	15.44	3.75	100
Others	100.00	0.00	0.00	100
Total	75.57	14.16	10.27	100

Conclusion

As with marriage, so too with mobility, the determining factor seems to be gender rather than either class, community, or region.

Differences on account of the latter, or indeed, due to education or economic independence, are relatively minor while the extent and pervasiveness of control are excessive.

The ideology of seclusion is all-pervasive in culture and society in India, and it has been the subject of voluminous research and analysis over the past few decades by sociologists, anthropologists, and feminists, in particular. It is not our purpose here to reiterate the familiar—and by now, well-known—features of such an ideology, simply to underline its principal characteristics as the context within which to present our survey findings. Primary among these is the need to control and regulate women's sexuality as a critical factor in maintaining the purity of the patriliny, ensuring the continuation of the patriarchal family, preserving its honour, and upholding the institution of marriage. In short, this implies retaining control over women's reproduction. The mean age of respondents in our sample is 34 years, but puberty is a watershed event in Indian women's lives; data from the MWS on girls' education, for example, reveal a significant correlation between attainment of puberty and higher drop-out rates for Muslim girls. This is also a major factor in arranging early marriages for them, and once married, the constraints on mobility are even greater, as we have seen. Seclusion, or limiting women's access to and presence in the public domain, entails a stern domesticity, confinement within the four walls of the house, with the circumference of activity limited to hearth and home. This sharp separation of private and public, and women's more or less completely dependent status, near complete divorce from their natal homes (and often living far from them), simultaneously reinforces patriarchal control and disables women. This control may even claim women as property, ownership of whom implies both control and the right of disposal, and is largely unchallenged; if ownership is unquestioned, authority will surely hardly ever be. In the ultimate analysis, what is regulated is not just women's sexuality, but their time and space; their labour; their income; their education; and, pre-eminently, their ability to choose or decide.

Given that the majority of women in our sample are so severely constrained, the findings with regard to their work participation as well as decision-making are not surprising. Although a paucity of jobs and lack of opportunities and skills are important reasons for women not to work, it is equally likely that, even if this were not the case, they would not obtain the necessary permission to do so, especially if the place of work is outside the home.

The freedom of movement index graphically illustrates the consequences of this control on women's educational status; on marriage; on their ability to work; and on their health. These several disabling restrictions, when combined with a fairly rigid sexual division of labour, serve to perpetuate women's dependent status as well as their seclusion, with the one reinforcing the other. This said, it bears repeating that a combination of factors, which includes low economic status (i.e., financial constraints), low educational attainment, scant opportunities, and a certain amount of conservatism, is responsible for the continuing absence of Muslim women in the public arena.

7

Domestic Violence

The systematic exposure by the women's movement of violence against women, and especially of sustained domestic violence, has focused attention on one of the most serious violations that women suffer at the hands of men within their own families, and in their own homes. Till recently, however, the issue has remained largely a 'women's issue', a problem that needed to be addressed by women's groups, activists, or other collectives within the community, because the 'domestic' nature of the violation precluded serious consideration by policy-makers, the law and, indeed, society in general. Even *To 'ards Equality*, the landmark report on the status of women published in 1975, did not include a section on violence. Largely as a result of tireless campaigning and lobbying by national and international women's movements, violence against women has begun to be taken seriously as a *social* crime, and a serious indicator of something terribly wrong in gender relations.

Any number of feminist theorists have indicated the importance of violence against women—actual or threatened—by men (and sometimes other women) as a critical instrument of patriarchal control. This violence includes physical and non-physical abuse and may extend right through the better part of a woman's life, all the way from female foeticide and infanticide to death by burning. Feminists in India have uncovered the endemic nature of domestic violence, but have also drawn attention to its structural and systemic underpinnings, whereby violence in the family and within the household is simultaneously sanctioned and silenced, and legitimized. Social institutions such as the police and the courts, while not endorsing it, nevertheless enable it to continue by not recognizing it as a crime in law (except in the case of dowry), or by not according it the serious attention it deserves while registering complaints. Indeed, a number of recent studies have identified the family/household as a major locus of violence against women and girls, raising important questions about women's vulnerability in the home—generally believed to be a safe haven.[1]

In India, socializing young brides (and from our Survey, we know that they can be as young as 13 years) into a family of consanguinally-related men often entails breaking them in through overt or covert violence. Humiliation, verbal abuse, insults, and back-breaking physical labour may (if she remains uncowed) extend to brutal physical abuse (often sexual), torture and, in extreme cases, outright murder in the form of bride-burning. Household studies carried out over the last decade by women's organizations, counselling and legal aid centres, and independent researchers have documented the range and extent of domestic violence in considerable detail, and established that it recognizes few economic or social barriers—it is pervasive in all classes and communities.[2]

The household also remains one of the most jealously guarded and inscrutable spaces as far as data collection on violence is concerned. Two recent national-level surveys, the National Family Health Survey (NFHS) (1998–9) and our own Survey have attempted to map the contours of domestic violence across the country, community-wise, class-wise, and state- or region-wise. The NFHS, in its second (1998–9) round of investigation on the status of family health in India, interviewed 90,000 women across the country on the incidence and nature of physical violence they experienced, and the reasons for it. The Muslim Women's Survey (MWS) similarly explored the scale of violence, correlating it with the respondents' standard of living, educational status, and age.

Respondents were asked about the incidence and nature of domestic/inter-spousal conflict; the reasons for it; whether verbal abuse had, on occasion, led to physical abuse; whether the respondent had ever been beaten or mistreated physically; and which family member perpetrated the violence. The question regarding reasons for conflict avoided the usual 'domestic' or household-related ones—such as dereliction of household duties by the woman; disrespect to in-laws; neglect of children; going out without permission; and so on. Rather, respondents were asked whether conflict leading to violence arose from disputes over land; sharing of property; her share of property being given to the daughter; husband's alcoholism; his frequent absences from the home; and forcible observance of purdah.

The MWS reported that approximately 20 per cent of respondents had experienced verbal and physical abuse in the marital home, over 80 per cent of it at the hands of their husbands. Figures for Muslims and Hindus are strikingly similar both in the NFHS and the MWS, although the MWS shows that *Hindu women experience greater levels of violence than Muslims in all four zones.* Rural women are worse off than urban women; poorer women, apparently, face greater levels of violence than better off ones (although, as we shall see, this is not necessarily the full story), the north and east zones of the country more violent than the south and west zones. The incidence of domestic violence appears to decrease with rising standards of living, but this may be because better educated, better-off women are less inclined to report violence in the home.

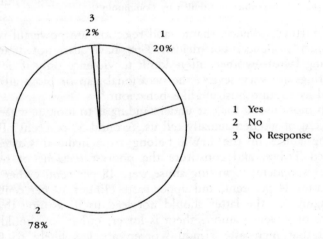

FIGURE 7.1: Can You Recall Any Time that Conflicts had Taken Place in Your Family?

But let us examine the MWS findings a little more closely. We should clarify at the outset that our data refer primarily to inter-spousal violence, mainly because the mean age of our sample is 34 years, but some general points about familial violence can nevertheless be made. The relatively 'low' figure of 20 per cent for women reporting violence should not distract us because, as mentioned earlier and noted by several researchers, under-reporting and reluctant acknowledging are common, especially when questions posed to women are part of surveys undertaken by anonymous enumerators.[3]

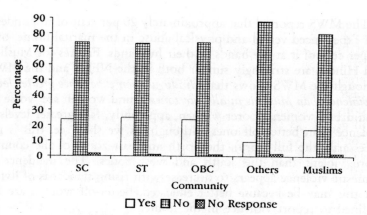

FIGURE 7.2: Reporting of Conflict by Community

Fear of further violence, shame, and rejection are powerful reasons for women's silence, but fieldworkers have also noted another interesting factor—women often admit to violence only if or when the beatings are very severe; the occasional slap or blow are often regarded as routine husband-like behaviour.[4]

Much more useful for our understanding is to look at what these 20 per cent of women actually tell us. Around 50 per cent of those reporting abuse in the MWS belong to Scheduled Castes and Scheduled Tribes, and constitute the poorest sections of society. Muslim respondents reporting abuse were 18 per cent, Other Backward Castes 24 per cent, and upper caste Hindus 10 per cent. The lower figure for the latter should not lead us to assume that the incidence of violence among them is lower; rather we should keep in mind that high-caste Hindu women are less likely to report violence, as Visaria and other researchers have noted.[5]

Regional Differences

Regional variations indicate that the west zone reports the lowest level of abuse, at 14.48 per cent, followed by the south zone at 16.12 per cent. The north and east zones have the highest levels of abuse, as shown in Figures 7.3–7.6. Not only are the figures lowest for the west zone, it also reports *roughly the same percentages for all women*, with the exception of Scheduled Tribes, thus erasing community and class differences. Much higher levels of violence in the north and east zones may be partially explained by at least three objective criteria, apart from gender, viz., poverty, low levels of education, and the lowest mean ages at marriage in the country. But there is one startling difference between the west and south zones, and that is in reporting by caste: Scheduled Tribes in the south zone return a zero per cent for domestic violence, whereas in the west zone they report the *highest* of all groups, in all zones, across the country—36.59 per cent.

Conforming to the overall pattern, Muslim women, too, are better off in the west and south zones, with the south zone reporting the lowest percentage—10.94. But the contrast between Muslim and

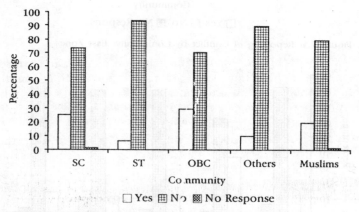

□ Yes ⊞ No ▨ No Response

FIGURE 7.3: Reporting of Conflict by Community: North Zone

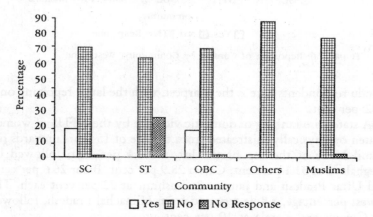

□ Yes ⊞ No ▨ No Response

FIGURE 7.4: Reporting of Conflict by Community: South Zone

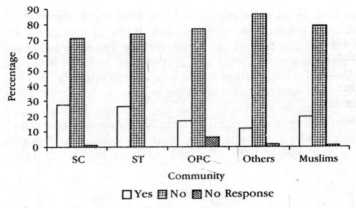

FIGURE 7.5: Reporting of Conflict by Community: East Zone

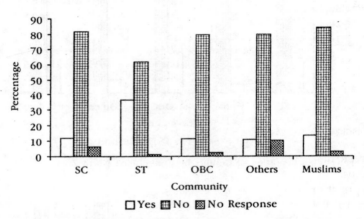

FIGURE 7.6: Reporting of Conflict by Community: West Zone

Hindu respondents here is the sharpest, with the latter reporting only 1.82 per cent.

A state-wise ranking of domestic violence by the NFHS of women beaten or physically mistreated from the age of 15 years upwards has Tamil Nadu at the top of the list, at 40.4 per cent; followed by Meghalaya at 31.1 per cent; Orissa 28.9 per cent; Bihar 26.6 per cent; and Uttar Pradesh and Jammu & Kashmir at 22 per cent each. The lowest percentage, 5.8, is reported from Himachal Pradesh, followed by Gujarat and Kerala at 10 per cent.

SES, Education, and Domestic Violence

A low socio-economic status (SES) apparently has a direct correlation to violence in the MWS data, with the poorest reporting the maximum violence (see Figure 7.7). A rise in class status seems to indicate a decline in violence, but this again begs the question: is this because women are less willing to report it as they climb up the social ladder? We may not ever be able to establish this conclusively, but the link

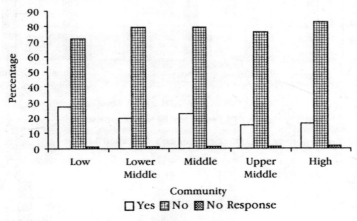

FIGURE 7.7: Reporting of Conflict by SES

between higher levels of education and reduced reporting is unambiguous, as Figure 7.8 indicates. However, this too, is open to interpretation. Higher levels of education among husbands similarly seem to have a positive (negative?) effect on women reporting violence; again this finding is ambivalent—social norms which require maintaining a public face and safeguarding family 'honour' may result in a willing acquiescence on the part of women *vis-à-vis* the men in their families, especially if they are otherwise reasonably secure.[6]

Women reporting physical abuse by their highly educated husbands dropped to one-fifth of that reported by women whose husbands were illiterate (see Figure 7.9), but this finding, too, has a surprise: *higher levels of physical violence and versal abuse were ascribed to men with secondary and higher secondary education*, though the reasons for this are unclear. Could it be that verbal abuse increases in direct proportion to better education? The figures seem to indicate as much (see Figure 7.9).

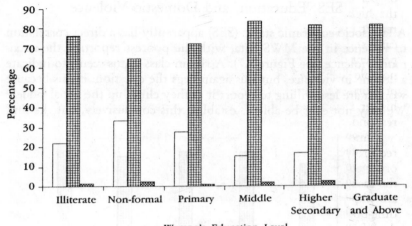

FIGURE 7.8: Reporting of Conflict by Women's Education Level

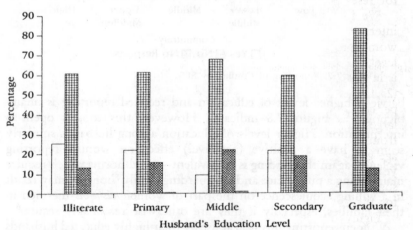

FIGURE 7.9: Nature of Abuse by Husband's Education Level

Forms of Abuse

The commonest and most prevalent form of conflict reported was verbal abuse, with the majority of women from all castes and communities citing it; in the country as a whole, it accounted for

63 per cent of all domestic abuse. Other Backward Castes reported the highest verbal and lowest physical abuse; and Muslim women report high levels of both compared to other groups. Verbal abuse can—and often does—escalate into physical abuse, as reported by 23 per cent of respondents who admitted to domestic violence. The most notable feature of this response is that, on further probing, overall proportions as well as community-specific proportions were slightly higher than in the initial responses, suggesting that more women responded to this probing.

Almost all researchers have noted that questions regarding violence require patient eliciting, and sometimes rephrasing or recasting, in order to obtain a more accurate picture, and this seems to have been the case with the MWS, too. Again, frequency or regularity of abuse are impossible to establish through a survey (which is necessarily time-bound), because of the nature of the experience. It is when we do a further disaggregation of violence and conflict by age, community, and region, however, that the general picture yields the most interesting variations, and throws up fresh questions and challenges for researchers.

We first look at reporting of conflict by age group. (The age-intervals in the following figures pertain only to currently married women, and it is to them that this discussion refers.) At the all-India level, the highest proportion of women reporting domestic conflict is in the 25–45 years age group (see Figure 7.10), which proportion (23.15 per cent) is also higher than the national average at 20.74 per cent. This figure reflects both the majority of our sample and the largest age interval—20 years. The next highest proportion is reported from the age group 20–5 years, followed closely by the 45–60 years age group. What is notable is that even in the age group above 60 years, conflict reporting only declines by a mere one per cent, suggesting that advancing age is a reason for significant reduction only for the age group 45–60 years.

Figures for women reporting physical abuse rise proportionately after the age of 18 years, peaking—again in the age group 25–45 years—at 24 per cent, and declining sharply by the time respondents are 60 years and above, to 5 per cent (see Figure 7.11). The peak years, however, report higher incidences of both physical and verbal abuse.

In rural India, this age group—25–45 years—reports the highest physical abuse at 26 per cent (see Figure 7.12), while the lowest figure is reported for the age group 60 years and above (1.34 per cent only)—

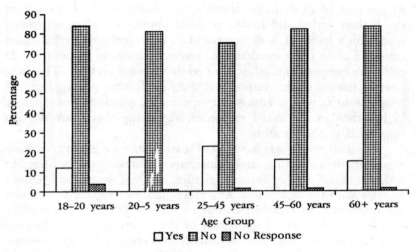

FIGURE 7.10: Reporting of Conflict by Age Group

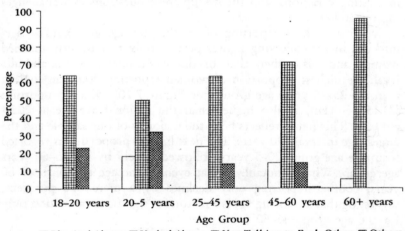

FIGURE 7.11: Nature of Conflict by Age Group

perhaps because most women are widowed by this age in rural areas. Yet exactly the opposite is the case in urban India, where the maximum physical abuse is reported by those who are 60 years and above at 37.12 per cent (see Figure 7.13), *100 per cent* of which takes place at the hands of their husbands.

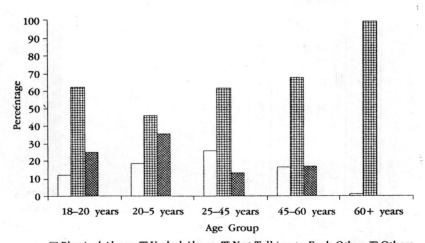

□ Physical Abuse ⊞ Verbal Abuse ▨ Not Talking to Each Other ▥ Others

FIGURE 7.12: Nature of Conflict by Age Group: Rural

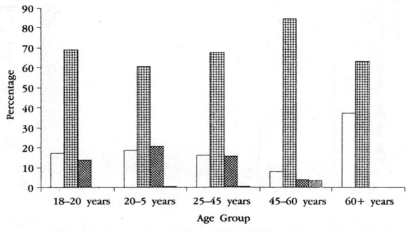

□ Physical Abuse ⊞ Verbal Abuse ▨ Not Talking to Each Other ▥ Others

FIGURE 7.13: Nature of Conflict by Age Group: Urban

Urban figures, overall, are lower than rural ones—15.71 per cent and 22.41 per cent respectively—reflecting the all-India pattern; what is different is that, here, the age group 25–45 years reports *lower* levels oɪ physical violence than both national and rural levels.

TABLE 7.1

Who was Responsible for Mistreatment by Age Group: Urban

Age group	Parents	Brothers	Sister	Husband	Mother-in-law	Father-in-law	Sisters-in-law	Sons	Others	Total
18–20	14.72	6.10	3.23	9.20	0.00	0.00	0.00	0.00	66.74	100
20–5	0.62	9.81	0.00	88.36	1.21	0.00	0.00	0.00	0.00	100
25–45	2.65	0.00	0.00	93.59	0.00	0.12	1.63	0.06	1.96	100
45–60	0.00	0.00	1.25	95.17	0.00	0.00	0.00	1.25	2.32	100
60+	0.00	0.00	0.00	100.00	0.00	0.00	0.00	0.00	0.00	100
Total	2.59	1.61	0.13	90.53	0.18	0.10	1.29	0.09	3.49	100

The most startling differences, however, are regional (see Tables 7.2–7.5). The north zone reports the greatest physical abuse among the age group 25–45 years; the south zone, among 20–5 year olds; the east zone, among 18–20 year-olds; and—shockingly and surprisingly—the west zone, in the age group 60 years and above, for whom the figure is 85.70 per cent! In sharp contrast the north, south, and east zones report very low figures for this last age group, at 0.41, 1.02, and 2.60 per cent, respectively. The west zone also reports the lowest figures for that otherwise more vulnerable age group—25–45 years—at 8 per cent. Maximum physical abuse, it would seem from the figures, takes place among the oldest and youngest age groups in the west zone. Notwithstanding these unexpected findings, it is worth noting again that the west zone, overall, reports the lowest physical abuse in the country, at 10.10 per cent, a good 8 per cent less than the next region, the south zone, at 18 per cent.

The north zone, again surprisingly, reports the lowest figure for physical violence in the youngest age group—indeed, it is significantly lower than all other regions—at only 1.86 per cent—and yet this zone,

TABLE 7.2
Nature of Conflict by Age Group: North Zone

Age group	Physical abuse	Verbal abuse	Not talking to each other	Others	Total
18–20	1.86	58.26	39.88	0.00	100
20–5	20.39	34.30	45.32	0.00	100
25–45	26.41	61.31	12.27	0.01	100
45–60	21.88	69.93	8.18	0.00	100
60 +	0.41	99.59	0.00	· 0.00	100
Total	23.83	59.23	16.94	0.01	100

TABLE 7.3
Nature of Conflict by Age Group: South Zone

Age group	Physical abuse	Verbal abuse	Not talking to each other	Others	Total
18–20	15.83	70.22	13.94	0.00	100
20–5	33.49	58.47	6.47	1.57	100
25–45	22.00	59.94	17.73	0.22	100
45–60	0.80	36.74	62.46	0.00	100
60 +	1.02	98.98	0.00	0.00	100
Total	17.94	59.47	22.29	0.23	100

180 □ *Unequal Citizens*

TABLE 7.4
Nature of Conflict by Age Group: East Zone

Age group	Physical abuse	Verbal abuse	Not talking to each other	Others	Total
18–20	27.63	67.15	3.64	0.00	1.58
20–5	12.89	85.83	1.27	0.00	0.00
25–45	23.11	56.54	19.67	0.68	0.00
45–60	6.67	88.67	4.66	0.00	0.00
60 +	2.60	97.40	0.00	0.00	0.00
Total	19.36	65.90	14.20	0.46	0.08

TABLE 7.5
Nature of Conflict by Age Group: West Zone

Age group	Physical abuse	Verbal abuse	Not talking to each other	Others	Total
18–20	20.13	79.87	0.00	0.00	100
20–5	11.95	63.45	24.60	0.00	100
25–45	7.75	91.88	0.22	0.15	100
45–60	10.84	78.33	0.48	10.35	100
60 +	85.70	14.30	0.00	0.00	100
Total	10.10	83.30	5.44	1.15	100

as we have seen, along with the east zone, records the lowest mean age at marriage—13.9 years for rural areas. If we go by the common finding that husbands account for the maximum violence against women, then this very low figure is remarkable. The east zone is more 'predictable' in this respect—here 18–20 year olds report the highest physical abuse.

Scheduled Castes (who account for 50 per cent of reported physical abuse), also report the highest violence in the youngest age group (67.43 per cent), but zero per cent in the 20–5 years and over 60 years age group (see Table 7.6). Scheduled Tribes similarly report no physical abuse among 20–5 year-olds, but this section is only represented by two age groups—20–5 and 25–45 years (see Table 7.7).

Other Backward Castes report *no* physical abuse in the oldest and youngest groups, but a high 34.29 per cent among 20–5 year-olds, almost *double* that among 25–45 year-olds (see Table 7.8). Departing from the usual pattern, however, the age group 20–5 years claims an almost equal incidence of physical and verbal abuse. Other Backward Castes report lower levels of physical violence, overall, than SCs and STs—18 per cent, as against 22.32 and 24.43 per cent respectively.

TABLE 7.6
Nature of Conflict by Age Group: SC

Age group	Physical abuse	Verbal abuse	Not talking to each other	Others	Total
18–20	67.43	32.57	0.00	0.00	100
20–5	0.00	44.16	55.84	0.00	100
25–45	26.58	59.64	13.51	0.27	100
45–60	23.27	73.83	0.00	2.90	100
60 +	0.00	100.00	0.00	0.00	100
Total	22.32	60.00	17.21	0.47	100

TABLE 7.7
Nature of Conflict by Age Group: ST

Age group	Physical abuse	Verbal abuse	Not talking to each other	Total
20–5	0.00	100.00	0.00	100
25–45	27.91	59.79	12.30	100
Total	24.43	64.80	10.77	100

TABLE 7.8
Nature of Conflict by Age Group: OBC

Age group	Physical abuse	Verbal abuse	Not talking to each other	Total
18–20	0.00	65.28	34.72	100
20–5	34.29	36.66	29.05	100
25–45	18.94	73.11	7.95	100
45–60	12.08	66.71	21.21	100
60 +	0.00	100.00	0.00	100
Total	18.01	67.38	14.61	100

Among upper caste Hindu women, *all those in the 45–60 years age group* who report violence, *report 100 per cent physical abuse.* But the next oldest, i.e., 25–45 year-olds, admit to verbal abuse, at 90 per cent (see Table 7.9). Overall figures for upper caste Hindu women reporting physical violence are higher than those for OBCs, at 22 and 18 per cent, respectively.

Muslim women are next only to Scheduled Tribes in admitting physical violence, at 23.59 per cent, but overall, the trend is similar to the national picture—rising upto age group 25–45 years, then declining to 15 per cent for the age group 60 years and above (see Table 7.10).

TABLE 7.9
Nature of Conflict by Age Group: Hindu Upper Caste

Age group	Physical abuse	Verbal abuse	Not talking to each other	Total
18–20	26.20	73.80	0.00	100
20–5	22.24	50.97	26.79	100
25–45	0.00	90.12	9.88	100
45–60	100.00	0.00	0.00	100
60 +	21.80	56.13	22.07	100

TABLE 7.10
Nature of Conflict by Age Group: Muslims

Age group	Physical abuse	Verbal abuse	Not talking to each other	Others	9
18–20	16.30	66.13	12.26	0.00	5.31
20–5	21.81	71.11	6.40	0.68	0.00
25–45	26.28	61.99	10.58	1.03	0.12
45–60	14.83	62.37	22.80	0.00	0.00
60 +	14.53	85.47	0.00	0.00	0.00
Total	23.59	63.93	11.42	0.79	0.27

Who Abuses?

Regardless of caste, class, and community, all women report the maximum physical abuse by husbands, no matter what their ages (see Table 7.11). But if not husbands, then fathers and sons step in, especially at the youngest and late middle age ·years—18–20 and 45–60 years. No significant rural–urban differences are evident here (see Tables 7.12 and 7.13), indicating again the more or less universal culpability of husbands across the country. (The one exception to this .is 18–20 year-olds in urban India, who report greater physical abuse by parents than husbands—15 per cent as against 9 per cent.) But some regional variations are notable. Husbands in the south zone account for less violence than their counterparts in the north zone—67 per cent compared to 94 per cent, respectively; but at least 14 per cent of respondents in the 25–45 years age group say they are abused by their brothers. A similarly high proportion in the east zone among 20–5 year-olds—22 per cent—report the same. One could put these percentages down to Muslim women, perhaps, who *did* report greater violence by brothers, but in that case the north zone, which has a sizeable Muslim population, is atypical, with a negligible 0.05 per cent reporting such abuse.

TABLE 7.11
Who Ill-treated by Age Group

Age group	Parents	Brothers	Sister	Husband	Mother-in-law	Father-in-law	Sisters-in-law	Sons	Any others	Total
18-20	4.72	0.9	0.48	83.23	0.82	0.00	0.00	0.00	9.85	100
20-5	0.18	2.88	0.00	94.78	1.20	0.00	0.00	0.00	0.97	100
25-45	2.53	1.84	0.00	88.81	2.07	0.02	0.43	0.01	4.28	100
45-60	0.00	0.00	0.20	96.95	0.00	0.00	0.00	2.49	0.36	100
60 +	0.00	0.00	0.00	100.00	0.00	0.00	0.00	0.00	0.00	100
Total	2.26	1.83	0.03	89.59	1.83	0.02	0.35	0.12	3.97	100

TABLE 7.12
Who Ill-treated by Age Group: Rural

Age group	Parents	Brothers	Husband	Mother-in-law	Father-in-law	Sisters-in-law	Sons	Total
18-20	2.98	0.00	96.05	0.97	0.00	0.00	0.00	100
20-5	0.00	0.00	97.44	1.19	0.00	0.00	1.37	100
25-45	2.50	2.30	87.62	2.58	0.13	0.00	4.85	100
45-60	0.00	0.00	97.28	0.00	0.00	2.72	0.00	100
60 +	0.00	0.00	100.00	0.00	0.00	0.00	0.00	100
Total	2.17	1.88	89.35	2.26	0.11	0.13	4.09	100

TABLE 7.13
Who Ill-treated by Age Group: Urban

Age group	Parents	Brothers	Sister	Husband	Mother-in-law	Father-in-law	Sisters-in-law	Sons	Any others	Total
18-20	14.72	6.10	3.23	9.20	0.00	0.00	0.00	0.00	66.74	100
20-5	0.62	9.81	0.00	88.36	1.21	0.00	0.00	0.00	0.00	100
25-45	2.65	0.00	0.00	93.59	0.00	0.12	1.63	0.06	1.96	100
45-60	0.00	0.00	1.25	95.17	0.00	0.00	0.00	1.25	2.32	100
60 +	0.00	0.00	0.00	100.00	0.00	0.00	0.00	0.00	0.00	100
Total	2.59	1.61	0.13	90.53	0.18	0.1	1.29	0.09	3.49	100

184 □ Unequal Citizens

TABLE 7.14
Who Ill-treated by Age Group: North

Age group	Parents	Brother	Husband	Mother-in-law	Sister-in-law
18–20	4.87	0.49	94.64	0.00	0.00
20–5	0.00	0.21	98.35	0.21	0.00
25–45	3.04	0.00	93.26	3.01	0.50
45–60	0.00	0.00	99.50	0.00	0.00
60 +	0.00	0.00	100.00	0.00	0.00
Total	2.62	0.05	94.24	2.38	0.39

TABLE 7.15
Who Ill-treated by Age Group: South

Age group	Parents	Brother	Husband	Mother-in-law	Father-in-law
18–20	0.00	0.00	0.00	7.72	0.00
20–5	0.00	0.00	95.31	4.69	0.00
25–45	3.94	13.53	68.64	0.00	0.18
45–60	0.00	0.00	100.00	0.00	0.00
60 +	3.64	12.51	67.36	0.43	0.17

Seven per cent of OBC respondents say they experience physical violence by their mothers-in-law, while *all* upper caste Hindu respondents name their husbands as perpetrators. Variations among Muslim respondents, however, are the most interesting and important. Close to 57 per cent—more than half—our respondents in the youngest age group, 18–20 years, reported that they were ill-treated physically by their *parents*, and 11 per cent said they were abused by their *brothers*. Husbands continue to be the ones responsible for maximum violence for the age-group 20–60 years and above, but a good 14 per cent of those between the ages of 45 and 60 years blamed their *sons* for physical violence. What this suggests is that male violence against women in the family, rather than being dissipated or centralized in husbands, is dispersed within the family, with all male members resorting to it at some stage or other.

The west zone is consistently outside the national pattern yet again, with the youngest women reporting *equal levels* of abuse from parents, brothers, *sisters*, and husbands—25 per cent each (see Table 7.16). This is so unusual that it demands further probing. Equally significant is the age group 45–60 years reporting very high levels of violence by sons, at 49 per cent (this is the only age group to do so);

but overall figures for husbands are the lowest in the country, at 49 per cent. This comparatively low figure is offset by an equal number of respondents—48 per cent in the 25–45 years age group—claiming that 'others' are responsible. This is intriguing, implying that male members other than those in the immediate family may be responsible, since all others have been accounted for. Whatever the cause and whoever the culprits may be for these 48 per cent of cases, the exceptional nature of the findings from the west zone are noteworthy.

TABLE 7.16
Who Ill-treated by Age Group: West

Age group	Parents	Brother	Sister	Husband	Son	Any other	Total
18–20	25.00	25.00	25.00	25.00	0.00	0.00	100
20–5	3.53	0.00	0.00	96.47	0.00	0.00	100
25–45	0.00	0.00	0.00	39.93	0.00	60.07	100
45–60	0.00	0.00	0.00	51.28	48.72	0.00	100
60 +	1.14	0.57	0.57	48.82	0.54	48.36	100

Reasons for Abuse

One of the most revealing aspects of our data has to do with reasons for conflict and violence, and an explanatory word about the questions asked in our Survey is in order here. As mentioned earlier, the following questions relating to women's primary activity were deliberately unspecified—housework, mothering, and looking after the family, which typically encompass the following: cooking; looking after children/parents/in-laws/; and looking after the house. Areas of potential conflict might include: suspected infidelity; inadequate receipt of gifts and money from the natal family; showing disrespect to in-laws; neglecting the house or children; leaving the house without permission; and not cooking satisfactorily. The question of conjugal conflict has seldom been raised in surveys, but it cannot be discounted as a major factor in domestic violence, because empirical studies have shown that women's resistance to sexual demands by husbands—or, for that matter, by other male members of the household—can result in swift and violent abuse.

The most frequently cited reason for violence across all classes and communities, was the husband's drinking habit, with the percentages for this being the highest for Scheduled Castes and Scheduled Tribes. This is followed by husbands going out without informing their wives and, most interestingly, sharing of property. This reason is especially significant for Muslim respondents who report a (comparatively) high 6.55 per cent on this finding, exceeded only by backward castes who report 7.55 per cent. The relative unimportance of disputes over *land* is not surprising—a primarily poor sample like ours is unlikely to have much land to dispute, in any case.

Purdah is not stated as a reason for violence by respondents in the MWS, except in the west of the country and, surprisingly, by Scheduled Tribes, for whom it is significant. The overwhelming number of women (64 per cent), however, reported 'other reasons' for the violence they experience, from which we may conclude that it is in the domestic/household arena that women are most vulnerable. Eighty-one per cent of Hindu, 69 per cent Muslim, and 68 per cent OBC women fall into this category; but figures for SCs and STs are appreciably lower, at 54 and 51 per cent, respectively, perhaps because alcoholism is more commonly reported by these two groups. In fact, the increase corresponds almost proportionally— 27 and 30 per cent respectively for both, as against 10.78, 6.23, and 10 per cent for OBC, upper caste Hindus, and Muslims, respectively. Poverty, violence, and alcoholism thus seem to have a clear correlation.[7]

Ninety-one per cent of respondents in the MWS said that the main perpetrators of violence were husbands, and for upper caste Hindu women, this percentage is 100 (see Table 7.19).[8] Muslim women reported the *lowest* figure for husbands, next only to OBCs, at 89 per cent; but they reported the highest percentage among all communities and classes for physical violence at the hands of their parents, and the second highest for mothers-in-law.

Muslim women are also unique for being the *only* group that reported some violence from sons, as well; while OBC women are the only ones to report violence by brothers. In both cases, it is only older women, in the age group 35–45 years for brothers, and 45 years and above for sons, who reported thus, and it may be that disputes over money or property-sharing are responsible for such violence. Hindu respondents apart, all groups also reported some violence from 'others' in the family—possibly other male members such as brothers-in-law, cousins, or uncles, all of whom may be responsible. The highest percentage here is reported by OBCs. This category of 'others' assumes significance in light of the finding that it is the next highest, after husbands, and twice as high as mothers-in-law, for instance.

TABLE 7.17
Who Ill-treated by Age Group: Muslims

Age group	Parents	Brothers	Sister	Husband	Mother-in-law	Father-in-law	Sisters-in-law	Sons	Any others	Total
18–20	56.97	10.89	5.76	16.42	9.97	0.00	0.00	0.00	0.00	100
20–5	1.55.	1.38	0.00	78.56	10.25	0.00	0.00	0.00	8.26	100
25–45	1.09	0.00	0.00	93.88	1.22	0.28	1.22	0.13	2.19	100
45–60	0.00	0.00	1.13	82.47	0.00	0.00	0.00	14.31	2.09	100
60 +	0.00	0.00	0.00	100.00	0.00	0.00	0.00	0.00	0.00	100
Total	2.93	0.54	0.29	88.49	2.53	0.21	0.90	1.28	2.83	100

TABLE 7.18
Reasons for Conflict by Community

Community	Land disputes	Sharing of property	Share of property given to daughter	Drinking habit of husband	Husband goes out without informing	Mother-in-law forces purdah	Others
SC	0.36	5.91	1.03	27.27	10.10	1.04	54.28
ST	1.89	0.00	0.00	29.81	5.52	11.05	51.73
OBC	3.83	7.55	0.24	10.78	7.16	2.15	68.29
Others	4.37	1.09	0.00	6.23	2.66	0.00	81.40
Muslims	2.79	6.55	0.56	9.95	7.39	2.23	69.21
Total	2.41	5.80	0.52	17.36	7.72	2.19	63.48

TABLE 7.19
Who Ill-Treated by Community

Community	Parents	Brothers	Sister	Husband	Mother-in-law	Father-in-law	Sisters-in-law	Sons	Any others	Total
SC	0.92	0.00	0.00	95.37	0.00	0.00	0.00	0.00	3.71	100
ST	0.00	0.00	0.00	96.21	0.00	0.00	0.00	0.00	3.79	100
OBC	0.00	4.99	0.00	82.56	5.31	0.00	0.88	0.00	6.26	100
Others	0.00	0.00	0.00	100.00	0.00	0.00	0.00	0.00	0.00	100
Muslims	2.93	0.54	0.29	88.49	2.53	0.21	0.9	1.28	2.83	100
Total	0.70	1.63	.03	91.02	1.93	0.02	0.37	0.13	4.18	100

Regionally, the north and east zones report the highest figures for violence by husbands, *with percentages for Hindu women being significantly higher than for Muslims in the north zone*. Despite this, however, and in contrast to the overall lower levels of violence in the south zone, the latter is the only region in the country where higher standards of living or SES actually report *higher* levels of violence, for urban Hindu women, and urban and rural Muslim women. The most glaring zonal variations, however, with regard to who perpetrates violence are to be found in the south and west zones; in the former, OBC women report a high degree of violence by 'others'— 21.78 per cent; and in the latter *100 per cent* Scheduled Caste women report the same. Could it be that Tamil Nadu (going by the NFHS finding) is responsible for this atypical picture?

Once again, it is necessary to emphasize that all data from the MWS only refer to women who admit to violence, and do not, by any means, indicate that an improvement in education, earning capacity, or standard of living will by themselves make for lower levels of violence; merely that it may just be shrouded in secrecy by women who wish to maintain a façade of respectability, dignity, and family honour.

Conclusion

The findings of the MWS are corroborated by other studies and by Police records which have shown a rising graph of crimes against women over the last few years. The latest report released by the Delhi Police shows that dowry cases are on the rise, as are cases of harassment of women by their husbands, which rose from 950 in the year 2000 to 1158 in 2001. The increase only indicates that more cases are reported to the police, not necessarily that violence itself has increased; but conversely, a drop in the number of cases reported does not mean that violent crimes against women have registered a decline. Indeed, serious under-reporting by women and a widespread reluctance to admit to domestic violence have meant that the few statistics that we have are gross under-estimations. The International Centre for Research on Women (ICRW), for instance, reports that 43 per cent of women in its survey of seven cities in India had experienced some form of physical, verbal, or psychological violence, ranging from threats to abandonment, at least once in their lifetime. Other studies put the figure at anywhere between 22 and 60 per cent.

Statistics released by the National Crime Records Bureau (NCRB) amplify this further. They reveal a shocking 71.5 per cent increase in cases of torture and dowry deaths during 1991-5, most of them within the home. According to Sharda Prasad, former director of the NCRB, there are three specific situations in which women are especially vulnerable: within the home; while in transit; and in the workplace. 'We could put in systems to handle such crime in the workplace—as the recent Supreme Court order of 1997 in the *Vishaka vs. the State of Rajasthan* case attempted to do. It's more difficult to handle crime perpetrated while women are in transit, on the streets, and in the public transport systems, but even this problem could be addressed to an extent by educating the public to intervene. But it is the crime perpetrated within the four walls of the home that is extremely difficult to address. This is one area where reporting is minimal and where the woman is often most exposed to peril.'

Extreme and chronic poverty, women's economic dependence, and lack of viable options outside marriage have combined with a deeply entrenched culture of male authority to make domestic violence endemic in India. Its full dimensions are only now beginning to emerge, but a few general observations can be made based on the MWS and other recent surveys and studies.

Although domestic violence is generally understood to refer to inter-spousal violence—and indeed, that is the prevalent and predominant form it takes—researchers and fieldworkers point out that it encompasses everything from female foeticide and extreme neglect of female infants and girls to girl-child abuse, verbal and physical battery, marital rape, deliberate deprivation, and psychological and mental torture. It is also, as is now coming to light, directed increasingly against the aged. Its endemic nature may be gauged by the fact that, often, research and fieldwork that set out to probe other issues such as health, autonomy, work, or decision-making, run up against the pervasive and sustained presence and experience of domestic violence, across caste, class, and community as an inhibiting factor. Recognizing the enormity of its occurrence, agencies like the World Bank and the World Health Organization, for example, have pointed to the serious implications of its impact on the overall health, capabilities, functioning, and demographic profile of countries, and of women in particular.[9] In India its endemic character is reinforced, structurally, by persistent, prescriptive gender subordination and, institutionally, through a range of highly discriminatory practices, policies, and prejudices that not only disable, but disempower, women.

In addition to the above, women's vulnerability stems from an array of prohibitions, denials, and severe constraints that make for an oppressive everyday reality in which the majority of women—and especially, poor women—lead their lives. Powerful social and cultural norms ensure that marriage is the primary life-choice for women, and equally powerful conventions and customs prescribe a range of practices that, ultimately, result in their being equipped for little else. We have seen how education and equal opportunity are denied or withheld; how mobility is severely curbed; entry into the workforce—and, hence a measure of economic independence—actively discouraged, prohibited, or simply made extremely difficult by other demands on women; and, finally, how state and society have failed to provide them with other alternatives that will enable them to break free of their disabilities.

This situation is compounded by the high level of tolerance in society for violence as a means of conflict resolution generally, and domestic violence in particular. Not only is the latter seen to be 'private', an intimate family matter not meant for public scrutiny or intervention, it also enjoys widespread social sanction. A little bit of wife-beating is seen to be desirable in order to discipline and control women, especially young brides—and the earlier the better, it would seem, going by the age break-up in our data. Eighteen to 45 per cent of husbands in Leela Visaria's study acknowledged that they physically abused their wives, and we may assume that the actual figure is higher. Their readily admitting to violence is itself an indication that social stigma attaches not to the crime, but to women's breaking the silence that surrounds it. The internalization by women of their low self-worth, as people of less value than men, is one reason for the shocking finding of the NFHS that 56 per cent of women justify physical abuse by men in the family, on one ground or another. By this they simultaneously reinforce and reproduce both gender subordination *and* patriarchal control, and contribute to maintaining the extreme power distortion in gender relations.

The gendering of domestic violence is readily apparent if one just looks at the 'causes', other than economic constraints, cited for inter-spousal violence: resistance to excessive control; husband's alcoholism; family socialization in violence; failure to carry out her domestic duties satisfactorily; sexual politics; a woman's infertility; failure to fulfil marital or domestic obligations and duties; fear of censure which may lead to further violence; extreme economic dependency on her husband; lack of viable alternatives. The dailiness of many of these activities, and the poverty that determines the existential reality of the majority of women means that the potential for violent domestic conflict is ever-present; at the same time, an extreme gender imbalance means that violence is visited upon them in the very domain to which they are more or less forcibly confined—the domestic and private.

In conclusion, if we were to step back for a moment from a primarily instrumentalist approach to domestic violence—which seeks only to establish the impact of violence on women's health-seeking behaviour or on their ability to participate 'effectively' in development programmes, for instance—and examine instead, the totality of women's lives, lived in an environment of deprivation, exclusion/seclusion, economic dependence, and overall violence in the marital domestic arena, we might be able to better determine the parameters and full extent of their powerlessness.

Endnotes

1. See especially Leela Visaria, Nishi Mitra, Veena Poonacha, and Divya Pandey, *Domestic Violence in India: A Summary Report of Three Studies*, vol. 1, International Center for Research on Women, Washington, D.C., 1999. Also the *National Family Health Survey (Second Round), 1998–9*; and assorted reports by the Centre for Women's Development Studies, Centre for Social Research, the Lawyers' Collective, and Sakshi (all New Delhi).

2. Malavika Karlekar, 'Domestic Violence', *Economic and Political Weekly*, 4 July 1998.

3. Thus, in Shireen Jejeebhoy's sample of 2000 women from two districts of Tamil Nadu and Uttar Pradesh, a high 50 per cent reported battery at their husbands' hands; and Leela Visaria's in-depth interviews with 450 currently married women in Gujarat revealed the same. Shireen Jejeebhoy, 'Wife-Beating in Rural India: A Husband's Right?' *Economic and Political Weekly*, 11 April 1998. Ranjana Kumari's study of 150 dowry victims in Delhi indicated that 61.3 per cent were thrown out of their homes by their husbands after prolonged periods of harassment and abuse, but it is more than likely that the women themselves would have admitted to this only after the event. Quoted in Leela Visaria et al., *Domestic Violence in India*.

4. Leela Visaria et al., *Domestic Violence in India*; Malavika Karlekar, 'Domestic Violence'.

5. Shireen Jejeebhoy goes further, in fact, arguing that Muslim women in

Tamil Nadu in her sample reported lower figures for domestic violence because of cross-cousin marriages and women remaining within the family.

6. Leela Visaria observes that of the women who maintain silence, 75 per cent emphasized a concern for their husbands' and families' honour as the main reason for keeping quiet. Leéla Visaria, 'Violence Against Women: A Field Study', *Economic and Political Weekly*, 13 May 2000.

7. As with the MWS, the NFHS too reports the highest violence among the poorest sections of society, with Scheduled Castes reporting 27.4 per cent; but the alarming detail revealed by their data is that the *maximum violence was experienced by women working for cash*—29 per cent; followed by those who work, but not for cash—24 per cent. This suggests two things: one, that poor women with incomes are especially vulnerable, either because they can be beaten into parting with their money; because they go out to work and cannot therefore be as strictly supervised; or because they are more assertive. Women who work, but not for cash, may also be vulnerable for some of the same reasons, including, in addition, neglecting the family or household while they work. While this may may be tolerated if the woman also happens to bring in some money, it is unlikely to be the case if she doesn't.

8. Empirical studies confirm survey findings on husbands as the chief perpetrators of violence. Fifty per cent of women in Shireen Jejeebhoy's sample reported battery by their husbands; 42 per cent in Leela Visaria's group of 450 women in Kheda district of Gujarat experienced physical beating and violent sexual assault; and 75 per cent Scheduled Caste women in rural Punjab spoke of regular beatings by husbands. Shireen Jejeebhoy, 'Wife-Beating in Rural India': A Husband's Right? Evidence From Survey Data, *EPW*, 11 April, 1998, pp. 855–62. Mahajan, quoted in Leela Visaria, 'Violence Against Women'.

8

Access to Basic Amenities and Awareness of Welfare Schemes

Social welfare objectives and allocation of publicly-provided goods were pre-eminent on the agenda of the state at the time of independence. Indeed, in most societies, the government or the state plays a critical role in providing public goods such as health and education. Access to public goods is a decisive factor, because without an acceptable standard of living for the masses, no political participation or legal equality would make sense. These services include, for example, safe drinking water, proper drainage, and sanitation. The generally inadequate availability of these basic public services in India is in itself symbolic of the extent to which these objectives have not been achieved. There is a serious deficiency in the accessibility and availability of basic amenities in the cities and rural areas.

· This chapter looks at the respondents' perception about basic issues and amenities in their area, awareness of government schemes and programmes, and access to various welfare services and facilities, and the benefits received from them. One set of questions pertained to various types of problems in the neighbourhood in terms of availability of services, and another set was on the distance and availability of health facilities. Finally, we asked questions on various types of development programmes run by the government, especially programmes directed towards women.

The MWS asked respondents to list the major problems faced by people in their neighbourhood. As both Muslim and Hindu respondents were selected from the same locality, the problems reported were common to both groups of the area. Overall, slightly over half the respondents reported drinking water as the major problem for both rural and urban areas, but going by proportions, it is a greater

problem for rural than for urban areas (see Figures 8.1 and 8.2).[1]
Town-level data from the Census depict a similar picture. At least 38
per cent of 3790 towns did not have a tap or tube-well, which means
a sizeable section of the population has to depend on sources that are
neither reliable nor hygienic.[2]

Within urban areas, non-availability of drinking water is the
biggest problem, followed by lack of sanitation facilities, again a
greater problem for rural than for urban respondents. Drainage is a

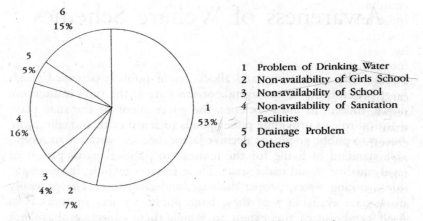

1 Problem of Drinking Water
2 Non-availability of Girls School
3 Non-availability of School
4 Non-availability of Sanitation
   Facilities
5 Drainage Problem
6 Others

FIGURE 8.1: Most Important Problems in the Neighbourhood: Rural

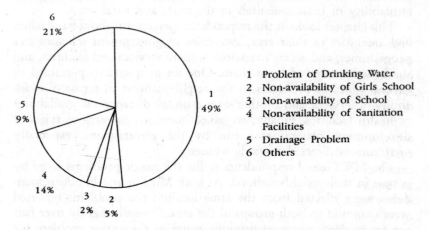

1 Problem of Drinking Water
2 Non-availability of Girls School
3 Non-availability of School
4 Non-availability of Sanitation
   Facilities
5 Drainage Problem
6 Others

FIGURE 8.2: Most Important Problems in the Neighbourhood: Urban

bigger problem in urban than in rural areas, at 9 and 5 per cent respectively. Non-availability of schools for girls is a much greater problem in rural than in urban areas.

The classification of problems by both communities is similar in rural areas. The proportions of Muslim respondents reporting non-availability of sanitation facilities and of schools for girls are marginally higher in urban areas. The non-availability of sanitation facilities should come as no surprise in view of the poor civic amenities and sanitation in Muslim dominated localities. Urban differences by community are insignificant and correspond very closely to the all-India urban proportions.

Drinking water seems to be a greater problem in the east (followed by west) zone, than in the north and south zones. The proportions for drainage in the west zone are significantly greater than the national average. By contrast, non-availability of schools for girls is significantly lower in the west than in other regions, particularly for Muslim respondents. Non-availability of schools is far higher in the north than in other zones, and is very low in the west and south, corresponding to the trends in low literacy and education in these regions. Non-availability of sanitation facilities is very high in the north, much greater than other zones, followed by the east, low in the west and the south. The majority of Muslim households have less access to civic amenities like water and electricity. Arguably the poor availability occurs due to lack of initiative or resources of state governments, especially the less developed states, Madhya Pradesh, Uttar Pradesh, Bihar, and Orissa.

One important set of questions was on health facilities, including Primary Health Centres, hospitals, and dispensaries or clinics. Data on utilization of facilities has been obtained from the following questions: Is there a government health centre/hospital in your area? Do you go to this centre if someone in your family is ill? If not, where do you go? Why don't you go to the health centre?

Health provisioning varies significantly between rural and urban areas, and between communities. Nearly half the respondents in the rural areas from both communities claim that a government health centre does not exist in their areas, as opposed to about 20 per cent in the urban areas. All those who answered 'yes' were further asked if they would take someone to the government hospital in the event of sickness. Sixty per cent (of those answering yes) said that they would, the remaining saying no. Those who answered 'no' to this and

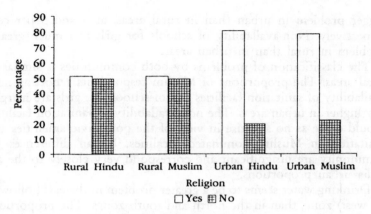

FIGURE 8.3: Availability of Government Hospital

the previous question were asked, if not, where do you go? Almost 65 per cent of all respondents said that they would go to a private doctor, 30 per cent to a private hospital, and the remaining 5 per cent divided between other providers. The rural–urban divide shows that, given the poor availability of various types of government health facilities in rural areas, people depended more on private facilities than government. In urban areas, however, dependence on government facilities is much greater than private. In the north zone, most of the respondents go to a private doctor in the absence of a government hospital, the rest to a private hospital. In the south, the proportions are reversed, with the bulk going to a private hospital and the rest going to a private doctor. Interestingly, a greater proportion of Muslims, as compared to Hindus, go to a private hospital in the south. The pattern and proportions in the east are similar to the north zone. In the west zone, Muslims are more or less equally divided between private doctor and private hospital. A small minority from both communities reported visiting a trust/NGO dispensary.

Respondents were further asked why they didn't go to the health centre. Long distance (37 per cent) and lack of adequate facilities (30 per cent) seem to be the two most important reasons for respondents to not use the government health centre (see Figure 8.4). The reasons were almost similar in rural and urban areas, and among members of both communities with some marginal differences.

Distance seems to be more important for Muslims than for Hindus, with the opposite being true in the case of lack of adequate facilities.

TABLE 8.1
Alternative Sources of Health Care: Hindu

	Private hospital	Private doctor	Ayurvedic doctor	Homoeopathic doctor	Unani doctor	Trust/NGO dispensary	Others	Total
Hindu	29.29	65.36	0.60	0.52	0.66	1.29	1.36	100

TABLE 8.2
Alternative Sources of Health Care: Muslims

	Private hospital	Private doctor	Ayurvedic doctor	Homoeopathic doctor	Unani doctor	Trust/NGO dispensary	Others	Total
Muslim	30.10	64.63	0.46	1.39	0.19	0.49	1.78	100

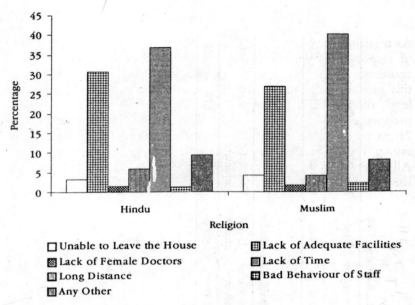

FIGURE 8.4: Reasons for Not Going to the Health Centre

About 3 per cent respondents cite inability, that is, restrictions on mobility, to leave the house as the reason for not going to the health centre, with no significant difference between the communities. In the north, long distance is an important constraint for Muslims in availing health centre facilities. Long distance is much more important for both communities than all-India (a little over half the respondents give that as the reason). In other words, not being able to use health facilities such as exist in the north zone could well be due to restrictions on mobility as well as lack of money for transport to the hospital and because government facilities are not readily available. Correspondingly, proportions citing lack of adequate facilities are lower than that for all-India. Here no responses are very high (36 per cent of the respondents did not give an answer). The trend is similar to the all-India pattern.

The proportions of respondents unable to leave their houses are significant, as is lack of time. Community differences are significant for long distance as well as for inability to leave the house; for the latter, slightly more proportions of Muslims, as compared to Hindus, women give that as the answer.

Utilization of *Balwadi/Anganwadi*

As regards the availability of balwadis and anganwadis, the majority of respondents report non-availability at the all-India level, with community differences being insignificant (see Figure 8.5). However, this picture is characterized by regional variation. At the regional level, the majority responds 'yes', except in the north zone. The proportions vary widely by region—from 86 per cent in the west to 21 per cent in the north. The low proportions in the north of those saying 'yes' are contributing to the overall low all-India proportions. All those who said 'yes' were further asked if their children went to the balwadi?

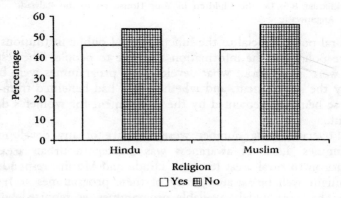

FIGURE 8.5: Availability of Balwadi/Anganwadi

The majority of the respondents who were aware of the existence of balwadis in their neighbourhoods did not send their own children to these. Here the community difference is significant. A far greater proportion of Muslims sent their children to balwadis than Hindus (see Figure 8.6). On the whole, this confirms the all-India trend, except that the proportions vary widely across regions. For those who send their children to the balwadis, the proportion varies from 44 per cent (highest) for east zone Muslims to 24 per cent for south zone Hindus (lowest).

Awareness of Development Programmes

Development programmes run by the government have played a major role in determining the availability of public goods to the urban

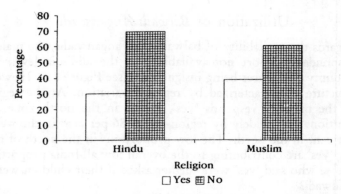

FIGURE 8.6: Do the Children in Your House go to the Balwadi/Anganwadi?

and rural poor. Crucial to the functioning of public institutions and welfare policies is the information available to people. The respondents were asked about what development programmes were being run by the government, and whether they had benefited from any of those being implemented by the government for women's development.

An overwhelming number were unaware of any development programmes. Lack of awareness was greater in urban areas in comparison to rural areas for both Hindu and Muslim respondents. This might well be because many of these programmes are rural-based. The most widely available programmes, as reported by the respondents at the all-India level, are the Jawahar Rozgar Yojana (JRY), followed by the Indira Awas Yojana and the Integrated Child Development Scheme Services (ICDS) (see Table 8.3). These three appear to be the most important programmes about which there is some information and awareness. The awareness level was even lower for developmental programmes run for women and children. The majority of Muslim respondents who were aware of some programme were, however, unable to name any of them. Inability to name government programmes, especially women's programmes, suggests that the respondents have not had access to them.

Non-awareness is close to 40 per cent in the north zone. The JRY appears to generate the greatest response, followed by the Indira Awas Yojana. Again, there is a very high proportion of non-responses. Here, the Integrated Rural Development Programme (IRDP) followed by Development of Women and Children in Rural Areas (DWACRA)

TABLE 8.3

Awareness of Development Programmes being Run by Government

	1	2	3	4	5	6	7	8	9	10	11	12	13	14	15	Total
Hindu	3.17	0.55	2.60	16.03	1.19	9.58	10.70	1.05	0.03	0.25	0.46	0.92	0.36	0.42	10.47	100
Muslim	2.93	0.24	1.28	12.78	0.60	10.29	8.37	1.60	0.05	0.34	0.50	0.35	0.41	0.26	10.58	100
Total	3.14	0.51	2.55	15.63	1.11	9.67	10.42	1.12	0.03	0.26	0.47	0.85	0.36	0.40	10.49	100

Note: 1–Integrated Rural Development Programme (IRDP); 2–Training of Rural Youth for Self-employment (TRYSEM); 3–Development of Women and Children in Rural Areas (DWACRA); 4–Jawahar Rozgar Yojana (JRY); 5–Nehru Rozgar Yojana (NRY); 6–Indira Awas Yojana; 7–Integrated Child Development Services (ICDS); 8–District Poverty Initiatives Project (DPIP); 9–Employment Assurance Scheme (EAS); 10–Scheme for Urban Enterprises; 11–Scheme for Urban Wage Employment; 12–Scheme for Divorced Women; 13–National Credit Fund for Women; 14–Labour Welfare Scheme; 15–Others.

seem to be the most well-known programmes. There is a similar pattern of non-responses. Here the ICDS followed by the Indira Awas Yojana seems to be the important programme about which women have some awareness. The non-responses are lower than in the east zone. The Indira Awas Yojana, followed by ICDS, are two important categories of programmes.

Awareness of development programmes directed towards women is even poorer, with only 3 per cent Hindu respondents and 2 per cent Muslim respondents aware of any such programmes.

The vast majority of respondents claim to be unaware of any programmes directed towards women, and the picture seems to be uniform across zones (see Figure 8.7). Large proportions of respondents claim no awareness of programmes directed towards women's welfare, irrespective of education level (see Figure 8.8).

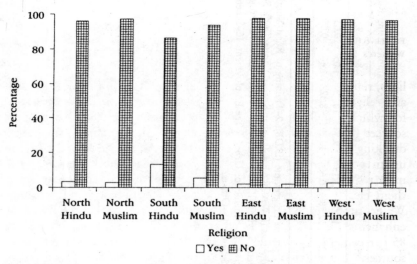

FIGURE 8.7: Awareness of Development Programmes Directed Towards Women by Religion

Conclusion

Going by the respondents' perception, the availability of basic amenities and public goods is most certainly unsatisfactory. Clearly, there are disparities in access to services and programmes along rural–urban lines and possibly along socio-economic status and community

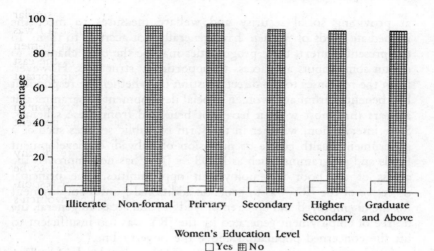

FIGURE 8.8: Awareness of Development Programmes Directed Towards Women by Women's Education Level

lines, reflecting discrimination in their provision on the basis of caste and religion.[3] By far the most important problem is drinking water, for which a sizeable section of the population has to fall back upon sources that are unsafe. The government is the principal provider of drinking water, especially in urban areas, nearly 72 per cent of the urban population obtaining water from government sources. That most respondents perceive drinking water as the main problem facing them clearly reflects the inadequacy of the public supply system. Water supply and sanitation expenditure are not only aimed at enhancing the quality of life, but also health conditions. Moreover, 85 per cent of the population dependent on water uses government sources.[4] In short, the vast majority of the respondents and their households seems to live in dehumanized conditions, as they have to do without safe drinking water and sanitation. This scarcity is despite the government's active involvement in the provision of drinking water through various programmes to cover a hundred per cent of the urban population by 1991.[5]

Again, going by the levels of awareness, it would appear that the benefits of most government schemes, which over the years have been made more specific to target women beneficiaries, by fixing the conditions of minimum participation (IRDP, JRY, EAS), and aimed at providing social security and welfare measures to meet the immediate needs of women, have generally not accrued to them. In the present context, these programmes may be the only channels to obtain some inputs and access to opportunity structures. However, from the responses to the direct question on whether the respondent had benefited from any women's social development programmes, it appears that most women have not benefited from these schemes. State intervention, whether in the form of public services such as a government health centre or provision of balwadi or development funds and programmes such as ICDS or JRY, has not improved the access of the poor to employment opportunities. The principal objective of the JRY was to generate additional gainful employment for the unemployed and underemployed in rural areas. In general, the degree of employment generated by the JRY was too insufficient to lift the concerned population above the poverty line.[6]

Lacking information and awareness, and given low levels of literacy and high levels of poverty, Muslim women lack the wherewithal to access the government programmes. The low levels of literacy that obtain in this sample can only partially explain lack of awareness of development programmes. As women from poorer classes and a minority, they are doubly disadvantaged in gaining access to government welfare programmes. It is clear that Muslim women are extremely marginal to the government programmes and welfare functions adopted by the state. However, these programmes are an important means of combating the impact of structural inequities that impede the access of the poor to socio-economic security. The case for social intervention in the provision of health and other facilities and services is strong for several reasons. There is a specially strong case for public involvement in the fields of health, nutrition, and education from the viewpoint of rights and equity.

Endnotes

1. The next big category is 'others', but we do not know what this consists of.

2. Amitabh Kundu, *In the Name of the Poor*, Sage Publications, New Delhi, 1993, p. 199.

3. For instance, Roger Betancourt and Susan Gleason show the existence of statistical discrimination in the outcomes of the allocation process for medical services on the basis of caste and religion. They suggest that a higher proportion of Muslims or Scheduled Castes in the rural area of a district leads to lowering

of the public input and this discrimination is the consequence of decisions by the state governments. 'The Allocation of Publicly-Provided Goods to Rural Households in India: On Some Consequences of Caste and Religion and Democracy', *World Development*, 28(12), 2000, p. 2177.

4. Amitabh Kundu, *In the Name of the Urban Poor*, p. 202.

5. More than 70 per cent of the urban population gets water from government agencies.

6. K. Seetaprabhu, 'Socio-economic Security in the Context of Pervasive Poverty: A Case Study of India', SES Papers, ILO, 2001.

9

Women's Participation in the Political Process

Women's participation in elections and political activities is an important means by which women gain status and autonomy, but their presence in party politics and leadership remains limited. Their low political representation, however, does not appear to have any correlation to their voter turnout or political awareness. Women are quite conscious of the importance of their vote and regularly exercise their franchise. Over the years, the number of women voters has shown a steady rise; while it is still lower than that of men, the gender gap has reduced from 16 per cent to less than 10 per cent over the past four decades. In the 1999 Lok Sabha elections, for example, 58 per cent female voters exercised their franchise.

This chapter seeks to understand and assess the nature of women's political participation. In particular, it disaggregates the participation related evidence in terms of region and social groups. While most analyses of political participation draw their inferences from aggregate voting data, this chapter uses awareness of major issues concerning the political system to understand women's participation in the political process.

To assess women's involvement in political activities, the MWS asked a number of questions regarding their participation during elections and their willingness to contest in elections. Respondents were asked about the age of voting. Overall, 53 per cent of them were aware that 18 years is the correct age for voting; 25 per cent gave no reply; and 9 per cent replied '20 years'. Comparatively more Hindu respondents from both urban and rural areas were aware of the correct age for voting. Among Muslims, about 51 per cent replied correctly but lack of response amongst Muslims was higher.

Voting Trends

If voting in elections is an indication of participation, then the participation level of our respondents is high by world standards. Most women in this sample exercised their right to vote. Overall, 85 per cent voted in the elections, which is remarkable. It shows a level of participation that has not only kept pace with the upward trend in voting since the 1991 elections, but is in fact at an even higher level. Generally, women as a group constitute the largest group of non-voters. This sample, however, indicates above-average participation. Interestingly, the question of voting elicited no non-responses; the significance of this becomes apparent when we compare it with the high proportion of non-responses for many other important questions in the survey. No clear community or rural–urban differences are evident in this case; however, both in rural and urban areas, voter turnout is higher for Muslim women than for Hindus (see Figure 9.1). This difference is significant, with rural percentages being marginally higher than urban for all respondents.

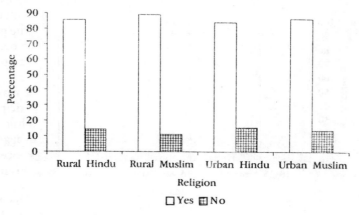

FIGURE 9.1: Voting in Elections

When asked whether they had voted in previous elections, the vast majority (around 90 per cent) replied that they voted every time. Here the rural–urban and the community differences are not significant; in other words, answers were independent of the respondents' location and religion (see Figure 9.2).

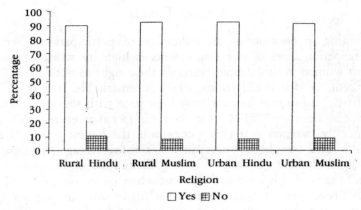

FIGURE 9.2: Do You Vote Every time?

Amongst age groups, the middle age group, 36–60 years, has the highest proportion of those voting every time (92 per cent); this proportion is the lowest (87 per cent) in the highest age group, 61–90 years (see Figure 9.3).

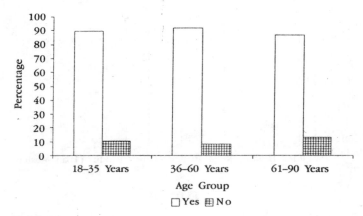

FIGURE 9.3: Age Group Versus Voting

Women's Autonomy in Voting

To assess the extent of autonomy in voting and to what extent the voting decision is made by women themselves, respondents were asked whom they consulted or who advised them to support a particular party or candidate.

As expected, members of their family and not people from outside advised the bulk of women. In fact, their husbands, and not others, advised about 60 per cent of the women. Nearly 30 per cent stated their family members (which could include husbands as well, as the option does not specify which family members other than husband) as their advisers (see Table 9.1). Notice that the role of party worker seems to be marginal: only about 3 per cent women reported voting under their influence. The impact of women's education level on who influences their voting preference is not very clear, as there is no discernible pattern across education levels. As this correlation was not very suggestive, we tried to see if there were significant community differences among women regarding voting decisions.

TABLE 9.1
Women's Autonomy in Voting by Education Level

	1	2	3	4	5	6	7	Total
Illiterate	30.31	59.28	1.59	2.92	1.51	3.30	1.07	100
Non-formal	64.09	33.60	0.00	0.34	0.00	1.98	0.00	100
Primary	17.56	74.52	3.43	0.15	0.04	0.50	3.56	100
Middle	19.64	69.67	0.73	2.70	0.03	5.74	0.58	100
Higher Secondary	41.15	56.02	1.40	0.14	0.00	1.23	0.06	100
Gaduate and above	21.00	76.95	0.28	1.49	0.00	0.28	0.00	100
Total	29.18	61.14	1.60	2.51	1.15	3.17	1.12	100

Note: 1–Family member; 2–husband; 3–friends; 4–community elders; 5–religious workers; 6–party workers; 7–others.

Interestingly, it transpires that a greater proportion of Muslim women consult their husbands in comparison to Hindus (see Table 9.2). Correspondingly, the proportion of Muslim women who consult family members is lower than that for Hindus, but there is no significant difference regarding consultation with party workers across communities.

TABLE 9.2
Women's Autonomy in Voting by Religion

	1	2	3	4	5	6	7	Total
Hindu	29.95	60.09	1.68	2.60	1.24	3.17	1.18	100
Muslim	24.06	68.22	1.10	1.90	0.50	3.21	0.75	100
Total	29.18	61.14	1.60	2.51	1.15	3.17	1.12	100

Note: 1–Family member; 2–husband; 3–friends; 4–community elders; 5–religious workers; 6–party workers; 7–others.

The proportion of respondents who consult their husbands is significantly higher in the uppermost socio-economic class (74 per cent) than in the lowest (52 per cent) (see Table 9.3). Likewise, the proportion consulting family members is highest among the poor respondents rather than the rich. Awareness of candidates and parties is high among Muslims, which is another indication of their strong interest in the political process. The proportion saying a 'sure yes' is higher amongst the Muslims. For Hindus, 'no' and 'uncertain yes' are almost equal; among Muslims, 'uncertain yes' is higher than 'no'. Thus, on the whole, based upon the responses to this question alone, political awareness seems to be higher amongst Muslims (see Figure 9.4).

TABLE 9.3
Women's Autonomy in Voting by SES

	1	2	3	4	5	6	7	Total
Low	35.22	51.76	3.38	5.12	0.78	3.64	0.09	100
Lower middle	23.69	67.93	0.43	2.54	2.46	1.61	1.21	100
Middle	29.23	57.31	1.40	1.23	1.18	6.20	3.44	100
Upper middle	27.54	69.77	0.21	0.41	0.02	1.33	3.44	100
High	23.55	73.86	0.89	0.23	1.13	0.26	0.13	100
Total	29.18	61.14	1.60	2.51	1.15	3.17	0.05	100

Note: 1–Family member; 2–husband; 3–friends; 4–community elders; 5–religious workers; 6–party workers; 7–others.

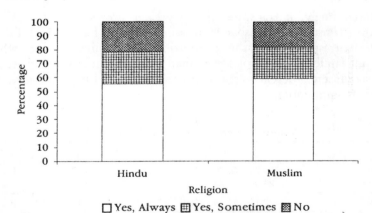

FIGURE 9.4: Awareness of Party and Candidate by Religion

Participation in Election Campaigns

An overwhelming proportion of 95 per cent respondents have not participated in an election campaign (see Figure 9.5). Nor does the picture change substantially according to the SES status of the respondents, as can be seen from Figure 9.6.

The same is the case with the respondents' marital status. About 4 per cent of currently married respondents answered 'yes', as

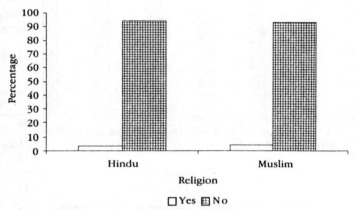

□ Yes ⊞ No

FIGURE 9.5: Participation in a Political Campaign by Religion

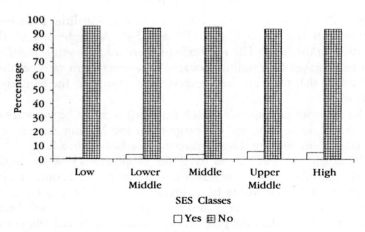

□ Yes ⊞ No

FIGURE 9.6: Participation in a Political Campaign by SES

compared to 5 per cent of widowed women (see Figure 9.7). It is not clear why the proportion of divorced women (0.27 per cent) or never married women (1.65 per cent) answering 'yes' to participation in a political campaign should be so much lower than that of separated (6.21 per cent) or deserted (9 per cent) women.

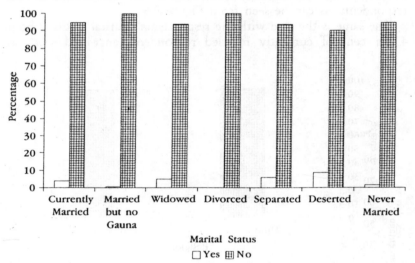

FIGURE 9.7: Participation in a Political Campaign by Marital Status

Political Awareness

Reservations for women in panchayats and municipalities have been written into law through the 73rd and 74th Amendments to the Constitution of India. The respondents were asked several questions in order to gauge their political awareness, among them whether they were aware that there are seats reserved for women in the panchayat elections.

The majority of respondents (69 per cent) seem to be unaware of such reservations, although the proportion for Muslim respondents is smaller than that for Hindu respondents (see Figure 9.8).

The north and south zones have 'no' proportions that are higher than the all-India figures. The east and west zones offer a contrast with awareness about reservations being higher (about 40 per cent) in these zones, those reporting being unaware (about 58 per cent) being significantly lower than the proportion in the country as a whole (see Figure 9.9).

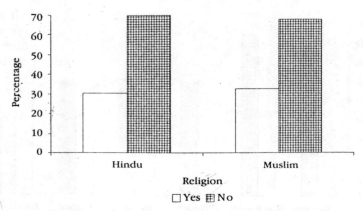

FIGURE 9.8: Awareness of Reservation for Women by Religion

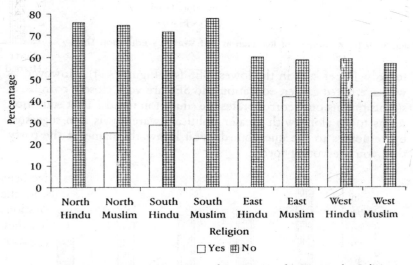

FIGURE 9.9: Zonal Variation in Awareness of Reservation for Women by Religion

Awareness of the existence of reservations rises sharply with a rise in women's education, with the proportion of highly educated women aware of it being more than double that of illiterate women (see Figure 9.10).

Although not as dramatic, a rise in the socio-economic status of the women clearly increases their awareness of reservations: about 47 per cent of women in the high SES class are aware of it as opposed

214 □ *Unequal Citizens*

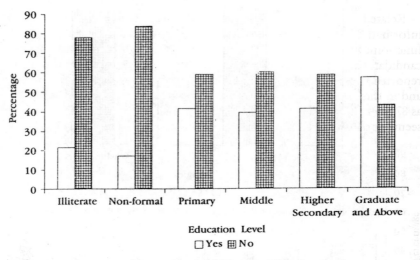

FIGURE 9.10: Awareness of Reservation and Women's Education Level

to only 12 per cent in the lowest SES (see Figure 9.11). However, as we have noted earlier, education and SES are very closely correlated, so this finding only corroborates the education trends. That education seems to go along with greater political awareness is also suggested by responses to the question: do you know the name of the party that you are voting for?

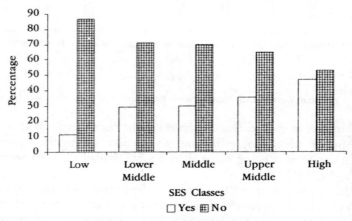

FIGURE 9.11: Awareness of Reservation by SES

Related to political participation in voting is the level of political information about candidates and parties, which is crucial to the functioning of democracy. Women do not lack information about candidates and parties. On the whole, about 56 per cent of respondents reported that they knew the name of the party they were voting for, and 'in the case of highly educated women the proportion was as high as 87 per cent (see Figure 9.12). Certain knowledge of the party's name seems to rise significantly with a rise in women's education level.

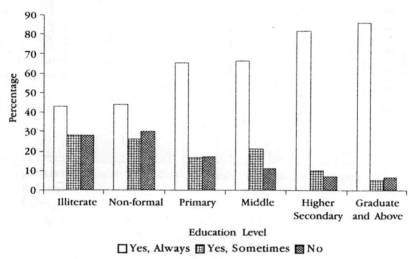

FIGURE 9.12: Awareness of Party and Candidate by Education Level

The extension of reservations to women in legislatures at higher levels has been under debate since 1996 when the Women's Reservation Bill was introduced in the Lok Sabha. The responses have been overwhelmingly in favour of extending reservations to legislatures. The majority of respondents, 76 per cent, support reservations at the state/national level election. While the difference in the 'yes' responses across communities is not significant, that in the 'no' responses is, with a higher proportion of Muslim respondents opposed to reservations at either level.

Looking at the two ends of the education spectrum, highly educated women demonstrate a greater support for reservations than illiterate ones. This does not, however, really translate into a linear pattern, as the proportions vary for the intermediate education classes, not necessarily according to the education level of respondents (see Figure 9.13).

Respondents were asked whether, given an opportunity, they would like to contest elections, to which an overwhelming majority, 78 per cent overall, responded in the negative, with the proportion of Muslims being significantly higher: 81 per cent as against 78 per cent for Hindus (see Figure 9.14). The north zone accounts for the highest

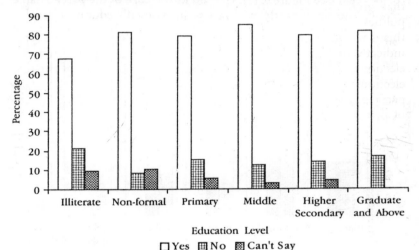

FIGURE 9.13: Support for Reservation by Education Level

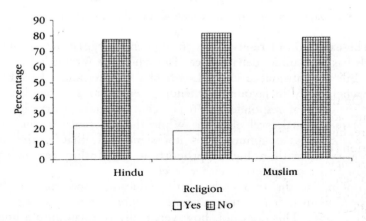

FIGURE 9.14: Desire to Contest Elections by Religion

proportion of negative responses, followed by the west, east, and south zones, in that order. Those who replied in the affirmative were further asked at what level they would like to contest elections.

To reiterate, only 22 per cent of the respondents replied to this question. Of them, 89 per cent would prefer to contest at the local level with the proportion dropping progressively at the state and central levels as the goal becomes more and more distant. It is clear that given an opportunity, women's participation in local level politics would be more intense than in the state or national levels; this is borne out by both non-empirical and empirical studies which indicate that since the 73rd Amendment was passed panchayat elections have elicited more enthusiastic women's participation than elections at the assembly and national levels. Clearly intensity of participation and awareness of issues varies by proximity of the tier of democracy to the citizen.

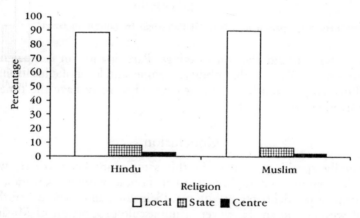

FIGURE 9.15: At What Level Would You Like to Contest?

On the whole, a minuscule proportion, about 4 per cent, of respondents admit to having participated in a political campaign, and even here, highly educated women have noticeably greater rates of participation (10 per cent) than less educated ones (see Figure 9.16). The small percentage of women participating in the campaign indicates that women have no exposure to election meetings. Participation in election campaigns presupposes a minimum level of involvement in politics. In the male-dominated politics of India, we should not be surprised that campaign participants are preponderantly men, and it

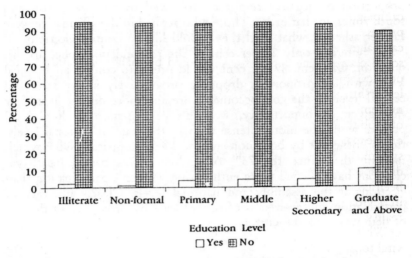

FIGURE 9.16: Participation in a Political Campaign by Education Level

is they who attend election meetings. Participation in campaigning positively correlates with mobility, income, and level of education, all in short supply, and hence women would scarcely have the time or opportunity to take part.

Conclusion

Generally speaking, women in this sample are keen voters, with Muslim women being keener than Hindu women. Overall, 85 per cent respondents reportedly cast their vote, and more urban than rural women did so. However, a minuscule proportion of Muslims and Hindus engaged in political activities beyond voting. Even though the majority of respondents were unaware of the 73rd and 74th Amendments, three-quarters supported reservations for women in legislatures; moreover, they expressed an interest in contesting elections, especially at the local level. The level of political awareness evident in the knowledge of candidate and party names is fairly high. These findings confirm trends from other survey data on voter turnout and political participation.

Is this trend confined to voting? Does it suggest anything more than a habit? While we cannot underestimate the importance of voting, nevertheless, their participation in even election meetings and campaigns is minimal, thus limiting their participation in the electoral process. The proportion of those who take no interest in election campaigns is uniformly high, with no substantial differences across social classes. One reason for this could be male domination of the political process and public sphere, the exclusion of women from leadership positions in party organizations, restrictions on women's movement outside the home, widespread illiteracy, and above all, lack of mobilization by political parties and organizations. Recent studies on the experience of women elected to reserved seats in the panchayat system have pointed to women's vulnerability to derision and disrespect, if not outright violence. Indeed, the threat of violence has been considered a major obstacle to women's political participation; in a vitiated political environment, this threat can easily become a reality.

While voting requires little education, in general, education is a vital tool for effective participation, that is, making informed choices, contributing to public debates, or signing petitions, for example. Education, for instance, 'increases their ability to demand economic and social policies that respond to their priorities', notes the 2002 edition of the *Human Development Report* of the United Nations Development Programme. Indeed, the MWS clearly shows that greater participation and political awareness are linked to higher education levels. Urban educated women are more aware of rights and policies, and are more likely to decide on their own as to which party they should vote for. Although most women in the MWS are illiterate and lack the means for active participation in the political process, they do not lack motivation. Illiteracy or low levels of education do not discourage them from looking for an active role in the political process, as indicated by nearly a quarter of respondents who expressed their desire to contest local elections. The very small participation in campaigns and meetings needs to be put alongside this keenness to contest local elections in order to assess the extent of women's political consciousness. Women show a keen awareness of the importance of democratic institutions and political participation but obviously have had little opportunity to contribute to them. While democratic rights are to be valued for themselves, yet, inadequate women's participation in these institutions, beyond voting, is one of the deficits of democratic governance in India. This is where issues other than elections and voter turnout become important in strengthening the links between democracy and social development. Even if it is self-evident, democratic governance facilitates human and social development only when institutions are accountable to people and the people themselves can fully participate (beyond voting in elections) in local and national debates and are involved in decision-making.

In the age of democratic politics we cannot overstate the importance of mobilization and voting, because the unorganized can raise their voices only at election time. Discrimination, which is institutionalized by society—in gender, community, and socio-economic status—means that participation in the democratic process can only be of symbolic value. The MWS and other surveys show that when it comes to exercising the right to vote, Indian women, including Muslim women, may show a greater determination than voters in more advanced democracies. Without this, women from the poorer classes or the minorities are victims of political vulnerability and are absent when the state's agenda is refashioned. But their experience with institutions of democracy is an increasingly unhappy one as it has failed in ensuring better economic outcomes. Viewing the low levels of literacy of this group of women in conjunction with the occupational and work participation, it hardly needs underscoring that the conditions for effective agency are absent.

10

Access to Mass Media

This chapter focuses on access to the mass media—television, radio, and newspapers. In low-literacy societies, non-print mass media—i.e. radio and television—are a more important source of entertainment and information than the print media, especially for women. This fact has assumed greater importance in the past two or three decades, with the marked increase in ownership of television across all classes, especially in urban areas. The mid-1980s and early 1990s witnessed a dramatic expansion of television to different parts of the country.[1]

To assess access and exposure to media, the MWS asked a number of questions on the print and electronic media: do you read or listen to a newspaper or magazine, do you watch television, do you listen to the radio, and how regular are these habits?

As mentioned earlier, around 34 per cent of Muslims belong to the low and lower middle SES categories, a proportion that is nearly double that of upper caste Hindus (18 per cent); that is, on the whole, Muslims have an average standard of living less than that of even the OBC, and well below that of upper caste Hindus. Data collected on ownership of household or consumer durables indicate that approximately 45 per cent households owned television sets and 40 per cent owned a radio. In fact, ownership of televisions far exceeds that of, say, refrigerators, which are owned by only 6 per cent of our sample in rural areas and 19 per cent in urban. Even so, low family income would be the reason that households do not possess television sets in most cases.

Print Media

Overall literacy in our sample is 43 per cent for Muslims and 59 per cent for Hindus, but only 20 per cent of respondents replied to our question on whether they read newspapers and magazines. A total of 730 Hindu women and 1905 Muslim women replied to the question on reading newspapers/magazines. Figure 10.1 indicates that roughly one-third of this 20 per cent—in other words, a very small percentage of the total sample—of respondents read them regularly.

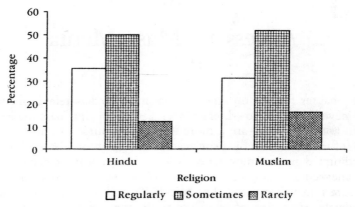

FIGURE 10.1: Reading Newspapers/Magazines by Religion

Not surprisingly, a greater proportion of Hindu respondents compared to Muslim reported reading newspapers/magazines regularly, and consequently a smaller proportion of Hindu respondents reported 'rarely'. The proportion of Muslim respondents reporting 'sometimes' is slightly greater. The community differences are not significant.

Television

Forty-five per cent of our sample replied to the question regarding watching television, that is a total of 1279 Hindu and 3360 Muslim respondents replied to this question. For both the communities, the proportion of respondents watching television is much larger than those reading newspapers/magazines. The number of women who watched television on a regular basis is over 40 per cent. About 45 per cent Hindu and 42 per cent Muslim women watch television regularly (see Figure 10.2). Regular viewership of television is higher amongst Hindus. A test for significance reveals that the community difference is statistically significant.[2] As mentioned earlier, the number of respondents watching television is much greater than those

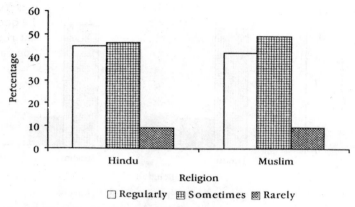

FIGURE 10.2: Watching TV by Religion

reading newspapers/magazines. This is not surprising given the reach of television and the low rates of literacy in the MWS.

Age intervals for both variables are noteworthy, with maximum readership/viewing in the younger age groups, but here, too, more women watch television than read newspapers, and more read or are read to, than listen to the radio. In fact, age differences with regard to the latter are almost negligible, with only the oldest age group, 50 years and above, indicating a significantly lower percentage.

Radio

A total of 583 Hindu respondents and 1589 Muslim respondents answered the question on listening to the radio. The proportions for both communities are very close to each other, but significantly much lower than the number of respondents answering the question on watching television. Overall 33 per cent Muslim respondents listened to the radio regularly and 53 per cent Hindus regularly (see Figure 10.3). Given that radio has unique advantages under Indian conditions, the low figures for radio are surprising. Unlike the printed word, the radio gets through to the illiterate population and over the years, the All India Radio has developed a formidable infrastructure for radio broadcasting. In fact, until quite recently, radio was the most effective channel for reaching the vast numbers of rural and urban poor. Compared to television, the radio is much cheaper. However, the rise of television has clearly reduced the importance of the radio.[3]

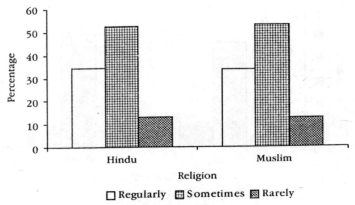

FIGURE 10.3: Listening to Radio by Religion

Media Exposure

Overall, media exposure is much greater in urban than in rural areas (see Figure 10.4), regardless of the type of media, and is greatest when women are more educated.[4] The relationship between highest grade completed and regularity of the newspaper habit is completely in the expected direction. As women become more educated, the frequency of their reading newspapers/magazines increases (see Figure 10.5).

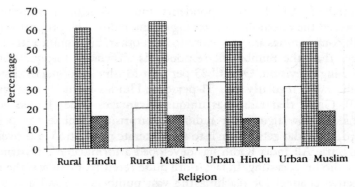

FIGURE 10.4: Media Exposure by Rural/Urban

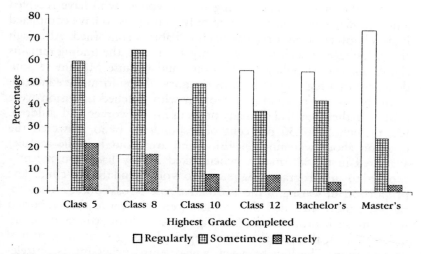

FIGURE 10.5: Regularity of the Newspaper Habit by Highest Grade Completed

The positive correlation between higher levels of education and increased exposure is evident in the case of newspapers and magazines, as shown in Figure 10.6. The rise is linear across education categories, except the second one, that refers to non-formal education.

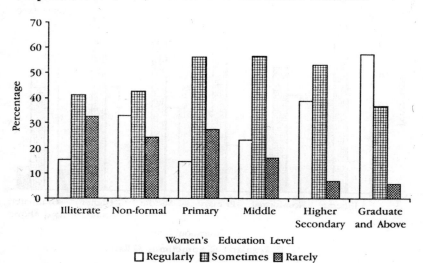

FIGURE 10.6: Regularity of the Newspaper Habit by Women's Education Level

226 □ *Unequal Citizens*

Here the most notable finding is that women who have received a non-formal education are second only to those who have completed high school, as far as a regular reading habit is concerned. Although the percentage of such women is only 2 per cent, the finding remains significant for its policy implications, and because Muslim respondents report a high figure for this category of non-formally educated.

In the area of programmes, women who watched television were asked whether they had seen any programme on women and children. On the whole, 67.30 per cent of respondents (who answered the question about watching television and are about half the sample) answered in the affirmative when asked if they had been recently exposed to any programming related to women and the girl-child. The proportion answering in the affirmative rose across education categories—the more educated the women were, the more they reported watching such programmes (see Figure 10.7). Proportionately more urban women than rural women reported seeing such programmes on television. The link between issue-oriented programmes on television and level of education is also clear, with viewership increasing as respondents climb the education ladder; this is true across communities. Programmes preferences confirmed common patterns. Respondents watched programmes on the girl-child, hygiene and nutrition, education, dowry, age at marriage, family size, immunization, and

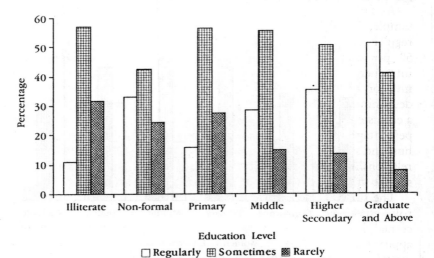

FIGURE 10.7: Regularity of the Television Viewing by Women's Education Level

economic independence for women. Almost equal proportions of respondents in urban and rural areas belonging to both communities had seen these programmes.

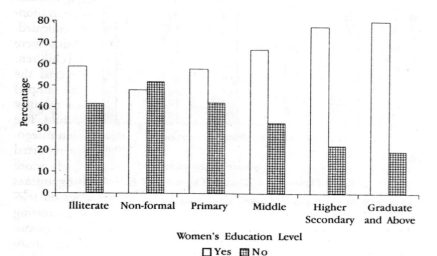

FIGURE 10.8: Viewership of Women Oriented Programmes by Education Level

As far as overall media exposure is concerned, roughly half our sample, 5686 women, responded; of them, 26 per cent reported regular exposure to newspapers/magazines, television, and/or radio; 58 per cent, sometimes; and 15 per cent, rarely. Occasional or infrequent exposure is the norm, whether the variables are community or education, which indicates that here, too, gender is the determining factor. Further, the figures for 'regularly' don't follow a consistent pattern with the husband's education level. However, the percentages for 'sometimes' more or less rise with the rise in husband's education level, but not unequivocally. On the whole, the relationship between husband's education level and women's exposure to mass media does not seem to be systematic.

The survey findings do suggest that education plays an important role, especially as far as reading newspapers and magazines is concerned, but the overall percentages are still rather low, and it would appear that residence, urban or rural, almost overtakes education with regard to media exposure. Younger women were more exposed to different types of mass media. The proportion that read newspaper/

228 □ *Unequal Citizens*

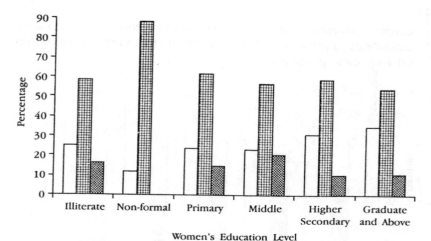

FIGURE 10.9: Media Exposure by Education: Hindu

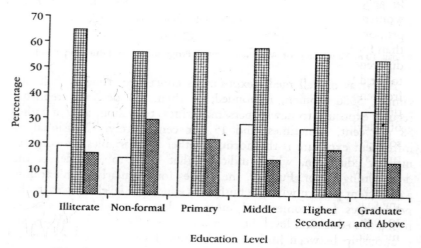

FIGURE 10.10: Media Exposure by Education: Muslim

magazine, listen to radio, or watch television decreased with the increase in age. But the proportion listening to radio did not vary much across various age groups, religion, and residence.

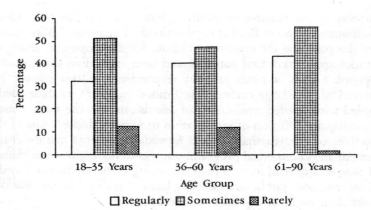

FIGURE 10.11: Regularity of Reading Newspapers/Magazines by Age Group

Conclusion

In general, mass media exposure was relatively higher for Hindu women in both rural and urban areas compared to Muslims. Also proportions reporting 'regular' media exposure are higher for Hindus than for Muslims. The bulk of this difference is accounted for by the difference in newspaper/magazine readership, which, in turn, is due to the difference in literacy levels; but for both communities, the most frequent response, irrespective of education level, is that of 'sometimes'. Part of this could reflect poverty in the sense that ownership of television or subscribing to newspapers is contingent upon the socio-economic status; it could be an indication of very little leisure time available to most women, most of the time. However, not just in the MWS, but in other surveys too, television viewership figures are always higher than the corresponding ownership figures, suggesting that exposure to mass media goes beyond the constraints of ability to buy.[5] The limited proportion of respondents listening to radio indicates that the potential of radio has gone untapped. Compared to television, radio is relatively cheap and thus within the reach of many more people with less formal education and lower socio-economic status. Yet, we find radio listening is not common among the respondents.

The infrequent exposure to mass media is a trend to be noted that defines the limited access of women to information in the MWS. We are not suggesting that exposure to mass media is unequivocally educative or informative or positive, but television has been found to influence the most fundamental individual activities.[6] Mass media have the potential for creating a climate for development, changing attitudes and behavioural patterns, and thus expanding the horizons of people's lives, a potential that respondents in this sample are deprived of to a large extent. The limited exposure to mass media coupled with limited availability of televisions was the main reason for inadequate diffusion of information to women. Indeed, one of the objectives of Doordarshan, which nowadays presents mainly entertainment and commercial programmes, was to highlight social change and women's development. However, going by access to mass media and information, public broadcasting has not realized its tremendous potential to perform a public service function.

Endnotes

1. Television viewing increased by 68 per cent between 1978 and 1983, and the number of women viewers rose by 33 per cent. Purnima Mankekar, *Screening Culture, Viewing Politics: Television, Womanhood and Nation in Modern India*, Oxford University Press, New Delhi, 2001, p. 6.

2. F test.

3. Arvind Singhal and Everett Rogers, *India's Communication Revolution: From Bullock Carts to Cyber Marts*, Sage Publications, New Delhi, 2001.

4. Media exposure: takes the value of 1 if regular for either newspaper/television/radio; 2 if sometimes; 3 if rarely.

5. Nilanjana Gupta, *Switching Channels: Ideologies of Television in India*, Sage Publications, New Delhi, 1998.

6. According to Gupta's study of the impact of television, respondents from lower income groups replied that television was a positive influence on society. According to them, access to news and information helped to raise awareness about society. Ibid., p. 116.

Conclusion

I

The Indian Constitution was a milestone for women's advancement; the right of non-discrimination on the basis of sex is guaranteed in the list of justiciable Fundamental Rights, as also protection under the law and equal opportunity in public employment. Yet, judging from the status of women in India, this has not always been the case.

The MWS presents a picture of glaring inequalities—social, economic, political—that consistently define and circumscribe women's lives—all women and Muslim women in particular. Trends in economic and social well-being reveal that, amidst all the celebration of cultural diversity, social improvement, and economic growth that has taken place in the country (more notably in some regions than others), women, and especially minority women, are lagging far behind. Group inequalities persist as a significant social division and this is apparent in at least three areas: socio-economic status, education, and work, even as gender inequality persists in marriage, mobility, and autonomy across the board. Although autonomy has been recognized as an essential component of empowerment, analysts and developmentalists have devised different gauges to measure its presence. The MWS posited freedom of movement and the capacity to make decisions independently as critical features of autonomy, and found that women's responses to detailed questions on these issues made for abysmally low scores on both. Material and group inequalities are thus compounded by an insidious—and sometimes difficult to quantify—gender disprivilege that is present even when some degree of economic or social advancement has taken place.

In some key areas Muslim women are not even equal to women in the Hindu community. The difference can be seen most sharply in the socio-economic status of Muslim households, occupational distribution, asset structure, and education. The standard of living of Muslims is generally poor and, in comparative terms, much below that of Hindu upper castes, lower even than that of OBC. Hindu–Muslim disparities in socio-economic status are statistically significant and constitute a major source of differentiation in women's status.

Significantly, there is much greater all-India similarity in socio-economic status among Muslims than among Hindus. Disparities in the status of Hindus across regions were relatively smaller, even though they were more polarized in terms of standard of living than Muslims. For example, upper castes were more evenly distributed across the SES spectrum in contrast to Muslims, who were concentrated in the lower and lower middle levels—that is, more than three-fifths of them belong to the low and lower middle categories. In other words, the extent of inequality varied significantly and the disparity between Muslims and Hindus is greater than among Muslims themselves. But this does not mean that there is no variability among Muslims across regions. Indeed, the MWS indicates striking class/economic variations among them in the south zone compared to the north zone. In the urban south and west zones, Muslims have a relatively higher standard of living, above the all-India average, and substantially so in urban areas; here they are concentrated in the middle and upper middle brackets. This is explained partly by higher levels of economic and social development in these regions, thus favourably impacting on Muslims as well; and partly by the fact that Muslims as a whole are generally better integrated in the south than they are in the north and east zones.

Muslims are poor in the north and very poor in the rural north, and they are also generally poor in the east where they are concentrated in the lower bracket. Their poverty becomes obvious from their asset structure: house ownership, land ownership, and ownership of consumer durables are all in short supply. This matches the National Sample Survey (NSS) estimates of per capita expenditure for specific groups, which clearly shows that tribals and Dalits in both rural and urban areas, and Muslims in urban areas, are over-represented amongst the poorest expenditure classes. Occupational distribution is another critical factor contributing to the generally poor economic status of Muslims; that is, they are mostly in the unskilled labour category or in small business or self-employment, and definitely not in or top-end occupations or employment, which are dominated by the upper castes. In short, Muslims are mostly self-employed in low-paying, often semi-skilled work, which is unable to generate income that would lift them out of poverty.

Community differences in education are also quite significant. Muslim women across the country are more illiterate than Hindus—59 per cent of them have never attended school, less than 10 per cent have completed it; in short, Muslim women fare more poorly than the average Hindu women in education. Very few Muslim women study beyond the primary stage and even fewer beyond the age of 15 years. The MWS findings demonstrate a strong connection between low socio-economic status and low schooling levels; in fact, financial constraints and a clear gender bias eclipse all other constraints on Muslim women's education. The north zone, with high levels of poverty and low levels of schooling, offers strong evidence of this unmistakable nexus—financial constraints are more crucial for Muslims and more so in the north than elsewhere, thus underscoring the subalternity of the Muslim population. But Muslims are not uniformly poor and uneducated; they are much better off in the south and also in the west and certainly better off than their counterparts in the north and east zones. The considerably better education levels of Muslims in the south, and to some extent in the west, belie the view that religion denies them education.

The MWS did not canvass information on gender disparity in educational attainment, but several studies have drawn attention to the low educational attainments of Muslim men. Significantly, as many as 26 per cent of educated Muslim women have illiterate husbands—a peculiar feature of the community, an indication of the generally low levels of Muslim male education, and symptomatic of the pressure to impose a ceiling on girls' education. Completing high school renders them ineligible for marriage, giving rise to an anxiety that surfaces across the community, across regions. Since Muslim boys frequently drop out, girls who manage to reach high school are made to discontinue, because an 'over-qualified' woman is unmarriageable.

A general devaluation of continuing education for girls is linked to the desirability of early marriage for them, as indicated by the mean age at first marriage which is a low 15.6 years all-India; in the rural north, it dips even further, to 13.9 years. However, even when, as in Kerala, the age at first marriage is much higher—20 years according to the NFHS—this does not readily translate into a tangible improvement in the status of Muslim women in terms of education levels comparable to women in other communities or greater autonomy and mobility. Early marriage or 'married off' was cited as an important reason for dropping out. Poor families with male and female children are likely to favour their sons' education over that of their daughters, especially because girls help at home with housework and the care of siblings. When money is scarce, even free schooling can be too dear, because travelling to school and clothes and books add up to an unaffordable cost. Moreover, early marriage is an effective brake on girls' education, factors that never come in the way of boys' schooling. Young girls are handicapped by distance from schools, especially once they reach middle school, when sex segregated schools are difficult to come by; this is often reason enough for girls to drop out. The sharpest community disparities are to be found in the high drop-out rates for Muslim women after the primary school level—when, in fact, their enrollment is equal to, and in some states even higher than, that of Hindus. This is the case even in the south and west—which otherwise perform better than the north and east zones as far as literacy and other indicators of educational attainment are concerned.

As noted, the MWS findings point to a marked improvement in women's prospects, at least as far as education is concerned, with delayed marriage—by which is simply meant marriage by the age of 20 years—but it is not difficult to calculate the benefits of delayed childbearing, the possibility of acquiring some basic skills, some measure of autonomy, and a real increase in self-worth. Currently, the age at which the majority of girls are married off remains a full two years below 18, all-India, and lower by as much as four to five years in some parts of the country.

Less than 15 per cent of Muslim women report themselves to be working. With the exception of those in a higher economic stratum, the regional picture, too, reflects the national trend of low women's work participation—the proportion of non-working women is huge, irrespective of place of residence or region. The one notable difference between Muslim and Hindu women in the MWS is that two-thirds of Muslims are self-employed, or engaged in home-based labour, probably the most exploited category of work other than bonded labour. Occupationally, they are in the informal sector, self-employed in low-paying often semi-skilled home-based work, casual labourers, and domestic workers, all of which would be characterized by poor working conditions and low wages.

The evocation of purdah and cultural restrictions have conventionally been a powerful explanatory motif for Muslim women's low rates of work participation, but it is clear that these restrictions are not significantly higher for Muslim women and, therefore, cannot explain their low work levels. We find that women themselves do not perceive these as the main reasons for not working. Should women have the option of working outside the house they face other obstacles, including extreme strictures on mobility: over 75 per cent of women across communities report that they need permission from their husbands to work outside the home. It is open to question whether husbands' control over them and refusal of permission account for the low work participation; or the lack of access to resources and work opportunities and discrimination that many women in the informal sector experience. In either case, many women opt for home-based work because it enables them to combine wage-earning with housekeeping responsibilities, and because children can help out if need be.

The more prosperous, socially advanced states would, one might expect, make for better female labour participation rates, but this is not necessarily the case. A World Bank study indicates that prosperous states like Haryana and Punjab share low female labour participation rates with Bihar and West Bengal where poverty is high; but Maharashtra, which ranks third in terms of per capita income, has the highest female labour participation, a fact borne out by the MWS, too. How is this to be explained, because all three situations seem to be counter-intuitive? In Punjab and Haryana, it would appear that greater prosperity means women are withdrawn from work as a mark of status; yet this consideration does not apply to Maharashtra. And if poverty is a driving force for employment, Bihar and West Bengal defy this logic. Thus, when even the compulsions of poverty do not release women in appreciable numbers into the workforce, we must acknowledge that a powerful combination of economic distress, lack of skills and opportunities, and the demands and restrictions of the private domain is responsible. For these reasons, it is probably more useful to look not at religion or purdah or conservatism for Muslim women's work status, but at low education, lack of opportunity, low mobility, and domestic responsibilities as important inhibiting factors.

Under these circumstances, the fact that hardly any Muslim women are aware of or able to access those welfare programmes and facilities that the government does provide, especially to the disadvantaged, is shocking. The most obvious target group of these schemes—such as JRY, IRDP, ICDS, and TRYSEM—should be poor Muslim women, the majority in this sample. Yet, even balwadis seem to be inaccessible to more than 75 per cent of them; and only three per cent of these were aware of development programmes run specifically for women and children. State intervention as a strategy to combat structural inequalities is a necessary input; when it is available (however inadequately or unsatisfactorily) but inaccessible for all sorts of reasons, it becomes equally necessary to examine the reasons for its failure.

It is obvious that lack of information is an important reason for most welfare provisions passing women by—most of them did not know of the existence of special loans and grants to widows, for example, or of credit facilities; but how are they to come by this information? Less than 20 per cent of our respondents have access to any printed media, but more than 50 per cent are illiterate, so even if they did, they would be unable to read; a much larger percentage (42 per cent), however, watch television, and the more educated women do report watching issue- and women-oriented programmes. This is an ideal medium for disseminating useful information and raising awareness; it should not be the case that so much welfare provisioning is unavailed of simply because women are not informed about it. Since so few women have the possibility of going out and obtaining the information for themselves, it is incumbent upon providers—government agencies, non-governmental organizations (NGOs), the public sector, and other institutions—to make a greater effort to reach them.

The MWS findings indicate that economic structures alone do not frame women's experiences of oppression and deprivation, nor is change in class structures and economic inequality sufficient to facilitate a just transformation. This suggests a need to identify the most important gender inequalities that constrain women. Indeed, the inescapable conclusion from patterns in marriage, decision-making, and mobility is that marriage, motherhood, and housework are women's primary occupation. The sexual/gender division of labour is organized around this central condition, and all major decisions for the majority of women are either a consequence of, or contingent upon, it. It assumes even greater importance when we see that close to 98 per cent of women remain married for the better part of their lives. Divorce, desertion, separation and widowhood accounted for less than 5 per cent of the single women in our sample, not including those who have never been married.

Extreme restriction on mobility is one of the most disquieting findings of the MWS, with over 75 per cent of women reporting that they need permission from their husbands for virtually every activity, including working outside the home. The process of discrimination and disadvantage thus comes full circle. Here again, community and regional variations are minimal, with even the relatively more favourable south and west zones conforming to the all-India pattern.

In most areas of decision-making, too, women are woefully dependent. Less than 10 per cent of respondents reported taking decisions on their own on major and minor matters, but a good 30–5 per cent did say that they decided jointly with their husbands; over 50 per cent said they were consulted on all decisions regarding the household; and Muslim women report greater consultation than Hindus for all categories of decisions. Older women are more likely to be involved in decision-making than younger ones; and Hindu–Muslim disparities are negligible, as are regional and class differences, indicating that the question of autonomy is gender, rather than community or class specific. The decision-making index (DMI), like the freedom of movement index (FMI), graphically illustrates this disability, that is, the limited autonomy of women in all spheres. Women in general have very little decision-making authority, especially when it comes to deciding about marriage, work, and major purchases and investments.

One issue on which almost all recent studies are agreed is the extent and pervasiveness of domestic violence in India. Its incidence cuts across caste, class, and community, and although it appears that the north and east of the country report greater levels of violence, this picture might change if actual, rather than reported violence alone, were assessed. The MWS is notable with regard to two findings: one, that over 50 per cent of reported violence is accounted for by Scheduled Castes and Scheduled Tribes, who comprise the poorest of the poor. Other Backward Castes are next at 24 per cent; Muslim women third at 18 per cent; and upper caste Hindus, 10 per cent. Second, over 80 per cent of those who admitted to violence identified husbands as the primary abusers. Younger women appear to be more vulnerable than older ones, less educated and poorer more vulnerable than better-off, better-educated women, but these differences may be due more to ready admission by these groups rather than to an actual decrease in the violence experienced. Inter-spousal violence is thus both widespread and endemic.

One of the positive findings of the MWS is the fact that women do exercise their franchise—85 per cent of our respondents reportedly vote, and do so of their own volition. Levels of awareness are high, even though a minuscule proportion actually engages in any kind of political activity beyond voting. But a high 75 per cent of our respondents support reservations for women, indicate a strong sense of social and civic responsibility in their choice of issues that are important for the community, and also locate themselves firmly in the local rather than the national arena. Here, again, community and regional differences are insignificant, but urban educated women are definitely more aware of rights and policies than less educated rural women. They are also more likely to make informed decisions about how to exercise their franchise.

The MWS also reveals a significant generational difference in attitudes towards co-education. Indeed the respondents' age plays a major role in the formation of attitudes with regard to these issues, indicating an important generational shift. Over 60 per cent of respondents from both communities are in the 18–35 years age group and, typically, a greater number of younger respondents favoured sending girls to co-educational schools. Men's education, too, positively influences educational opportunities for women. Over time, men's education and economic development in the north and east zones may conceivably bring about much-needed change and improvement in women's lives.

II

Indian culture is strongly gender stratified, characterized by cultural and social practices that exclude women, with hierarchical patriarchal relations in which fathers or husbands have authority over family members. Yet, there is a pervasive belief that Muslim women have less autonomy and mobility than Hindu women, and are more likely to be denied education and work opportunities, owing to restrictions imposed on women's freedom by Islamic codes.[1]

The MWS does not report significant community variations in decision-making, mobility, and access to public spaces; in fact what it shows is that most women have very little autonomy and control over their own lives across communities and regions. Women's participation in decision-making was limited in all spheres and very partial in even routine household matters, with the majority of women from both communities having no role at all in decision-making. However, these findings must be interpreted keeping in mind that autonomy levels in the subcontinent as a whole remain the lowest in the world.[2]

Hindu–Muslim differences in marriage, autonomy, mobility, and domestic violence are so insignificant that they point to the similarity of cultural practices and pervasiveness of patriarchal control across communities, even as better education and single status, and regional location may ease the controls somewhat. Not all women experience restrictions to the same debilitating extent, just as all women do not experience similar economic pressure. By focusing on the link between gender and class, on the one hand, and between gender and regional location, on the other, we can explain why some women manage to surmount patriarchal controls and others do not. Poverty underpins and reinforces patriarchy; conversely, an improvement in class/economic and educational status moderates and tempers it. Taken together, a higher SES and regional location create differences that allow women to transgress or go beyond bounds set by overwhelming patriarchal control. This can be seen from the differential impact on marriage trends, for instance, of place of residence, urban or rural, and regional location. Even though marriage is a universal norm, nevertheless one-fourth of upper caste Hindu women and one-fifth of Muslim women in the rural south have never married, and the percentage rises in direct proportion to higher socio-economic status. The rural south also reports the highest incidence of second marriages. Women in urban India with medium or high levels of education are less likely to be married below the legal age than women with low levels of education; and awareness of the legal age at marriage rises dramatically with an improvement in women's educational status. Also significant is the rising graph for later marriages, which indicates a gradual improvement in socio-economic status and education.

In other words, regions have distinct socio-economic patterns and cultures that influence the status and well-being of women. That is why a poor Scheduled Caste woman's lived reality is qualitatively different from that of a poor Muslim woman; and a poor Muslim woman in Uttar Pradesh or Bihar is rather differently situated than her counterpart in Kerala or Tamil Nadu. Because these have had a high investment in social development, they are more likely than states at the other end of the spectrum to protect the entitlements of the poor and secure minimum welfare for all. South India is characterized by a weaker enforcement of female seclusion and less strict adherence to patrilocal residence rules. Literacy rates and educational levels are higher than in the north, life expectancy for both males and females is better, infrastructure has been built and maintained, the disadvantage of being born low caste is less of an obstacle in advancement than elsewhere in the country. Above all, the south is a place of deep-rooted traditions of co-existence among religious communities, where the prejudice and bigotry that have flourished in the north and west find little quarter. All women, including Muslim women, thus have a better chance of availing education and accessing infrastructure resources like health and social welfare in the more progressive and developed regions. Again, states like Tamil Nadu, Maharashtra, and Kerala, that have had a history of social reform and progressive political movements, have also made a greater contribution to improving women's status. This is borne out by all studies, including the MWS, which reports the highest educational attainment for women, including Muslim women, in the south and west. By contrast, West Bengal, which also has a history of social reform and progressive politics, has not invested nearly as much in the social sector over the last few decades, with the result that, together with Bihar and Orissa, it makes for a very low educational attainment for women in the east. Here, however, community differences are very sharp, with poor Muslim women accounting for the very low figures.

Regional development appears to be a better predictor of the status of women than Muslimness or religion *per se*. Path dependence in the north (poverty, patriarchy, and hardly any social development initiatives to speak of have combined to practically erase community differences) constrains Muslim and Hindu women, and both are more or less equally disadvantaged as far as education and quality of life is concerned. This point is crucial to understanding the status of women in the north, which is distinguished by unequal gender relations: extreme female powerlessness, restricted freedom of movement, limited inheritance rights in practice and access to economic resources, and inadequate opportunities for sustained employment. However, the jury is still out on the soundness of its explanatory potential across the board, even for the north. The more important point is that regional, group, and gender disparities can be reduced through public policies, and that it is possible to address the problem of social development to a great extent.

III

In order to appreciate the extent of Muslim women's disadvantage generally, let us recapitulate the stark reality of her life as revealed by the MWS. She is typically among the poorest, whether she lives in urban or rural India, and is illiterate for the most part; if educated, she seldom progresses beyond primary school; she is married by the age of 15 years, usually has three children by the time she is 20 years old, and is plagued by ill-health for most of her life. Low skills and education, as well as seclusion and a severe lack of mobility, limit her chances of paid work outside the home, making for almost complete economic dependency on her husband—who is likely to be poor and disadvantaged himself. Violence, or the threat of violence within the home—where she spends the greater part of her life—and the lack of any viable options to it keep her in a highly subordinated and often abusive relationship, while cultural and social norms, suffused with a pervasive patriarchy, allow her little choice or decisional autonomy in practically every aspect of her life.

In this context how best is women's status to be assessed? Some analysts have focused on education levels, and economic activity, others on autonomy in decision-making, and yet others on delayed marriage. The MWS findings highlight the central role of education, work participation, marriage, mobility, and autonomy in determining women's status. For the most part, our results indicate that the shortage of three essentials: knowledge (measured by literacy and average years of schooling), economic power (work and income), and autonomy (measured by decision-making ability and mobility) are among the chief defining features of women's low status. These deficits certainly pinpoint many fundamental things that are wrong with Muslim women's situation, but we must note that the shortage of these three essentials is not restricted to Muslim women—in reality, they define the condition of the majority of women in this sample, irrespective of community.

How then does one account for Muslim women's disadvantage and deprivation? Class, gender, and the state are the grid on which women's status ought to be mapped. Moving beyond debates on the explanatory primacy of class over gender (and others) we have

242 □ *Unequal Citizens*

emphasized their mutual constitution and intersection. The axes of class, gender, and community are contingent on each other for they are constructed and experienced simultaneously, and thus create overlapping and mutually reinforcing forms of disadvantage and deprivation, most apparent in the subordination of Muslim women. They are disadvantaged thrice over: as members of a minority community, as women, and as poor women. While their lives are similarly positioned at the intersection of gender, class, and community within the dynamic context of Indian society, polity, and economy, their minority status qualitatively transforms their experiences in very distinct ways. Gender discrimination coalesces with class inequalities in perpetuating a *structured disempowerment of Muslim women*.

Four factors must be considered before we concede the proposition of structured disempowerment: poverty, communal politics, patriarchy, and personal laws, all of which mediate and structure disempowerment. Poverty would be an obvious explanation for their low status, but not poverty as an abstraction, nor as enumerating the large numbers of respondents in the low to lower-middle SES classes, or indeed the larger number of Muslims in these categories than upper caste Hindus and OBCs; rather, poverty that constrains one's abilities and capabilities. Associated with poverty is continuing illiteracy and low levels of schooling that make a mockery of the government's commitment to total literacy and universal schooling till the age of 14 years. Illiteracy is a proxy for the poor, as illiterates also tend to be very poor. Finally, inequality is itself shaped by the larger context: the persistence of relationships that emphasize difference between communities, classes, and sexes at all levels of society. All these take their toll on the well-being of women because gender inequality is strongly correlated with poverty.

Sex discrimination, as Martha Nussbaum says, is such a pervasive factor in most poor women's experience of poverty that 'it would be wrong to say that any aspect of their poverty is fully understandable without taking it into account'.[4] Feminist analyses and empirical studies have demonstrated that, like most things, the experience of poverty, too, is gendered. When, for example, food consumption has to be drastically reduced as a consequence of poverty it is women and female children who eat less. When household incomes fall and prices rise, it is women's and girls' access to education and health that is immediately affected. When economies are privatized as a consequence of structural adjustments, it is women who are dismissed from wage labour and pushed into piece-rate work. When resources are scarce, women's limited access to them is further curtailed. This is one reason why the increasing feminization of poverty has caused alarm bells to ring because, as Noeleen Heyzer notes, when women persist in poverty it has long-term consequences for society. Poverty is transferred inter-generationally to children—especially female children—through malnourishment, the substitution of women's work by young girls in household maintenance, and low investment in their health and education, particularly if a trade-off has to be made against the survival needs of the household.[5] But why sex discrimination should almost always work exclusively in women's disfavour—after all, men are poor, too—is because poverty intersects with patriarchy to perpetuate gender hierarchies and systemic discrimination based on sex, and caste and community. The sexual division of labour, whereby men are producers and providers and women are reproducers and carers, not only obscures women's significant contribution to both production and national economies and the survival of their households, it does more than that—it endorses social and cultural barriers to women's full participation, as equals, in the social and economic life of the country.

Notwithstanding the differences between Hindu and Muslim women, it is necessary to reiterate that the overall economic backwardness and disadvantage of Muslims in India combines with social and cultural norms regarding the role of women and patriarchal control to entrench the subordination of Muslim women and reinforce their oppression. These are further exacerbated by state inaction which institutionalizes discrimination through religious personal laws, but it should be noted that personal laws represent only one aspect of women's subordination; even if all such laws were reformed or changed, Muslim women's material conditions would continue to be oppressive.

There is one respect in which personal laws are of crucial significance, however, and that is in highlighting the dichotomy between private and public, a binary that we have referred to earlier. A clear articulation of the separation of the public sphere from the personal or private domain was made by colonial law which proceeded to enact a common criminal code for India, but codified customary practices with regard to marriage, inheritance, adoption, divorce, and maintenance in accordance with religious precepts. By implication—and also by law—the public space was designated as secular, the personal as governed or regulated by tradition, convention, or religious injunction. The post-colonial state retained this legal separation of private and public through the continuation of personal laws, even though they are in direct contradiction of the Fundamental Rights of citizens guaranteed by the Constitution.

The implications of this for women are evident and have been extensively commented upon, but let us consider what all this tells us about private and public. For all practical purposes, private signifies the familial or marital space and, by extension, the household sphere where male authority is not only socially and culturally sanctioned, but protected by law.[6] By removing the traditional family or household unit from the purview of customary practice, personal laws have privatized and sanctified the institution of marriage and the family, rendering them unamenable to public intervention of most kinds, including progressive action by the state. As Ratna Kapur and Brenda Cossman argue, 'The legal regulation of women is informed by, and serves to, reinscribe familial ideology' with all its constraints and rigid gender hierarchies.[7] The private domain is where a majority of Indian women spend the greater part of their lives. For them, public space simply does not exist, or exists mostly in the abstract, for two important reasons: one, because their entry into the public sphere is strictly regulated by male authority, as the MWS findings demonstrate so clearly; and two, because even those very few women who do access it rarely do so as true equals. For most women, then, the public is often just an extension of the private, with all its hierarchies and biases. Just as the guarantee of equality remains unrealizable for most women, so too the right to freedom of mobility, of association, and of travel are severely circumscribed by patriarchal control. This is also why, for women in the subsistence and non-monetized sectors of the economy, the domestic and non-domestic spheres exist as a single system, and why home-based labour for women is usually merely an extension of domestic work, what they do anyway. Thus public and private patriarchies align, albeit unintentionally, to keep women in their place—subordinated.

IV

How then is the goal of equity and empowerment to be achieved for Muslim women? Given the pre-eminence of the discourse on gender,

development, and empowerment in India and the marginal status of
Muslims in general and Muslim women in particular, one answer
would be to engage with the secular discourse of development and
empowerment, as we have tried to do. The current articulation of this
discourse in a climate of neo-liberal economics, however, has
unidimensionally reduced gender disadvantage to poverty and is all
about reaching out to the desperately poor, namely, Scheduled Castes
and Scheduled Tribe groups. Although we have demonstrated that
Muslim women do fall in the category of the poor, very rarely have
mainstream policy makers acknowledged their poverty. This is why
one thrust of state policy has been to emphasize community identity,
so that being a Muslim takes precedence over a host of other identities,
such as class and even gender. This may be promoted deliberately,
as in the example of 'protection' of minority rights through the
Muslim Women's (Protection of Rights in Divorce) Act, 1986; or
it may be fostered in more indirect ways, as a consequence of the
injunction to render other modes of description—i.e., religion—
irrelevant in the operation of public life.

Over the past two decades, this has brought questions about
cultural difference to the fore. When attention is paid to Muslim
women, the focus has been on how they are different from Hindu
women. This emphasis on difference invariably leads to two issues—
lack of female education and restrictive purdah—and how they are
linked to religion as ideology. Thus it has been widely argued that
cultural norms and the relationship of women to Islam are at the core
of Muslim women's status; and that low status is a consequence of
the 'traditional way of life'—that is, Islamic restrictions on women's
freedom. Indeed, the way in which Muslim women are discussed in
the popular discourse suggests that such debates are centrally about
the merits or demerits of religion or Muslim culture, seldom about
the actual status of women, and even less about the effect of
differences of class, ethnicity, and local/regional cultures on women's
status. The MWS findings, however, demonstrate that religion per se
does not influence the status of women, even though there are
community-specific disadvantages which arise out of poverty; social
and economic class, urban or rural residence, and regional factors are
far more important, as we have argued above.

So what could equity and empowerment possibly mean or encompass for Muslim women? Are they to be gained through education,
work opportunities, the generation of and control over income, good

health, and greater participation and representation in public life? Is empowerment about women being in decision-making roles, and intervening in public policy and processes of social change? Or is it simply about women speaking for themselves, making their own choices, controlling their own lives? Some feminist analysts believe that empowerment can be seen as 'a change in the context of a woman or man's life that enables her/him increased capacity to lead a fulfilling human life, characterized by external qualities such as health, mobility, education and awareness, status in the family, participation in decision-making and level of material security, as well as internal qualities such as self-awareness and self-confidence'.[8] Others advocate that women increase their power, where power is identified less with domination and more with women's ability to increase their self-reliance and strength to determine their life-choices, influence the direction of change, and have control over crucial resources.[9]

The United Nations Development Programme (UNDP) introduced the Gender Empowerment Measure (GEM) which evaluates the progress women have made at the political and economic levels. It critically scrutinizes whether men and women are able to actively participate in economic and political life and in decision-making. The components of this measure are: the percentage of women in parliaments, among administrators, managers, professionals, and technical workers, and women's earned income share as a percentage of that of men. Where the GDI focuses on an expansion of capabilities, the GEM is concerned with the use of those capabilities to make the most of opportunities that life has to offer.

Both the GDI and GEM have been critiqued by feminists and development analysts as being inadequate measures, as reflecting the biases of assessors, and as insufficiently allowing for disparities between developing and developed countries. The variables used to judge GEM are problematic as they are unable to capture the complexity of empowerment within a context defined by glaring class inequalities, socially sanctioned gender biases, and inequality. Naila Kabeer goes further when she says that though these indicators are preconditions for empowerment, they do not, in themselves, constitute a process for empowerment. For her, empowerment is inextricably tied up with *the condition of disempowerment* and refers to the 'processes by which those who have been denied the ability to make choices acquire such ability. In other words, empowerment entails *a process of change*'.[10] Especially as far as women are concerned, empowerment refers to the expansion in their ability to make strategic life choices in a context where this ability was previously denied to them.

At the core of empowerment lies the contested issue of power and the agency–structure relationship, and how it has been interpreted. Decision-making ability, as mentioned earlier, is an essential component of agency, and the extended discussion on it with regard to women's decision-making capacity in the MWS is a reflection of its importance. The very low scores on the DMI for over 70 per cent of our respondents indicates very low—low or no—levels of autonomy *as a norm*, for implicit in their responses is the embeddedness of social and cultural mores and practices that obviate *the need to decide* as far as most women are concerned. The issue of marriage is one such—women are socialized, groomed, and sometimes compelled into acquiescing with or consenting to a decision that has already been made by elders, by social pressure, and cultural expectation. The question of the number of children to have or whether to continue one's education are also critical life-choice decisions over which women have virtually no autonomy, for all the reasons already discussed. Overall, one can say that these indicators are about capturing outcomes and have very little to say about processes that give rise to these outcomes. The ability to make choices can be directly affected by socio-economic status, education, and work and income, or indirectly by social structures and economic development. Taking all of the structural constraints, decision-making, and mobility behaviour into consideration, one may then expand the scope of autonomy to include knowledge, economic participation, decision-making ability, and physical mobility.

It is evident that four decades of development planning and targeting women in particular, and now a dominant market economics, have not resulted in increasing either their economic autonomy or their sense of empowerment. The MWS is more or less unequivocal on this. Yet it would be a mistake to think of the reality of Muslim women's lives as forever unchanging and unchangeable; the MWS itself provides us with some clues for thinking otherwise. This can be seen from the open-mindedness on girls' education; on co-education; the desire for higher age at marriage; and political participation. (Indeed, we cannot overestimate the importance of political participation because the only activity for which permission is not required is going to public meetings.)

Further indications of positive change are found in school enrollment figures which show that, up to primary level, Muslim girls are
enrolled in more or less the same proportions as Hindus. The MWS
shows that there is a generational change as far as age at first marriage
is concerned—though still deplorably early (at 15.6 years) it is rising
gradually. More significantly, though, women themselves seem to
favour later or delayed marriage for daughters, thus indicating that
they are aware of the desirability of observing at least the minimum
legal age norm, even if they are not often in a position to act on that
realization. A glimmer of some form of consensual decision-making
is also apparent in the finding that at least one-third of our respondents reportedly decided on important family and other matters
jointly with their husbands. This may only mean concurring with
them or deciding under pressure, but mediation or negotiation cannot
be ruled out; in other words, behind-the-scenes influence may be more
common than we think.

The fact that women exercise their franchise in large numbers is
another positive finding, but even more important for our analysis
is the level of political awareness exhibited by them: more than two-
thirds of them support affirmative action in the form of reservations
for women, and they support it at the local level—where they live
and may work. This is amplified by their willingness to contest
elections, and by their choice of projects, programmes, and services,
should they come to power. To put it differently, despite being poor,
disadvantaged, discriminated against, and disempowered in any number of ways, they are able to articulate their preferences and express
agency—given an opportunity, they display a readiness to take up the
challenge and to alter their material condition through political
action. All these are, potentially, hugely empowering and where they
have occurred, they have indeed effected major change.

An agenda for initiating the process of positive change is thus
possible, once areas of critical concern have been identified. The
acceptance of literacy for women as an end in itself, desirable and
necessary, is now taken for granted, but literacy alone cannot be a
sufficient means for enabling the process of change to retain its
momentum. Continuing and higher education are required for a
substantive improvement in status; these in turn require a combination of state, governmental, and individual community action to take
place. We have seen how affirmative policies and programmes on the
part of governments in several states—Kerala, Andhra Pradesh, Madhya

Pradesh, and Tamil Nadu, for example—have dramatically altered women's educational status, but these need to be supplemented by changes in attitudes as far as girls' education and marriage are concerned, in order to effect a real difference.

We cannot emphasize enough the importance of maintaining the legal age of marriage for girls in India. Currently, the average age of marriage remains a full two years below 18 years, all-India, and lower by as much as four to five years in some parts of the country. Practically every gender-specific disadvantage can be attributed to early marriage, from declining health as a result of poor nutrition and early child-bearing, to withdrawal from education and the workforce, and from most public spaces. Consequent on this are extreme economic dependence, physical vulnerability, a crippling lack of autonomy and, ultimately, a devaluation of women themselves.

An improvement in women's status does not necessarily have to proceed sequentially, from literacy to education to health and work, and so on, in a linear trajectory. Without in any way underestimating the importance of all these as ends in themselves, recent experiments demonstrate that education, empowerment, and development are multifaceted and co-dependent, and can proceed simultaneously. Functional literacy can fulfil some functions, but it may not always educate women into recognizing their capabilities and claiming their rights; the attempt of the Education for Women's Equality (EWE) programme, for example, was to instil critical awareness and impart practical skills to women to enable them to deal with their everyday realities, and to confront and resist local power hierarchies and interests. In other words, it educated them in social action.

The success of the Self-Employed Women's Association (SEWA) demonstrates the effectiveness of organizing and bargaining—an old trade union principle—even for those who are self-employed and working in the unorganized sector. The collective empowerment that this results in has exponential gains, as illustrated by both SEWA, Ahmedabad and Lucknow, who now have huge memberships, run their own schools, banking and credit facilities, communication, and sundry other projects. The MWS, like the NIUA, the NSS and the Census, confirms that over 90 per cent of women are self-employed, with the MWS putting the percentage for Muslim women higher than that for Hindus. The potential for organizing, therefore, is considerable; it remains one of the most effective strategies for making working women visible, in the absence of a recognition of women's labour and their contribution to the national economy.

V

As we hope is clear from the foregoing Survey and findings, our principal purpose has been to delineate the multi-dimensional aspects of Muslim women's status. We began this study with the need to understand their status within a framework of social inequality and inter-group disparity. We have explored the interactive processes of diversity and disadvantage, within which the differences of class and community have been impossible to overlook. The MWS findings do reveal group-specific socio-economic inequalities on several important indicators; at the same time, gender biases are evident, both within and between communities. Outcomes for women in many respects result from the fact that they have less control than men over decisions that shape their lives.

Taken as a whole, the MWS findings point to the need for a new unmarked conception of community, going beyond assumed notions that are either caught up in special group recognition and the cultural rights argument, or are bogged down by the controversy over minority claims of enhanced representation in government jobs and legislative bodies. The first assumes that a group's distinct identity must be maintained; the second believes that job quotas or greater presence in public institutions can address all problems. Neither is concerned about the social and economic disadvantage of religious minorities, whether gender- or class-based. Given that a distinct group identity does exist for Muslims and for women within the community (and seems likely to continue as no government is prepared to confront a legal change of personal laws), does a commitment to equality require us to go beyond the principle of group recognition of religious identity or discrimination suffered by Muslim women under the regime of personal laws, to accommodate specific measures of economic and social well-being?

We do not offer any specific view of discrimination in Indian society and Muslim women within it, except to indicate that social injustices are widespread, whether deliberate or otherwise, in the allocation of public services or in discrimination against socially and economically marginal groups. Given that Muslims have been a significant presence in electoral democracy, it would be extremely difficult to show that the material and social inequalities that characterize Muslim women are a product of Muslim discrimination, rather than a vestige of poverty and lack of education, as well as the social and economic processes that confront marginal groups. Nevertheless, the pattern of social stratification that emerges from the MWS findings would seem to warrant special recognition, and a strong claim that government and non-governmental organizations be attentive to the ways in which government neglect and majoritarian practice can disadvantage Muslim women. In sum, then, we should be concerned about the need to reconcile the principle of equality with the fact of community-specific disadvantage, and about the full citizenship of Muslim women within Indian democracy.

Endnotes

1. Shireen Jejeebhoy and Zeba Sathar, 'Women's Autonomy in India and Pakistan: The Influence of Religion and Region', *Population and Development Review*, December 2001, p. 687.

1. Shireen Jejeebhoy and Zeba Sathar point out that women's autonomy in India, including in Tamil Nadu where women enjoy greater autonomy than their northern counterparts, is far more limited than that of women in other parts of Asia (Malaysia, Philippines, and Thailand, for example). Ibid., p. 690.

3. Ashutosh Varshney, *Ethnic Conflict and Civic Life: Hindus and Muslims in India*, Oxford University Press, New Delhi, pp. 95–100.

4. Martha Nussabaum, *Women and Human Development: The capabilities Approach*, Cambridge University Press, Cambridge, 2000.

5. Noeleen Heyzer and Geeta Sen (eds), *Gender, Economic Growth and Poverty*, Kali for Women, Delhi, 1995, p. 23.

6. Maratha Nussbaum, in Zoya Hasan, E. Sridharan and R. Sudarshan (eds), *India's Living Constitution: Ideas, Practices and Controversies*, Permanent Black, New Delhi, 2002, p. 258.

7. Ratna Kapur and Brenda Cossman, *Subversive Sites*, Sage, New Delhi, p. 13.

8. *Human Development in South Asia 2000: The Gender Question*, Mahbub ul Haq Human Development Centre, Oxford University Press, Karachi, 2000.

9. Moser, 1989.

10. *Development and Change*, p. 9.

Appendix
Questionnaire

Muslim Women's Survey
Woman Schedule

State _____   ☐☐

District _____   ☐

Block _____   ☐

City/Town/Village _____

Rural/Urban [Rural: (–1), Urban: (–2)]   ☐

Household number

Name of woman _____

Line no. of woman in the household schedule   ☐☐

Result codes

Completed: 1, Women not at home: 2, Refused: 3, Incomplete: 4, Others: 5

Name of interviewer _____

Date of interview _____

Time of start of interview   ☐☐ Hours ☐☐ Minutes

Back checked by_____

Date _____

Edited by_____

Date _____

Namaste, My name is .... and I am working with ORG Centre for Social Research—a research organization that conducts largescale surveys at national level from time to time. We are at present conducting a survey on lives of women in the entire country. Today we have come to meet some people in your village/area. We are fortunate that we are meeting you also. We would very much appreciate your participation in the survey. Kindly spare some time and give us your responses one by qne. We promise that we will keep all the information provided by you utmost secret and it will be utilized only for research purpose. Your name will not be divulged at all. Hope you will cooperate with us.

Q. No.	Question	Answer	Skip to
	Type of household	Muslim _____ 1 Hindu _____ 2	
	Type of locality of household	Muslim dominated _____ 1 Hindu dominated _____ 2 Both equal _____ 3	
1.	EDUCATION		
1.1	How old are you?	Age in completed years _____ ☐☐	
1.2	Have you ever attended school?	Yes _____ 1 No _____ 2	→ Q. 1.6
1.3	Which type of school have you attended?	Govt./private _____ 1 Madrassa _____ 2	
1.4	What is the highest grade you completed? (Write 00 if less than one year completed)	Grade _____ ☐☐	
1.5	Are you currently studying?	Yes _____ 1 No _____ 2	→ Q. 1.8a
1.6	Check Q 1.2 and Q 1.5 If stopped studying (Q 1.2=1 and Q 1.5=2) Why did you not continue further studies or if never attended (Q 1.2=2), why did you not go to school at all?		

Q. No.	Question	Answer	Skip to
	(Do not prompt) (Multiple Answers)	School too far away ____ 01 Transport not available ____ 02 Education not considered necessary ____ 03 Failed ____ 04 Required for household work ____ 05 Required for work on farm/ family business ____ 06 Required for outside work for payment in cash or kind ____ 07 No proper school facilities for girls in the village/ locality ____ 08 Financial constraints ____ 09 Family objected ____ 10 Death of father/mother ____ 11 Not interested in studies ____ 12 Married off ____ 13 Attained puberty ____ 14 Required for care of siblings ____ 15 Others (specify) ____ 77 Do not know/Can't say ____ 88	
	Check Q. 1.2. If Q. 1.2 = 2, ask Q. 1.7; otherwise skip to Q. 1.8a		
1.7	Some people without going to school also get educated. What about your case?	Learnt at home ____ 1 Went to non-formal education centre ____ 2 Did not learn anything ____ 3	→ Q. 1.9a → Q. 1.9a
1.8a	Did you face any problems, which you overcame to continue your studies?	Yes ____ 1 No ____ 2	→ Q. 1.9a
1.8b	If yes, specify the obstacles that you overcame?	Financial constraints ____ 1 Death of father/mother ____ 2 Parents' opposition ____ 3 Others ____ 7	
1.9a	What is your mother-tongue?	☐☐	

Q. No.	Question	Answer	Skip to
1.9b	Please tell which languages you can speak, read, or write? (Yes: 1, No: 2)	Language Read Write Speak Code □□ □ □ □ □□ □ □ □ □□ □ □ □ □□ □ □ □	
1.10	In your opinion, up to what standard/grade/class should a girl study?	Grade □□	
1.11	In your opinion, up to what standard/grade/class should a boy study?	Grade □□	
1.12	In your opinion, should the girl be sent to co-educational school?	Yes _____ 1 No _____ 2	→ Q. 2.1a
1.13	In your opinion, up to what standard/class/grade the girl-child should be sent to co-educational school?	Grade ____ □□	
2.	ACCESS TO MEDIA		
2.1a	Do you read or listen to newspaper or magazine?	Yes _____ 1 No _____ 2	→ Q. 2.2a
2.1b	Which newspaper/ magazines do you mainly read or hear?	Hindi newspaper/magazines ___ 1 Urdu newspaper/magazines ___ 2 English newspaper/magazine ___ 3 Other language newspaper/ magazine _____ 7	
2.1c	How regular is the habit?	Regularly _____ 1 Sometimes _____ 2 Rarely _____ 3	
2.2a	Do you watch TV?	Yes _____ 1 No _____ 2	→ Q. 2.3a

Q. No.	Question	Answer	Skip to
2.2b	How regular is the habit of watching TV?	Regularly _____ 1 Sometimes _____ 2 Rarely _____ 3	
2.2c	Can you tell me whether you watched any programme or advertisement related to women or the girl-child recently?	Yes _____ 1 No _____ 2	→ Q. 2.3a
2.2d	If yes, what was the message?	Hygiene and nutrition of children _____ 01 Education of children _____ 02 Education of girl-child _____ 03 Evils of dowry _____ 04 Immunization of mother/children _____ 05 Advantage of small family size _____ 06 Age at marriage _____ 07 Health of mother _____ 08 Economic independence of women _____ 09 Others (specify) _____ 10	
2.3a	Do you listen to radio?	Yes _____ 1 No _____ 2	→ Q. 3.1
2.3b	How regular is the habit of listening to radio?	Regularly _____ 1 Sometimes _____ 2 Rarely _____ 3	
3.	MARRIAGE		
3.1	What is your current marital status?	Currently married _____ 1 Married but gauna not performed _____ 2 Widowed _____ 3 Divorced _____ 4 Separated _____ 5 Deserted _____ 6 Never married _____ 7	→ Q. 3.6a

Q. No.	Question	Answer	Skip to
3.2	Have you been married only once or more than once?	Once _____ 1 Twice _____ 2 More than 2 times _____ 3	
3.3	At what age did you get married (first) time?	Age (in years) ☐☐	Skip to 3.6a (If Q. 3.2 = 1)
3.4	At what age was your first marriage dissolved?	Age (in years) ☐☐	
3.5	At what age were you married the last time?	Age (in years) ☐☐	
3.6a	In your opinion what is the ideal age at marriage for boys?	Age (in years) ☐☐	
3.6b	Why do you say so?	_____	
3.7a	In your opinion what is the ideal age at marriage for girls?	Age (in years) ☐☐	
3.7b	Why do you say so?	_____	
3.8	Are you aware of the minimum legal age at marriage for boys and girls?	Yes _____ 1 No _____ 2	→ Q. 3.12
3.9	What is minimum legal age of marriage for boys?	Age (in years) ☐☐ Do not know _____ 88	
3.10	What is minimum legal age of marriage for girls?	Age (in years) ☐☐ Do not know _____ 88	
3.11a	Is this norm followed in your community?	Yes _____ 1 No _____ 2	→ Q. 3.12
3.11b	If not, why is it not followed?	To reduce the burden on parents _____ 1	

Q. No.	Question	Answer	Skip to
		Lack of education _____ 2 Availability of good match at younger age _____ 3 To avoid chances of love affairs _____ 4 It is customary _____ 5 Others (specify) _____ 7	
3.12	Have you found any increase in age at marriage for girls in your community in recent times?	Yes _____ 1 No _____ 2 Can't say _____ 8	
	Inter-Spouse Communication on Family Size and Family Planning		
	Ins.: Ask Q. 3.13 to 3.17c to currently married woman only, i.e. Q. 3.1=1, otherwise skip to Q. 4.1		
3.13	How often have you talked to your husband about family planning in the past year?	Never _____ 1 Once or twice _____ 2 Frequently _____ 3	
3.14	Have you or your husband ever discussed the number of children you would like to have?	Yes _____ 1 No _____ 2	
3.15	Who decides in the family about the number of children you would have?	Husband _____ 1 Wife _____ 2 Both jointly _____ 3 Parents-in-law _____ 4 Others _____ 7 Nobody _____ 8	
3.16	How many children do you have?	Male ☐ Female ☐ Total ☐	
3.17a	Are you currently using any family planning method?	Yes _____ 1 No _____ 2	→ Q. 4.1

Q. No.	Question	Answer	Skip to
3.17b	Which method?	Vasectomy _____ 1 Tubectomy _____ 2 IUD _____ 3 OP _____ 4 Condom _____ 5 Any other _____ 6	
4.	WORK/EMPLOYMENT/INCOME		
4.1	Are you self-employed, wage worker/employee, salaried, or unpaid family worker?	Self-employed _____ 1 Wage worker/employee _____ 2 Salaried _____ 3 Unpaid family worker _____ 4 None of these _____ 5	→ Q. 4.7 → Q. 4.4 → Q. 4.3 → Q. 4.8
4.2	Have you ever worked for earning cash or kind in the past?	Yes _____ 1 No _____ 2	→ Q. 4.20
4.3	What exactly did/do you do?	Embroidery/tailoring _____ 1 Milching _____ 2 Agricultural work _____ 3 Unskilled work/casual labour _____ 4 Skilled job _____ 5 White collar job _____ 6 Others _____ 7	
4.4	At what age did you start working?	Age in years ☐☐	
4.5	Was/is it full-time or part-time?	Full-time _____ 1 Part-time _____ 2	
4.6	Are/were you paid in cash or kind/not paid at all?	Cash only _____ 1 Cash and kind _____ 2 Kind only _____ 3 Not paid _____ 4 Line missing _____ 5	Skip to 4.9
	Check If Q. 4.1 = 1, ask		
4.7	If self-employed, what do/did you do as self-employed?	Professional (doctor, lawyer, architect, teacher etc. _____ 1 Vocational (tailor, beautician etc.) _____ 2	

Q. No.	Question	Answer	Skip to
		Petty business (fruit vendor, vegetable vendor, milk, ghee etc.) _____ 3 Large business (runs her own school or company etc.) _____ 4 Small business (papad, agarbatti, craft/artisan) _____ 5 Social work _____ 6 Others _____ 7	Skip to 4.9
	Check: If Q. 4.1 = 4, ask		
4.8	As an unpaid family worker, what do/did you do?	Work in the family farm ____ 1 Work in the family profession (milk, etc.) _____ 2 Work in the family business (petty business) _____ 3 Family craft _____ 4 Others _____ 7	
4.9	Are/were you working throughout the year/ seasonally/occasionally?	Throughout the year _____ 1 Seasonally _____ 2	→ Q. 4.11
4.10	How many days in a year do you work?		
4.11	Since how long have you been working/For how long did you work?	No. of years _____	
4.12	Do/did you do any other job/work besides this?	Yes _____ 1 No _____ 2	→ Q. 4.13b
4.13a	If yes, what work are you engaged in?	Agricultural labour _____ 1 Tailoring/embroidery _____ 2 Milching/animal products ____ 3 Unskilled work _____ 4	
4.13b	What prompted you to work?	To support the family _____ 1 To supplement the income ____ 2 To utilize time _____ 3 Others _____ 7	

Q. No.	Question	Answer	Skip to
4.14	What is your average monthly income?	Rs _____ ☐☐☐☐☐	
4.15a	'Generally how much do/did your earnings contribute to total family income?	Almost nothing _____ 1 Less than half _____ 2 About half _____ 3 More than half _____ 4 All _____ 5	→ Q. 4.16
4.15b	If contribution is not full, what will you do with your earnings? (Multiple response)	To meet self's aspiration _____ 1 To meet household needs _____ 2 To meet children's aspiration ___ 3 To save money _____ 4 Health needs _____ 5 Others _____ 7	
4.16	Who mainly decides/used to decide about how money earned by you will be used?	Respondent decides _____ 1 Husband decides _____ 2 Jointly with husband _____ 3 Parents/in-laws _____ 4 Elders _____ 5 Jointly with someone else _____ 6 Family's/Joint decision _____ 7	
4.17	Do you manage to save some money out of your earnings?	Yes _____ 1 No _____ 2	→ Q. 4.19
4.18	Where do you keep that money? (Multiple answers)	Myself _____ 1 In the bank _____ 2 In the post office _____ 3 With the husband _____ 4 With Father-/Mother-in-law ___ 5 With parents _____ 6 Convert it into gold _____ 7 Any other _____ 8	
4.19	Check Q. 4.1 = 5 If currently not working, what are the reasons for not working? (Multiple answers)	No need to work _____ 01 Disinclination _____ 02 Family responsibilities _____ 03 Child bearing/rearing _____ 04 Lack of education _____ 05 Lack of skills _____ 06	

Q. No.	Question	Answer	Skip to
		No permission from husband/parents _____ 07 Lack of employment opportunities _____ 08 Got married _____ 09 Lack of mobility _____ 10 Purdah _____ 11 Any other _____ 77	
4.20	If no to Q. 4.2. Sometimes we do not consider such activities like working on our own farm, sitting in our own shop, participating in our own family business, or selling products like ghee, milk, flowers, fruits or vegetables, papad, etc. as gainful employment as there may not be direct cash earning or it may not be a regular job. Please recall whether you have ever engaged in such activities?	Yes _____ 1 No _____ 2 Do not remember _____ 9	→ Q. 4.23 → Q. 4.23
4.21	If yes, what was the nature of the job/work?	Petty business _____ 1 Work in own field _____ 2 Work for family business _____ 3 Embroidery _____ 4 Tailoring _____ 5 Others _____ 7	
4.22	How long did you work (months)?	_____ ☐☐	
4.23	Who decides whether a female member in the house should work outside or not?	Self _____ 1 Husband _____ 2 Father _____ 3 Mother _____ 4 Father-in-law _____ 5 Mother-in-law _____ 6 Others _____ 7	

Q. No.	Question	Answer	Skip to
5.	ACCESS TO WELFARE		
5.1	What are the three most important issues/ problems according to you that your neighbourhood is facing?	Problem of drinking water ___ 1 Non-availability of school for girls ___ 2 Non-availability of school ___ 3 Non-availability of sanitation facilities ___ 4 Drainage problem ___ 5 Others (specify) ___ 6	
5.2	Is there a government health centre/hospital in your area?	Yes ___ 1 No ___ 2	→ Q. 5.4
5.3	Do you go to this government health centre/ hospital if someone is sick in your family?	Yes ___ 1 No ___ 2	→ Q. 5.6
5.4	If not, where do you go?	Private hospital ___ 1 Private doctor ___ 2 Ayurvedic doctor ___ 3 Homoeopathic doctor ___ 4 Unani doctor ___ 5 Trust/NGO dispensary ___ 6 Others ___ 7	
5.5	Why do you not go to the health centre?	Unable to leave the house ___ 1 Lack of adequate facilities ___ 2 Lack of female doctors ___ 3 Lack of time ___ 4 Long distance ___ 5 Bad behaviour of staff ___ 6 Any other ___ 7	
5.6	Is there a balwadi/ anganwadi in your neighbourhood/village?	Yes ___ 1 No ___ 2	→ Q. 5.9a
5.7	Do the children in your household go to the balwadi/anganwadi?	Yes ___ 1 No ___ 2	→ Q. 5.9a

Q. No.	Question	Answer	Skip to
5.8	What are the reasons for not sending your children to the balwadi?	Lack of adequate facilities _____ 1 Lack of time _____ 2 Long distance _____ 3 No child to send to balwadi _____ 4 Do not want to send _____ 5 Family members objected _____ 6 Other (specify) _____ 7	
5.9a	What development programmes are being run by the government? (Multiple answer)	IRDP _____ 1 TRYSEM _____ 2 DWACRA _____ 3 JRY _____ 4 NRY _____ 5 Indira Awas Yojana _____ 6 ICDS _____ 7 DPIP _____ 8 EAS _____ 9 Scheme for urban enterprises _____ 10 Scheme for urban wage employment _____ 11 Scheme for divorced women _____ 12 National credit fund for women _____ 13 Labour welfare scheme _____ 14 Other (specify) _____ 15	
5.9b	Are you aware of any developmental programme in your area directed to women?	Yes _____ 1 No _____ 2	→ Q. 6.1
5.10	If yes, please tell me what are these programmes?	_____ _____ _____	
5.11	Do/did you benefit from any of these women's development programmes?	Yes _____ 1 No _____ 2	→ Q. 6.1
5.12	Which are the programmes you have benefited from?	_____ _____ _____	

Q. No.	Question	Answer	Skip to
6.	**PARTICIPATION IN VOLUNTARY WORK**		
	Now I will ask you about voluntary work. Sometimes people form voluntary organizations, do some social work, join mahila mandals or religious groups to help the people in the neighbourhood/ locality.		
6.1	Are you active in any organization or group in your neighbourhood?	Yes _____ 1 No _____ 2 No response _____ 9	→ Q. 6.3 → Q. 6.3
6.2	In which organization/ groups are you active? (Multiple answers)	Mahila mandal _____ 1 Community groups _____ 2 Religious groups _____ 3 Political group _____ 4 NGOs _____ 5	
6.3	Do you do any kind of voluntary work?	Yes _____ 1 No _____ 2	
7.	**MOBILITY**		
7.1	Do you require permission (please do not mistake intimation as permission) to go outside the home for the following purposes? Going to work Going to market Going to doctor/ health centre Going to election meeting For a religious meeting For social or cultural gatherings For work-related activities For demonstration Going to cinema/theatre For natal home visit To meet friends		

	Yes	No
Going to work	1	2
Going to market	1	2
Going to doctor/ health centre	1	2
Going to election meeting	1	2
Same for a religious meeting	1	2
For social or cultural gatherings	1	2
For work-related activities	1	2
For demonstration	1	2
Going to cinema/theatre	1	2
For natal home visit	1	2
To meet friends	1	2

Q. No.	Question	Answer	Skip to
7.2	If yes to any in Q. 7.1, whose permission is required? (Multiple answers)	Father ____ 1 Husband ____ 2 Brothers ____ 3 Mother ____ 4 Father-in-law ____ 5 Mother-in-law ____ 6 Other family members ____ 7 Others ____ 8	
7.3	In your family, who makes the major decisions on the following? (codes as below in each category) Father/Father-in-law: 1, Mother/Mother-in-law: 2, Jointly with parents/parents-in-law: 3, Husband: 4, Self: 5, Husband and self jointly: 6, Brother: 7, Whole family: 8.	Household expenditure ☐ Children's education ☐ Marriage ☐ Birth ceremonies ☐ Death ceremonies ☐ Treatment of major illness ☐ Travel ☐ Major purchases—land, property, gold ☐ Major investment—business bonds/shares ☐	
7.4	Please read these items. Are you consulted usually with regard to them? (Yes: 1, No: 2)	Household expenditure ☐ Children's education ☐ Marriage ☐ Birth ceremonies ☐ Death ceremonies ☐ Treatment of major illness ☐ Travel ☐ Major purchases—land, property, gold ☐ Major investment—business bonds/shares ☐	
8.	POLITICAL PARTICIPATION		
8.1	Which is the dominant party in your area?	Congress ____ 1 BJP ____ 2 Janata Dal ____ 3	

Q. No.	Question	Answer	Skip to
		CPI _____ 4 CPM _____ 5 Any other (specify) _____ 7 Do not know _____ 8	
8.2	At what age does a person acquire the right to vote?	Age (in years) _____ ☐☐ Do not know _____ 88	
8.3	Did you vote in the election?	Yes _____ 1 No _____ 2	→ Q. 8.8
8.4	Do you vote every time when there is an election?	Every time _____ 1 Sometimes _____ 2	
8.5	Do you vote on your own or follow someone's advice to support a party or candidate?	Vote on own _____ 1 Follows someone's advice ____ 2	→ Q. 8.7
8.6	Whom do you consult/ who advises to support a particular political party or candidate?	Family members _____ 1 Husband _____ 2 Friends _____ 3 Community elder _____ 4 Religious workers _____ 5 Party workers _____ 6 Any other _____ 7	
8.7	Do you know the name of the candidate/party you vote for?	Yes, always _____ 1 Yes, sometimes _____ 2 No _____ 3	
8.8	Have you ever participated in a political campaign?	Yes _____ 1 No _____ 2 No response _____ 9	→ Q. 8.10 → Q. 8.10
8.9	If yes, specify the election for which you participated in a campaign. (Multiple answers)	For local election _____ 1 For Panchayat election _____ 2 For Assembly election _____ 3 For Lok Sabha election _____ 4 Zila Parishad election _____ 5 Municipal Corporation election _____ 6 Any other _____ 7	

Q. No.	Question	Answer	Skip to
8.10	Are you aware that there is reservation of seats for women in the panchayat election?	Yes _____ 1 No _____ 2	→ Q. 8.12
8.11	Do you support such reservations in the state/ national level election?	Yes _____ 1 No _____ 2 Can't say _____ 8	
8.12	If you were given an opportunity to contest, would you like to contest?	Yes _____ 1 No _____ 2	→ Q. 9.1
8.13	At what level would you like to contest?	Local _____ 1 State _____ 2 Centre _____ 3	
8.14	If you get elected, what kind of work would you like to do?	School in the locality _____ 1 Medical facilities in the locality _____ 2 Pucca road/ Street construction _____ 3 Job opportunities for the women _____ 4 Sanitation facilities _____ 5 Income generation activities ____ 6 Help widows/divorcees/ aged women etc. _____ 7	
9.	VIOLENCE		
9.1	Was there ever a communal riot in your area or nearby area?	Yes _____ 1 No _____ 2 Do not remember _____ 3	→ Q. 9.6 → Q. 9.6
9.2	If yes, when did it take place last?	Years before _____ ☐	
9.3	After the last communal riots, have people moved in or moved out of your neighbourhood?	No change _____ 1 Hindus moved out _____ 2 Muslims moved out _____ 3 Christians moved out _____ 4 Hindus moved in _____ 5	

Q. No.	Question	Answer	Skip to
		Muslims moved in _____ 6 Christians moved in_____ 7 Any other _____ 8 No response _____ 9	
9.4	Do you know the reasons why the riots took place?	Yes _____ 1 No _____ 2 No response _____ 9	→ Q. 9.6 → Q. 9.6
9.5	If yes, what according to you were the three main reasons of communal riots that had taken place in your area? (Multiple answers)	Religious reasons _____ 1 Social reasons _____ 2 Economic reasons_____ 3 Political reasons _____ 4	
9.6	How are people affected by riots? (Multiple answers)	Not affected at all _____ 01 Psychologically traumatized __ 02 House looted and property damaged _____ 03 Forced to shift the house _____ 04 Physical attack on some members _____ 05 Sexual attack on some members _____ 06 Social restrictions on mobility of female members _____ 07 Children's education affected_____ 08 Any other _____ 09 No response _____ 10	
9.7	What role do women play during riots? (Multiple answers)	Women do not do anything ___ 01 Run away for safety _____ 02 Morcha against police arrest of their men _____ 03 Helping people escape _____ 04 Participating in preparation of attack on other community ___ 05 Participate in the looting _____ 06 Safe-keeping neighbours's property_____ 07	

Q. No.	Question	Answer	Skip to
		Sheltering people in their house _____ 8 Join peace morcha _____ 9 Attempt to stop riots _____ 10 Participate in relief activities __ 11 Any other _____ 77 Do not know _____ 88	
	DOMESTIC VIOLENCE		
9.9	Sometimes within family, conflict takes place among family members. Can you recall any time conflicts had taken place in your family?	Yes _____ 1 No _____ 2 Not response _____ 9	→ Q. 10.1 → Q. 10.1
9.10	If yes, can you tell me the nature of conflict?	Physical abuse _____ 1 Verbal abuse _____ 2 Not talking to each other _____ 3 Others _____ 7	
9.11	What are the reasons for these conflicts?	Land disputes _____ 1 Sharing of property _____ 2 Share of property given to daughter _____ 3 Drinking habit of husband _____ 4 Husband goes out without informing _____ 5 Mother-in-law forces daughter-in-law into purdah _____ 6 Others (specify) _____ 7	
9.12	Can you recall any time these conflicts led to physical violence? In other words, have you ever been beaten or mistreated physically?	Yes _____ 1 No _____ 1 No response _____ 9	→ Q. 10.1 → Q. 10.1
9.13	Who had beaten you or mistreated you physically?	Parents _____ 1 Brother _____ 2 Sister _____ 3	

Q. No.	Question	Answer	Skip to
		Husband _____ 4 Mother-in-law _____ 5 Father-in-law _____ 6 Sister-in-law _____ 7 Son _____ 8 Any other _____ 9	
9.14	What did you do after you were beaten or mistreated?	_____ _____ _____	
10.	**BACKGROUND INFORMATION ON HUSBAND** (check Q. 3.1, if never married, end the interview)		
10.1	How old was your husband on his last birthday?	Age in completed years ☐ Unmarried _____ 98	END
10.2	Did your (last) husband ever attend school?	Yes _____ 1 No _____ 2	→ Q. 10.4
10.3	What is the highest grade he completed?	Grade ☐☐	
10.4	What kind of work (does/did) your (last) husband mainly do?	Agriculture _____ 01 Agricultural labour _____ 02 Unskilled labour _____ 03 Skilled labour _____ 04 Doctor/Engineer/Lawyer _____ 05 Small business _____ 06 Large business _____ 07 Driver _____ 08 Teacher _____ 09 Clerical job _____ 10 Class IV service _____ 11 Others _____ 12